CONSCIENTIOUS THINKING

Georgia Review Books

EDITED BY STEPHEN COREY

Conscientious Thinking

Making Sense in an Age of Idiot Savants

DAVID BOSWORTH

The University of Georgia Press
ATHENS

Publication of this work was made
possible, in part, by a generous gift
from the University of Georgia Press Friends Fund.
Published by the University of Georgia Press
Athens, Georgia 30602
www.ugapress.org

Designed by Erin Kirk New
Set in ITC New Baskerville
Printed and bound by Sheridan Books
The paper in this book meets the guidelines for
permanence and durability of the Committee on
Production Guidelines for Book Longevity of the
Council on Library Resources.

Printed in the United States of America
17 18 19 20 21 C 5 4 3 2 1

Library of Congress Control Number 2016958180
ISBN: 9780820350653 Hardback
ISBN: 9780820350646 E-book

If we know in what way society is unbalanced, we
must do what we can to add weight to the lighter scale.

—Simone Weil

Contents

Essaying/Assaying America

David Bosworth's Magnum Opus

STEPHEN COREY

DAVID BOSWORTH first came to the attention of *The Georgia Review* more than a quarter-century ago with "Hard Being Good: Reaganomics, Free Expression, and Federal Funding of the Arts," a controversial essay that ran in the fall 1991 issue. I was in my eighth year with the journal, serving as associate editor and having the privilege of working with then-editor Stanley W. Lindberg on Bosworth's manuscript. Since that time Bosworth has published another ten essays in the *Review*, more than any other writer, and he was one of the first who came to mind when I was formulating the Georgia Review Books series with the University of Georgia Press.

I did not think of Bosworth because we have featured so much of his work but because of that work's scope, value, and durability. During the current period of rapid globalization and the proliferation of all manner of complexities, too many of America's writers have narrowed rather than broadened their sights. The personal essay and memoir dominate—sometimes to powerful effect, but often giving the impression (giving *me* the impression) that too many of our best wordsmiths are retreating from the most important fronts, unwilling or unable to do some of the more difficult essaying (the trying/attempting/weighing/analyzing/arguing) the world needs from them.

David Bosworth has been and remains a welcome and vital exception. He has as little direct interest in David Bosworth as is possible, having chosen instead to study the state of the world from every imaginable interrelated angle. An incomplete alphabetical list of his crucial topics includes art, business, celebrity, economics, history, literature, medicine, movies, mythology, philosophy, politics, psychology, and science. This book, four of whose eight main sections appeared first in *The Georgia Review*, has been more than two decades in the making—a fact that will not surprise you at all once you begin to be caught up by its thoughtful, instructive, and often brazen arguments.

Brazen: *to face with defiance or impudence*. For a quick taste of Bosworth's readiness to engage large matters, consider the titles of a few of his *Georgia Review* essays that did not end up in *Conscientious Thinking*: "The Cult of the Adolescent: Commercial Indoctrination and the Collapse of Civic Virtue"; "The Pharmacy of Pain Dissuasion: America's Addictive Faith in Psychoactive Drugs"; "Killing the Covenant: The Savage Idolatry of the New World Order."

No grousing from David Bosworth about parents or spouses who didn't or don't understand him . . . no strolls down the memory lane of childhood or climbs up the cliffs of the great outdoors . . . no ranting or whining born of an unwillingness or inability to step away from the mirror and *think*, carefully and humanely, about the rest of the world.

I have been fortunate to witness the growth of this book over many years and privileged to contribute to certain elements of its refining. Now, I am greatly pleased to place it before your eyes, that you may assay its essaying.

Acknowledgments

PORTIONS OF THIS BOOK first appeared, in an altered form, as essays in the following publications: *Georgia Review, Salmagundi,* and *Raritan.* I am indebted to their editors for providing a public forum for testing the narrative and analysis that follow.

CONSCIENTIOUS THINKING

A Key to the Map

Hope is not the conviction that something will turn out well,
but the certainty that something makes sense, regardless of
how it turns out.

　　　　　　　　　—Václav Havel

THIS BOOK has been motivated in part by the most pressing and perplexing of contemporary conditions: the flagrant failure of our nation's
meritocracy to manage our affairs effectively. The explosion of high-tech
invention during the digital era has been paradoxically simultaneous with
a widespread managerial meltdown. Finance, politics, medicine, scholarship, art: no field, it seems, has been immune to the contagion of rank
ineptitude under the guise of a supremely confident expertise.

We have endured since the 1980s a catastrophically incompetent
foreign policy that, misconducting two wars, has squandered blood and
treasure (up to $4 trillion) for negligible or even detrimental results. We
have suffered the application of a catastrophically false economic philosophy, whose toxic mixture of arrogance and greed led to the collapse
of the financial markets and to a recession so severe and unequal in its
punishments that it has threatened the survival of the nation's middle
class. Following the diagnostic advice of the medical profession (the virtual clerisy of our therapeutic society), we have been dosed with many
billions of dollars of antidepressant drugs that have proven to be scarcely
more effective than the placebos they were tested against.[1] For fifty years
now, the visual arts scene has been dominated by either pop kitsch or
agitprop, while the humanities have submitted to a series of reductive theories whose dominance flares then fades with a rhythm resembling the
facile turns of the fashion cycle. Even NASA, once the supreme example
of American can-do, has declined into an agency that too frequently *can't*,
one characterized by fatal accidents, busted budgets, and cancelled projects—a literal and metaphorical "failure to launch."

More worrisome than the existence of these examples per se has been the habitual absence of corrective action. The algorithms of our smart machines are supposed to learn from experience, but our leaders, it seems, too rarely do. The collapse of the financial markets and the belated exposure of Bernie Madoff's Ponzi scheme in December of 2008 were preceded from 1988 to 2002 by the savings and loan, Asian market, high-tech bubble, Long-Term Capital Management, Enron, and WorldCom crises and scandals, yet leaders on Wall Street, in Congress, and in our regulatory agencies proved deaf, dumb, and blind to the warnings they supplied. In the aftermath of a crisis caused by the deregulation of financial institutions "too big to fail," the reforms to date have resulted in both the consolidation of even larger firms and (in an egregious instance of political chutzpah) a revived resistance to financial regulations by the very corporations whose reckless behavior required federal intervention. Prior to the promiscuous prescription of Prozac and its kin, postwar America suffered two earlier rounds of infatuation with a family of legally prescribed psychoactive drugs—the tranquilizers Miltown and Equanil in the mid-fifties, and then Librium and Valium in the sixties and seventies—each of which also proved far less miraculous than initially advertised.[2]

One is strongly tempted when reviewing such a list to focus indignation on those "elites" who traverse the corridors of power, shuttling between their classrooms and labs at Harvard, Yale, and Stanford to their offices on Wall Street, First Street, and Pennsylvania Avenue. I understand the sentiment and wouldn't discount the claim, cogently made by Christopher Lasch in his final book, *The Revolt of the Elites*, that our meritocracy has been sliding for years now into something more like a self-interested oligarchy.[3] Certainly, with the exception of a few notorious fall guys, there has been little in the way of lasting consequences for incompetent leadership. A sexual indiscretion made public may force an American official to resign, but gross managerial ineptitude does not. Failing CEOs are still rewarded with Midas-scaled pay packages. Wall Street's mainline institutions voted themselves some $18 billion in bonuses in the very year that their gross incompetence required a government bailout. Economic advisers who were instrumental in killing attempts to regulate the disastrous market in real estate derivatives were later rehired to mend the system that their own recklessness had helped to ruin. The same talking heads whose wisdom endorsed the invasion of Iraq have continued to stream their dubious analyses into our mobile devices while the same doctors who prescribed the last overhyped drug have moved on to the next.

The primary problem with the populist critique is not its indictment of our elite leaders, then, but its failure to admit our broader complicity in their malfeasance or mismanagement. We do still live in a democracy, however compromised by the infusion of big money, and at least some of the disastrous policies cited here were initially popular, endorsed in polls or at the ballot box. The national indebtedness that so enraged Tea Party patriots was generated in part by irresponsible tax cuts that they themselves continued to support. The broader public as well as the federal government went on a spending spree during the aughts, remortgaging houses, running up credit card debt, reducing the national savings rate to near zero by 2005. And even a cursory review of a popular culture that is characterized by lottery mania, casino construction, prosperity theology, and "reality TV" shows scripted to enact fantastic scenarios of wealth and fame refutes the pat claim that a prudent citizenry has been betrayed by an elite as deficient in common sense as it is in common decency.

Still, although the failure in commonsense thinking has been widespread, the mistakes of those in power have been far more consequential and, for my purposes here, diagnostically revealing. Given the freedoms they license, representative democracies are especially dependent on the good judgment of their leaders in all fields to check the spread of those mass manias and phobias that can destabilize the social order. Yet in the two decades that preceded the financial collapse of 2008, the temper of America's leadership was as problematic as the content of their thought. The boom-bust cycle of the deregulated market—"irrational exuberance" flipping into reactionary panic and then back again—was mirrored by the whipsawing switch from vainglorious euphoria at the collapse of Communism to the xenophobic panic that followed 9/11. In a little more than ten years, "hyperpower" boasts about the triumph of freedom and the "end of history" were succeeded by orange alerts, domestic surveillance, and hysterical rants against the global threat of "Islamofascism." (The calamitous decision to invade Iraq in 2003 irrationally drew on both excessive moods: a paranoid inflation of Saddam Hussein's danger combined with a hubristic expectation of swift and certain victory.)

Despite many individual exceptions, wherever one turns when surveying the recent performance of our professional classes—the prescriptions of our doctors, the policies of our politicians, the projections of our economists, the sermons of our preachers, the theories of our critics, the productions of our age's most influential artists—the same urgent and perplexing question arises: *Why has it been the case* (to cite a line from Sophocles) *that our "thinking men should think so wrongly"?*[4]

Such a worrisome claim will seem deranged to those who are justifiably impressed by the progress of our sciences, and especially to those techno-optimists who feast on the prospects of Silicon Valley's latest release. Although anti-utopian, my argument here is not "declinist" in the usual sense. It would be foolish to deny that, due to the digital revolution, we are experiencing a virtual explosion of new knowledge, or that thanks to the accessibility of our smart machines the average American is far more competent in certain ways—geographical navigation, information retrieval, mathematical calculation—than ever before. But on further examination, this apparent coincidence of technological mastery with managerial ineptitude makes a lot of sense. A review of the historical record reveals that periods of rapid material or mental progress (such as the Renaissance, spurred by the invention of the printing press) can also induce social regress (the civil and religious wars of the seventeenth century). Once broadly applied, the new capacities introduced by a transformative technology (whether agriculture, writing, the stirrup, the book, or the Internet) are likely to disturb the intricate web of checks and balances that has kept the social order stable and its thinking coherent. Unintegrated, rapid infusions of new knowledge generate confusion and dissension, spurring those bitter battles we call culture war, even as the new powers produced by that knowledge invite their misuse, heightening the risk of actual war, whether civil or foreign.

In the deeper past, such technologically induced revolutions in consciousness and culture were rare. But since "the invention of invention" during the seventeenth and eighteenth centuries, the pace has increased dramatically, and with it the associated dangers of confusion, dissension, and social upheaval. Characteristic of the West and of America most purely, this scientific cast of mind naturally generates the unnerving mix of progress and regress, cleverness and cluelessness, that we see all around us. Expert at rational analysis and material manipulation (how-to and can-do), this mind is deficient in emotional and ethical reasoning (whether-to and what-for). Its capacity to focus intensely makes it highly adept at certain kinds of problem-solving (mechanical innovation and the "technical fix") but also renders it insensitive to the sort of collateral damages that such immediate fixes can sometimes cause.

This is the mind that invented the pesticide which, in solving the mosquito problem, threatened the survival of whole species of raptors, and designed the urban renewal project whose construction destroyed the social ties of the very community it was meant to save. Of more recent concern, this is the mind that created those mathematically complex investment instruments whose immediate profits masked their toxic impact on the integrity of our financial system.

Utilizing the literary devices of personification and hyperbole, I have been calling this combination of intellectual strengths and weaknesses the Idiot Savant. Referring as it does to a person who, though exhibiting exceptional mental ability in a specific area, also suffers from a broader ineptitude, this label obviously implies a severe critique. My intention in selecting it, however, was to diagnose and not demean. The etymology of *idiot* suggests, in fact, a plausible etiology for our current discontent. As derived from the ancient Greek *idios*, meaning "private" or "one's own," the deeper history of the word links a failure in intelligence (an ignorance or idiocy) to a radical separation of the one from the many. We are at risk of slipping into gross misconceptions, that verbal history suggests, when the individual thinker or particular line of thought becomes too removed from the collective guidance of the social or psychological whole. As we shall see repeatedly in the chapters that follow, it is precisely the over-specialization of the modern mind—its inclination to atomistic reasoning and linear projection, its disingenuous faith in its own objectivity—that has proven so dangerous.

The four chapters of part 1, "Idiot Savants: Case Studies in the Demise of Modern Reasoning," closely examine a set of significant Americans, über achievers whose careers have exhibited that peculiar combination of savvy and idiocy defined above. Entrepreneur Henry Ford, visual artist Andy Warhol, literary critic Harold Bloom, and a small cast of scientists led by Nicholas Negroponte at MIT's Media Lab: these are, I will insist, representative men. Insomuch as each was or is a leader in his field, their accomplishments do reflect the prevailing quality of thought in their separate professions—and, taken together, the quality of their professions is broadly representative of the nation's decision-making at the highest levels. Each exemplifies in his own site-specific way how our thinking men have been thinking wrongly.

Further, these four case studies have been arrayed in a rough chronological sequence that implies a historical process long at work. As the father of the consumer economy, Ford remained at the apex of American commerce from 1908, when the first Model T rolled off the assembly line, until well into the forties. Warhol dominated the arts scene in the sixties and seventies, and his work remains, arguably, the most influential since World War II. The Yale-centered Bloom eventually turned away from the esoteric monograph to engage a wider audience and become America's most popular literary critic, achieving something close to celebrity status in the 1990s. Finally, the Media Lab—founded to enhance and exploit the merger of the computer, communications, and entertainment industries—remains an active and influential research facility today. Ford's disingenuous idealism, with its "ideas . . . for the good of all" that included a toxic campaign of anti-Semitism; Warhol's aesthetic of *an*esthesia; the solipsism of Bloom's criticism; the science of self-deception evident in the fantasies of immortality touted at the Media Lab: in all cases, the "idiotic savvy" of the works or claims analyzed in these four chapters preceded—and, in the character of their folly, predicted—the broader managerial meltdown of the aughts.

Given the multiple and often messy meanings that certain terms acquire through common usage, a further clarification is in order here. When using *modern* or *modernity*, I am referring solely to that revolution in Western thought which, superseding medievalism, led to both the scientific worldview and the Industrial Revolution—at its best, to a revival of democracy; at its worst, to the utopian delusions of the Idiot Savant. I am not referencing that avant-garde movement of the early twentieth century most commonly called Modernism; nor am I using *modern* in its most general sense, as loosely signifying anything that is contemporary. Yes, because the logic of modernity has calibrated America's core institutions, it remains powerfully present in our lives. But not only is that logic in decadent decline, as exemplified by the managerial meltdown we have been suffering; it is also being fiercely contested by an emerging set of post-modern methods, measures, and values.

Post-modern is itself, of course, a problematic term, much associated with and tainted by our culture wars. Here, I have used typography to distinguish between two distinct but still related senses of the word. When unhyphenated, postmodern does refer to the work of those artists and authors who have rejected the key claims of liberal modernity, dismissing its linked beliefs in individuality, originality, objectivity, and progress, and who insist instead on a radical subjectivity that denies any stable standards for goodness, truth, or beauty. The extremity of their stance seems unsupportable to me and too temperamentally akin to the modern mind-set it aims to critique, claims I will fully address in chapters 2 and 5. Nevertheless, the overall shape and persistence of these postmodern works are diagnostically revealing, the character of their opposition exposing the failures and follies of the modern mind-set.

More commonly, though, I have employed a hyphenated spelling of the term. The aim is to escape the partisan associations of our culture wars by heightening the literal and, initially at least, neutral meaning of *post-modern*. Worldviews do pass. Whether for good or for ill, we have been moving away from many of the presumptions of our foundational past as the first modern society, caught up instead in an ambiguous transition between ruling common senses now a century in the making. We are indisputably *post*-modern in that we are living *after* the height of the modern era, but we are doing so without possessing as yet a coherent consensus as to what ought to replace it.

The aim of part 2, "Reality Check: Plotting a Map for Post-Modern Reasoning," is to imagine a desirable alternative to the modern mind-set: how, in the wake of its decline, might we find a commonsense way of gauging the world more applicable to our changing place and time? After establishing the deeper origins of modern thought and practice, those chapters closely examine the conditions that have been undermining their once-prevailing logic; they chart an emerging grammar of perceptions and interactions that, beneath or behind any aesthetic revision or political reform, is being shaped by the post-modern machinery that now mediates our lives. We do "make sense" through the evidence of our senses, and our radically upgraded technological devices have changed the ways that evidence is arrayed. Accelerating a process that began a century ago with the first electronic media, our daily use of desktops, laptops, mobile phones, and tablets with their search engines, shareware, and wiki-empowered social networking sites has been revising our default expectations as to what seems natural, right, and pleasing to behold—and it has been doing so in ways that repeatedly conflict with modernity's beliefs about the true, the good, and the beautiful.

In a deliberate play on *science*, I have been calling these post-modern ways of assessing the world *conscientious* thinking. As with *idiocy*, the etymology of the word—marrying a prefix (*con*) meaning *with* or *together* to a root (*scientia*) meaning *learning or knowledge*—clarifies both the kind of reasoning it describes and how that reasoning consistently contrasts with the default operations of the modern mind. Whereas the science of modernity strove to know the world through isolation and specialization, post-modern thinking now aims to know *with*. It stresses *con*-scientious measures that can account for the "togetherness" of experience, naturally preferring relation over isolation, hybridity over purity, and the authority of consensus (the hive mind) over the sovereignty of individual expertise. Collaborative, interdisciplinary, multisensory, multicultural: in various ways, the conscientious mind strives to marry thought *with* feeling, the sciences *with* the arts, the visual *with* the auditory, the familiar *with* the foreign, the present *with* the past, this medium or genre *with* that. In contrast to modern reasoning, whose primary metaphor was the *atom* (including the social atom of individualism), the post-modern mind prefers to attend an entire *field* of interrelated effects.

This ongoing shift in the organizing grammar of authoritative thought can be traced in every discipline, from art and anthropology to physics and genetics, and the conflicts it has spurred have not been limited to the spheres and feuds of intellectual pursuit. The contention between modernity's scientific and post-modernity's conscientious modes of reasoning has erupted in every precinct of American life, challenging and often changing the ways classrooms are run, friends relate, money is made, crimes are committed, mates are chosen, children are raised, and the dead are memorialized. Our default conceptions of space and time, and of the proper relationship between self and society, have been shifting at an ever-accelerating rate. To survive this new environment, we will have to reimagine the inner workings of a democratic culture that has been powerfully informed by modern values.

And along with reforming the old, we will need to refine the new: what we *can do* through using our digital technologies will have to be disciplined by new communal understandings as to what we *should do*. In the seventeenth century, the challenge confronting the West's moral imagination was how to both license and tame the new social and intellectual atomism spurred by the printed book; the crisis today is how to express and restrain the emerging togetherness of the digitally interconnected field.

Such an argument clearly requires further substantiation. This summary is only intended to clarify in advance the logical link between the detailed case studies in part 1, which chart the demise of one commonsense way of mapping the world, and the speculations in part 2, which strive to imagine an effective replacement: those new or renewed mental tools that might help us to think rightly again.

In fairness, too, something should be said about the character of the mind that has made those speculations. I am the author of two books of fiction, who, after long supporting his writing habit through blue-collar work, won some literary prizes and reentered the academy. Not long thereafter, I began to suspect that we were living in a profoundly transitional era, one in which the underlying premises of Western consciousness and culture were rapidly shifting. Putting aside my fictive manuscripts for what I presumed to be a brief exploration of that intuition, I soon found myself committed to an ever-ramifying study of the cultural transformation that was indeed under way. The fruit of those efforts has included multiple essays published here and abroad, an unexpected run as a think-tank consultant, a substantial book on ethical change—*The Demise of Virtue in Virtual America: The Moral Origins of the Great Recession*—and, climactically, the companion volume you now hold in your hands.

When I look back, it now seems natural that I chose to tackle such a wide-ranging project. I have always been avidly, one might even say promiscuously, curious. During my grammar-school days, my parents would frequently find me parked in front of our one small bookcase, reading the *World Book Encyclopedia* for fun. In college, wandering from philosophy to psychology to literature, I delayed choosing a major as long as I could and, after graduation, didn't select a so-called career track more specific than an abiding desire to engage the world through the written word. Even when my writing focused solely on fiction, I wasn't pursuing "art for art's sake," and never imagined that I should, or even could, fully separate my literary ambitions from the rigors of analysis, the burdens of parenthood, the duties of citizenship, or the inequities imposed by my low-status jobs.

Such a stubbornly holistic approach to life and letters has deeply influenced the book that follows. The chapter on Henry Ford, for example, is not only based on extensive research into the man and his times; it is also informed by the two years I spent working on an assembly line—including an intimate, bone-deep recollection of the dehumanizing costs of the industrial efficiencies pioneered by Ford—and, too, by an abiding love of literature which insists that F. Scott Fitzgerald may have as much to say about the nature and impact of the great industrialist as Freud, Marx, or Milton Friedman.

In the end, though, no advanced degree, professional seat, or Purple Heart earned for "romantically" suffering the slings and arrows of blue-collar work can pre-validate the analysis to come. Drawing on the widest array of evidence, I have made the best case I can. And although I strongly believe in the conclusions drawn, I don't present them here as some final "theory of everything"—that holy grail of the modern mind-set, whether in physics, philosophy, or political science—but offer them instead as a preliminary sketch, with an open invitation to those who engage it to revise its shape as they see fit.

That help is doubly needed. By its very nature, any successful revision of commonsense thinking can only occur through the richest forms of collaboration. And too, I freely confess that, as someone raised on the tacit presumptions of modern reasoning, I have yet to assume a task more elusive than freeing myself from the comfy confines of a common sense whose default calibrations of the good, the true, and the beautiful—however dated—still *seem* natural.

Whether or not I have succeeded here in escaping those confines, I can't conceive of a more urgent mission. Rather than the threat of Islamic terrorism or even the rise of China's authoritarian capitalism, the greatest long-term challenge to the survival of American democracy is the necessity of our nation's reforming itself for a post-modern age that its own inventions have been generating.

Will our collective wisdom ever catch up with our accelerating cleverness? Can we achieve a civilizing conscientiousness appropriate to the age without imploding first into yet another round of anarchic fury? The historical record is littered with the wreckage of societies that failed similar tests, and as the violence of its annals vividly reminds us, failures of the communal imagination eventually have to be suffered in the flesh. Nevertheless, these pages do proceed hopefully, if in Václav Havel's stoic revision of that overused word. They have been charged with the conviction that we *can* "make sense" of this latest incarnation of the human predicament. To a modern mind weaned on the grandiose scale of utopian dreams, that may seem a paltry ambition. To do so, though, would be the first crucial step in a successful reclamation of the American experiment, for only when the sensible has been reliably sketched can new forms of the desirable begin to be imagined.

PART I
Idiot Savants

Case Studies in the Demise of Modern Reasoning

To think that thinking men should think so wrongly!
—Sophocles, *Antigone*

CHAPTER 1

Our Lord Ford

The Commerce of Disingenuousness

One who brings
A mind not to be chang'd by Place or Time.
The mind is its own place, and in it self
Can make Heav'n of Hell, Hell of Heav'n.
—John Milton, *Paradise Lost*

Today

"History is more or less bunk," Henry Ford said, in what is often presumed to be the purest expression of American anti-intellectualism on record.[1] Ford *was* an adamant anti-intellectual, someone who actively disdained what he called "living in books," but the dismissal of history, the antsy and often arrogant itch to escape its claims on both our cultural and individual sovereignty, has also been an animating force among some of the West's most influential intellectuals, people whose minds—having designed our marketplaces as well as our morality, having fashioned the very boundaries of perception and restraint—do enclose our "Place [and] Time."[2] People whose books, for good and for ill, we have indeed been living inside.

The certainty of closure can lure the questing vessel of human thought with the lethal sweetness of the Sirens' song. Even an apparently remorseless determinist like Marx needed to imagine a time when his relentless machine of history would stop, a victorious endgame through which the state would wither away, all social divisions peacefully dissolve. And when Communism collapsed, some of its ideological antagonists, in an eerily ironic reflection of Marx's Pollyanna prediction, were not shy about making an equivalent claim. Not only could there be a millennial "end of history," but we were in fact nearing that end, a climax signaled by the failure of Communism itself. According to the triumphant theory of American political scientist Francis Fukuyama, first pronounced in 1989, capitalist democracy rather than the workers' paradise was the "final form of human government." In this new "posthistorical" era that we were entering, human events would continue but because "all the big questions had been settled" and the glorious "end point in mankind's ideological evolution" had been reached, the basic nature of social organization was now complete. The ideal system of human governance had already been achieved and was none other than our own.[3]

Although far more learned, nuanced, and self-questioning than any argument by Ford, Fukuyama's thesis was still tinged then with the same missionary nativism (our way of life not only *is* but *ought* to be the universal way) that characterized the automaker's supremely self-confident attempts at social reform on a global scale some seventy years before—in a period during which, as we shall see shortly, Ford began using his enormous wealth and heroic reputation to proselytize a series of so-called ideals that ranged wildly from the admirable to the asinine to the utterly appalling. At some deep and (for him) inarticulate level, as much temperamental as intellectual, Ford's brusque dismissal of history as bunk is allied with Fukuyama's assertion that history can be settled or solved, that the human story not only has a logical, necessary, and predictable end but one that we can, somehow, live beyond. Each man's thinking emerges from a characteristically American disingenuousness that, in its delusionary excesses, can endanger the very democracy it idealizes. Each reflects an irrepressible belief that, perfection and completion close at hand, our cleverness will soon render us immune to the dangers of the past, to ruinous chance and self-induced folly.

During the decade preceding the financial meltdown of 2008, for example, mainstream politicians and the pundits who advised them evinced the belief that we had freed ourselves at last from the whipsawing swings of the business cycle. In an extension of Fukuyama's post–Berlin Wall triumphalism, prize-winning economists on both the left and the right were claiming then that the stock market would never crash again. As guided by a new cast of native geniuses—Bill Gates, Andy Grove, and Alan Greenspan replacing Andrew Carnegie, Henry Ford, and J. P. Morgan—our postindustrial expertise had fixed forever the glitches and bugs of the industrial era, upgrading our economy into a perpetual motion prosperity machine, and this confidence was shared by millions of average citizens who were buying both houses and stocks at rates shockingly unrelated to their historical value.

Such purchases were fueled by a species of hope deeply encoded in the national character. As first applied on American shores by European emigrants determined to free themselves from their oppressive pasts, it was a temper that drew on one of the core presumptions of liberal modernity: its belief that, over time and with effort, "things" (economies, personalities, technologies) do get "better and better" and the "new" will necessarily be "improved." This predisposition, as confirmed by the ever-increasing powers of our high-tech machines and co-opted by our consumer economy's investment in planned obsolescence, has led us as a people to tacitly accept Ford's overt rejection of history's claims. We may not know that we believe it, but we behave as if we do, tossing out old clothes, cars, credos, jobs—old families, too. To note this is merely to observe that our minds *are* changed by our place and our time: we do live in a throw-away society, a junk culture, and a junk culture not only invests in the notion but also operates on the principle that history is bunk.

Yet if we step outside our labs and malls and corporation conference rooms, if we turn down the sound and take a look around free of the schedules that tutor us daily, history seems less like bunk and more like a *bunker*. Even in an age of giddy high-tech progress, the recollected past remains our bastion, our basis, our bias; for good and for ill, it is the star chart that guides us. We are always, in some sense, living inside it: its systems, its forms, its buildings, its metaphors, and—all too often—its plots of revenge. Just as death is, quite literally, our physical home, providing the earth we stand on, the food we eat, the cloth and the wood that shelter us, so history is our mental home, providing the syntax and the substance, the methods and the memories without which we cannot think at all.

Henry Ford's innovative use of mass production, the orderly incrementalism of his Model T's assembly line, was already implied in Descartes' revolutionary *Discourse on Method*, first published in 1639.[4] Even Ford's scorn of history was preceded by that method's procedural skepticism. History's "bunk," including the very idea that history might be bunk, helped to underwrite both Ford's fortune and what passed for his philosophy. Nevertheless, when trying to tidy up his infamous quote, Ford still clung to the delusion of a personal immunity, the unshakable belief that *his* mind at least could be its own place. "I didn't say [history] was bunk," he corrected. "It was bunk to me. . . . I didn't need it very bad."[5]

Like most dubious ideas, the notion that any person or society can be posthistorical is a delusion, then, with a history of its own, and as my references to Descartes and Milton suggest, this delusion reaches back to modernity's roots in the scientific revolution and the Protestant revolt. Some of the sources of our current discontent can be traced, that is, to the very movements that gave birth to our democracy. Fukuyama's vision does bear a distant relation to Winthrop's "city upon a hill," with the spiritual mission of a chosen people converted into a political imperium on a global scale. The sovereign self, whose narcissistic claims are so prevalent today, was always a potential corruption of democracy's ideal, the self-reliant citizen.

Henry Ford proves to be an especially pivotal figure in these conversions and corruptions of liberal modernity's democratic ideals. Although he was one of the dominant leaders of the late industrial age, we can see in his persona both the vestigial remains of older American identities and the legible shadows of a new one encroaching. As his Model T became the prototype for a whole new kind of mass-marketed product (the literal and figurative engine for our debt-driven consumer economy), Ford's life of protean self-invention, self-deception, and media manipulation was one of the earliest examples of the new character being shaped to serve that economy. At the core of this apparently puritanical and plain-speaking leader stirred the makings of a now all-too-familiar figure. Narrowly savvy, morally suspect, and relentlessly disingenuous, he was an early corporate version of that character I have been calling the Idiot Savant.

Yesterday

Missionary Hate: Making the World Safe for Anti-Semitism

> Imagine for a moment that there were no Semites in
> Europe? Would the tragedy be so terrible, now? Hardly!
> —Henry Ford, *Eternal Jew*

Henry Ford did need history. Not only would a historical awareness have revealed all he truly owed to those who came before him; it also might have prevented him from inciting and endorsing the most dangerous political prejudice of his age. At the very height of his authority in the early 1920s, when he was the richest man in the world by far and so popular that a college student survey placed him, just after Jesus and Napoleon, as the third greatest figure in human history, Ford directed his privately owned weekly magazine, the *Dearborn Independent,* to publish a series of virulently anti-Semitic articles.[6] Let there be no mistake: despite Ford's later attempts to deflect blame by pretending he was unaware of its content, the campaign was both initiated on his orders and a true reflection of his bigoted thinking. Imagining himself to be a great global reformer and educator, a kind of mass-market moral missionary, Ford purchased the magazine with the specific intention of making it his personal propaganda organ—an ambition bluntly stated when he first announced his publication plans. "I am very much interested in the future, not only of my own country, but of the whole world, and I have definite ideas and ideals that I believe are practical for the good of all, and intend giving them to the public without having them garbled, distorted, or misrepresented."[7]

Highlighting his personal endorsement of the magazine's content, the editorial spaces were simply named "Mr. Ford's Own Page."

Ford tried to stress the high-minded nature of the project by refusing to sell advertising, by forbidding any coverage of his own multiple enterprises, and by a series of editorial positions that criticized war profiteering, jingoism, and corporate monopolies. Yet included among these "practical [ideas] for the good of all" was a revival of the notorious *Protocols of the Learned Elders of Zion*, a forged document "proving" that the Jews were secretly plotting to take over the world. For ninety-one straight weeks, despite substantial financial losses on the magazine itself, a Jewish boycott of his cars, principled opposition from mainstream Christian organizations, the best advice of friends he admired, and the protests of his son, Ford persisted in his campaign of ludicrous but dangerous vilification. The cause for all things bad, great and small, from World War I to short skirts to the decline in the quality of the candy bar, was laid at the feet of what he repeatedly called "the international Jew." According to this theory as it was elaborated weekly in the *Independent*'s pages, Judaism was not a religion but a race and a would-be nation, whose members were united globally in a conspiracy against all other nations and races. These conspiring Jews were somehow, at one and the same time, the secret financiers of capitalism (usurers who sucked the profits from productive gentile industrialists) and the authors of the Bolshevik revolution. They controlled the press, dominated the union movement, and had imposed the gold standard—three aspects of early twentieth century life that Ford especially despised.[8]

The magazine was only the beginning of Ford's proselytizing on this poisonous subject. Many of the anti-Semitic articles were collected into a book, *International Jew*, which eventually sold as many as ten million copies in America. True to Ford's aim of bettering the "whole world," this publication, most of whose copies listed Ford as the actual author, was then translated into sixteen languages, including German—there, under the title *Eternal Jew*.[9] Although scholars actively dispute whether Ford actually contributed financially to the Nazi cause, there can be little doubt that his racist ideology both influenced the movement intellectually and helped win it support.

The calendar here is extremely important. At the time when Ford's anti-Semitic notions were flooding Europe in 1921, Hitler had just assumed leadership of the new and still tiny Nazi party, and although clearly a racist, he hadn't fully formulated his ideology. According to Albert Lee's book-length study of Ford's campaign, "the connection between *Mein Kampf*—the blueprint for Hitler's murderous reign, which he dictated while imprisoned in 1923—"and Henry Ford's *International Jew* is blatantly clear. Hitler plagiarized from Ford and sometimes the very words that appeared in the *Dearborn Independent*." Ancillary evidence abounds: Ford was the only American mentioned in *Mein Kampf,* his life-size portrait hung above Hitler's desk in his Munich headquarters, and the Nazi leader later told a Detroit newspaper reporter, "I regard Henry Ford as my inspiration."[10]

He wasn't alone. Ford had become an extraordinarily popular figure in Germany, especially with the poor rural *Volk* who would eventually provide Hitler his base of support—so popular, in fact, that his autobiography became Germany's number-one bestseller. At Nuremberg, the leader of the notorious *Hitler Jugend,* Baldur von Schirach, claimed that Ford's anti-Semitism had been a major factor in his own conversion to the cause at the age of seventeen, and he recalled that the youth movement had used Ford's articles in its propaganda campaigns. American pro-Nazi groups and racist organizations, whose number and membership exploded throughout the 1930s, continued to cite Ford's articles even after he was forced by a legal suit to publicly disown them in 1927. (In fact, Ford refused even to read the recanting statement written by his aides.) The Nazi leadership itself so valued his contributions to their cause and took so little stock in Ford's retraction that in 1938, just a year before they plunged Europe into war, they awarded him their highest honor for a foreigner, the Grand Cross of the Supreme Order of the German Eagle. Created by Hitler himself, the cross had only been offered to four other men, including Mussolini. And shortly later, in an act that seemed to stress the specific reason for their gratitude, the *Reich* leaders presented their second highest award to Ernest Liebold who, as Ford's personal secretary and general manager of the *Dearborn Independent,* had been the primary organizer of the anti-Semitic campaign.[11]

All of this poses the very serious question of Henry Ford's culpability for one of the greatest debacles in human history. Although anti-Semitism had long existed in the West when Ford boldly assumed the role of global moral missionary, his *Independent* campaign boosted that baneful prejudice with the new ways and means of publicity and celebrity that were to characterize the electronic age. Even if we dismiss as unproven Albert Lee's reasonable suggestion that the very content of Hitler's racist thinking was influenced by Ford's, no one can deny that his global reputation as industrialist savior and friend of labor lent an aura of heroic authenticity to the rank resentments, paranoid plots, and vicious scapegoating that characterized both *Eternal Jew* and *Mein Kampf.* Ford's work, in essence, prepared an audience to receive the Nazi message and made the party's

extremist agenda appear more respectably mainstream. Recalling that
Hitler's assumption of power was by no means assured and only marginally
attained, we are obliged to ask whether the Nazis would have ever achieved
the authority to send the world to war without their implicit ideological
resemblance to the West's most famous and admired man at the time.

That is not to say that Henry Ford endorsed a policy of internment or
extermination in America. He continued to employ Jews in his factories
and offices, his exposure of the "plot" was never accompanied by proposals of active intervention, and the editorial policy of the *Independent* was
"that the cleansing must come from within Judah itself."[12] This much can
and should be said, however: the ideas that Ford so energetically broadcast were, in fact, an implicit invitation to political violence. If Jews were
maliciously controlling the press and the banks, if they were behind all
wars and were in the habit of seducing gentile children into drugs, drinking, and illicit sexuality, would a responsible society converted to those
truths really wait for the offenders to reform themselves? And to pose the
rhetorical question cited at the start of this section—would it be so terrible
to have a Europe emptied of Jews?—was to necessarily invite, from some
quarters at least, the toxic answer of ethnic cleansing. Nevertheless, however coercive the circumstances and dubious Ford's sincerity, he did publicly recant his anti-Semitic views, and although his corporate rule became
exceptionally autocratic, he never suggested the sort of violence that was,
from the very start, an essential ingredient in the Nazi mentality.

More germane here, Ford's performance in the 1920s supplies a partial answer to the most frequently asked question about the Holocaust—
how could so many civilized people collaborate in the implementation of
a truly evil policy? The example of this highly accomplished and distinctly
American industrialist moves us away from easy generalizations about
German character toward a more disturbing and transnational alliance of
mind-sets. No, Ford was not a Nazi, but like the Nazis he was an ethnocen-
tric anti-intellectual who nevertheless wanted to model the future after his
own ideas. Ford was not a German, but he was, like too many Germans, a
genuine anti-Semite as well as a highly gifted professional, and one can see
in that mix of subjective prejudice and objective cleverness—in that "idiotic savvy"—a psychological potential that would actualize into the Final
Solution.

In Germany, thousands of engineers, architects, and doctors applied
their professional expertise to the exercise of infamy. Given the right political context—a people humiliated in war, threatened by cultural change,
and buffeted by economic anarchy—the same might have happened in

America. Merging the opinions expressed in *Eternal Jew* with the organizational talent evident in Ford's corporate empire, one can easily imagine the design of a Michigan (dis)assembly line whose final tally of productivity would be Jews killed and not cars made.

The Pacifist Fascist

In one of the many revealing ironies that animate his life story, the likely source of Ford's bigoted beliefs was the frustration of his own adamant if ignorant idealism. The same moralist fervor that eventually led him to build model schools and villages, and that fueled his campaigns against jazz, drinking, and sexual licentiousness, had been expressed earlier through his well-meaning if naive opposition to World War I. Genuinely appalled by the waste of lives and resources, Ford spoke out against the conflict while America was still neutral, resisted converting his factories to armaments and, when he was forced to convert, made a very public and widely admired promise to return every dollar of personal profit that he made from the war. As the climax to this highly publicized and well-financed pacifist campaign, Ford commissioned a "peace ship," which, loaded with anti-war luminaries such as Thomas Edison and Guglielmo Marconi, sailed to Europe with the actual ambition of mediating a truce. The goal, Ford announced with characteristic grandiosity on November 24, 1915, was not only to "have the boys out of the trenches by Christmas" but also "to stop war for all time."[13]

Buoyed in equal measure by the good intentions and self-esteem of its participants, who in essence thought the publicity of their presence sufficient to reverse the course of war, this peace mission accomplished nothing, of course. Rocked by dissension, ignored by the belligerents, and much mocked in the press, this was Ford's first and most ignominious public failure. Accustomed to making the boldest of promises—unthinkable speed records, wage hikes, production schedules—which he would then not only redeem but moralize in the quasi-religious terms of the American dream, Ford suddenly had to confront the unique and indisputable fact of his own ineffectuality. Yankee can-do couldn't this time. And like many a true believer, rather than doubt his own doctrine—which, like all of Ford's missionary causes, had become inseparable from an overweening sense of moral sovereignty, his inalienable right to be right all the time—he would search for an excuse, would grasp for an exceptional reason why.

Later, Ford claimed that it was on the peace ship itself that a journalist (and a Jew no less) first explained to him how the war was being orchestrated by a group of Jewish financiers. The killing's continuation, against all common sense and Ford's own heretofore invincible will, was necessary for Jewish profiteering. The journalist later sued Ford, but what matters here is less the true initial source of his bigoted theory than Ford's own irrational will to believe it. In the absence of an intimate understanding of the past, which complicates and implicates, which invites a humility in the face of so many good intentions gone tragically astray—in lieu of the historical education he supposedly didn't "need," America's leading industrialist quickly embraced a paranoid conspiracy theory: the *reductio ad absurdum* of rationalized certainty.

That the man who didn't want to live "in books" would choose instead to live inside the pinched confines of a conspiracy's plot is not so surprising. The human mind does require its explanations, a way to gauge, to catch and then grade the messy flux of human affairs; and a mind trained to believe in its own neatly configured utopian schemes is most in need of a scapegoat to scathe when, once again, the millennium it designed fails to arrive on the predicted date. And so it was that the pacifist idealist came to inspire the belligerent fascist, and that "practical" ideals "for the good of all" became implicated in a poisonous doctrine, deadly to millions.

Front Man: Radical Materialist as Virtual Puritan

That Ford could become a pacifist who supported fascists did not exhaust the paradoxes cultivated by the purblind rule of his idiotic savvy. Further elaborations would include the "anti-historical historian," the "agrarian industrialist," and the source and shaper of them all: the "modest, no-nonsense publicity hound." There is no real contemporary equivalent to the public standing that Henry Ford managed to achieve through the teens and into the twenties. To approximate it in our age, we would have to imagine some amalgam of Bill Gates, LeBron James, Oprah Winfrey, and Rick Warren. This enormous popularity, of the influential sort normally reserved for martyred leaders or military heroes, was rooted in the tangible achievements of his industrial genius, including the first affordable car, the first five-dollar-a-day wage, and the first employee profit-sharing plan. But it was also the self-conscious product of a never-ending publicity campaign, a self-mythologizing in which vanity donned morality in the greater service of profit-taking.

Not just any myth would do. To market his Model T, Ford cast himself as a model man of a special yet familiar sort. He was "just" a plain-speaking, hard-working, straight-laced, hands-on, can-do, adversity-overcoming farm boy. Following the formulaic fantasy of a Horatio Alger plot, this public image told the story that Americans then, caught up in the stresses of industrialization, were most eager to hear: that of small-town virtue defeating urban evil even as it earned astounding wealth. His mythologized past reliably reenacted the enduring gospel of American disingenuousness, that paradoxical narrative where the virtuous man, rather than eschewing the life of plenty, actually and "innocently" achieves it. Where goodness gets the gold and still remains good.

Although Ford's genuine accomplishments, especially in the earlier years, should not be discounted, the falsities of his public persona and the hypocrisies of his moralistic preaching were multiple and often extreme. Borrowing the romantic notions of rural adversity and misunderstood genius, Ford claimed, for example, that his farmer father had forbidden him to practice his mechanical skills—a challenge to his advancement which, as his sister later testified, never happened.[14] Nor, as the myth had it, was the Ford Motor Company's success primarily attributable to his genius as a hands-on inventor or even to his skill as a day-to-day manager. As might be expected, the company hired excellent engineers from the very start, and although Ford was a true corporate visionary in his insistence on the large-production, low-cost, universal-consumption model of doing business, the initial triumph of the company over its many competitors arose in large part from its unsurpassed dealership-and-distribution system, which was developed by one of Ford's savviest partners, James Couzens.

Newspapers and newsreels loved to emphasize Ford's innate modesty—a key feature to the moralistic side of the public image he honed. As with many of the attributes that constituted the myth of the man, there was an initial kernel of truth to this compliment. Ford began as a relatively shy and inarticulate man who, having tasted the fruits of publicity, eventually became so addicted to adulation that he would peremptorily fire employees who attracted public praise: as all blame must deflect to the international Jew, all credit must accrue to the boss himself. And as we have already seen, his stubborn faith in the virtue of his pet ideas eventually assumed an arrogance of cataclysmic proportions.

Ford's discovery of the uses of publicity, however, also constituted his most unique contribution to his company's success. He was among the very first to realize the commercial potential of personal celebrity: that new variety of instant and all-consuming fame being ushered in by the age's revolution in information technologies, including telegraphy, photography, motion pictures, and radio. Many cite Charles Lindbergh as the first modern celebrity, and the sheer suddenness of his reversal from near anonymity to global renown after his cross-Atlantic flight in 1927 does provide a compelling example of the transformative power of electronic

communications. But Ford became nearly as famous more than two decades earlier when he set the world's speed record in one of his company's cars. And although he and Lindbergh shared an almost identical
public image—each was perceived to be a shy, solitary, can-do pioneer, a
new Natty Bumppo for the industrial age—the actual differences between
them were profound; while "Lindy" set out to break the record for a solo
flight largely for its own sake and then was stunned to find himself the
center of public acclaim, Henry chased the speed record with the specific
intention of generating publicity for his automobile.

As the man and the product merged in the single word, *Ford*, the
boosting of one automatically lent its luster to the other, and the owner of
both quickly recognized that egregious self-promotion held untapped potential as a sales technique. With his separate desires for self-glorification
and self-enrichment now merged into one, the automaker became the un-
matched maestro at generating what we now call buzz. David Lewis, who
wrote an entire book on Ford's public image, estimated that through the
twenties Ford's company received more than twice the press coverage of
any other corporation, and that Ford himself bested the coverage of major
magnates like the Rockefellers by at least a factor of five—a stunning difference. In fact, only Calvin Coolidge, who was president for almost seven
of those years, had more stories written about him.[15]

And unlike the company's achievements in engineering and management where the myth of his mastery concealed contributions by many
others, this remarkable triumph in public relations was almost solely due
to Ford's own genius at media manipulation. What he intuitively grasped
and then quickly mastered was the set of simple rules that would dominate
marketing in the coming era of mass communications. Ford was among
the first to realize that celebrity could equal profitability, that any attention in the press was better than no attention, that the outrageous and exciting "played" better than the merely factual, and that the fastest route to
winning the public's admiration was to hold up a mirror to their favorite
pieties so that in praising you they could applaud themselves.

Like Ronald Reagan long after him, Ford created an attractive image
for himself by trial and error. Whatever worked, whatever drew attention
and admiration in the press, true or not, became a new feature in the leg-
end of leadership he was inventing—or rather co-inventing with a press
that was always avid for copy and with a public who so clearly wanted the
Algeresque myth to be true. As Reagan could grow teary-eyed recalling
his visit to a liberated death camp when, in fact, he never left Hollywood
during the war, Ford could turn the minor embarrassment of wearing mis-
matched shoes into a fetching ritual of humble remembrance, informing

the reporter who noted the error that the accident was intentional: he wore the older shoe to remind himself of his childhood poverty.[16]

More than merely distorting his biographical past, these conjurings of a fictive self served to mask the most disturbing implications of Ford's commercial activities in the present tense. The very life of rural virtue that his character supposedly embodied, and whose principles he so stridently proselytized, was in fact being actively undermined by the product he sold. Few inventions have more radically changed the social and economic structure of the nation than the automobile. The desertion of the small community, the factory employee's supersession of the independent farmer and small shopkeeper, the continued subversion of plain-speaking and honest dealing by salesmanship and publicity, the material economy's shift in value from thrift to credit, and the moral economy's parallel shift from self-restraint to self-indulgence—all these crucial revisions of American life and character, which constituted the very sources of Ford's own success as automaker, he finessed and displaced with the image he staged of wealth achieved through the compass of moral simplicity. But if he (and the rest of corn-fed America through him) couldn't be faulted for the darker aspects these changes wrought, someone else must be to blame. Enter the Jew—alien, ugly, and all-corrupting—onto Ford's moral stage.

What constellation of abhorrent qualities defined this all-powerful yet paradoxically subhuman creature? The Jew was urban, when Ford's own factories were helping urbanize America. The Jew was decadent, a moral tempter, when Ford's own cars were providing the youth of America with a portable bar and bedroom apart from parental eyes and community censure. The Jew's ambitions were expansively international, when Ford himself had ambitions, commercial and ideological, not just for his "own country, but [for] the whole world." The Jew was a war profiteer, when (contrary to his very public claims) Ford never actually returned any of the profits he made from armaments manufacture in World War I.[17] Above all the Jew was a usurer, tempting others into indebtedness, when Ford's entire industrial empire was based on tempting America's middle class into the new habit of borrowing to buy.

Ford has been called a Puritan for his moralizing ways, but it is crucial to understand that he was not. A true Puritan would have searched for moral accountability within himself. Lacking what those early Americans believed to be the most essential grace—humility—Ford became instead a virtual Puritan, a man who assumed the rhetorical semblance but not the ethical substance of their spiritual life. He became, in fact, the very type of man whom the original Puritans most feared: the apparent proponent of the righteous way who, lacking grace, sinned against its light.

A common theme in the *Dearborn Independent*'s analysis was the "gentile front": groups of non-Jewish businesses and civic organizations that supposedly provided a cover for those nefarious yet rarely seen international financiers. Actually, though, Ford's own public image as Virtual Puritan was the real front. His moralizing persona provided a cover of attractive conservative plausibility that concealed a scarier series of radical actualities then overtaking American life. His image helped to mask, from himself and others, the real sources of change as, for good and for ill, modern capitalism revised the economy from rural agrarian to urban industrial and worked to convert the national character to the values required for mass-market consumerism.

As I Like It: The "Community" of Solipsism

> When Ford said "history is bunk," he meant other people's versions of history. . . . Toward his own history he was pious, not only personally but in a public way.
>
> —Gary Wills, *Reagan's America*

Ford's capacity to believe in the extreme contradictions that defined his self-conception was supported in large part by the extraordinary power he had come to wield, an actual commercial sovereignty on an unprecedented scale. After duping his partners into selling out to him in 1919, brilliantly manipulating the press to broadcast his bluffs and bully his opponents into compliance, Ford and his family became the sole owners of the age's largest industrial empire. He was reported to have danced a jig in delight when he heard the news that the sale had gone through, but from the perspective of history Ford should have gone into mourning. Although his populist image would survive through his death, most of his actual achievements as a uniquely worker-friendly corporate leader were now behind him, and the purchase, when combined with Ford's humiliating performance in a libel trial the very same month, spurred a series of ultimately destructive decisions, including his public campaign of anti-Semitism.

Ford was suing the *Chicago Tribune* for an editorial that, in attacking his pacifism, had accused him of being both an anarchist and an "ignorant idealist." Owing in large part to his own successful pursuit of celebrity, the trial became a spectacle on an order only later matched by the Scopes and O. J. Simpson cases; and when Ford testified in July of 1919, the *Tribune*'s lawyers succeeded in ridiculing him before an audience of reporters by repeatedly exposing an ignorance that would have been unbecoming of an average citizen, much less someone who aspired to be a global reformer and educator. This was the occasion when Ford's earlier statement that history is bunk, revived for ridicule by the *Tribune*'s lawyers, entered the national vocabulary. The millions of readers who followed the trial also learned that Ford didn't know the date of the American Revolution, that he couldn't identify Benedict Arnold, and that he was completely clueless as to the causes or the conduct of the War of 1812. In an extreme example of a Pyrrhic victory, Ford actually won the case, but he was awarded only six cents in damages, less than a penny for each of his seven long days of public humiliation on the witness stand.[18]

That was an unacceptable return for a man who had transformed a minimal investment into a billion-dollar empire in less than twenty years, nor did the image of class dunce sit well with someone who had sold himself as a native genius. The coincidence of the trial and Ford's assumption of complete ownership over his company proved disastrous. Rather than inspiring him to empower his genuinely idealistic nature with a real education, his experience on the stand only reinforced his already overweening desire for control, and now he had the actual authority to position himself so that his opinions could never be questioned again. This was the moment when Ford turned the *Independent* into his personal propaganda organ: if large newspapers were going to be permitted to criticize him unfairly, then he would create his own and, beating the press lords at their business, communicate his ideas directly to the people. This was the moment, too, when he began ridding the company of independent-minded executives, replacing them with a narrow circle of fierce loyalists, like Ernest Liebold and Charles Sorenson. As the dominant figure of his age whose celebrity had indeed raised him to the iconic status of royalty, Ford had already been dubbed the Flivver King (*flivver*: a small cheap automobile).[19] But now, free of any partners and employees who might check his opinions, and hiding behind lackeys who would reliably censor all countervailing news, the richest man in the world retreated inside a self-sealing kingdom of his own design, a Potemkin village of the mind, where he could reassuringly presume that his own will was equal to, and generative of, the way of the world.[20]

Shortly after wresting sole control of the company, the automaker chose to make that village into an actual locale. Returning from the mockery of the *Tribune* trial one day, Ford told Liebold that he wanted to build a museum, a place where American history—history as *he* knew it to be and not the bunk of intellectuals—could be fairly represented.[21] The germ of the idea grew exponentially, and soon Ford began construction of an entire ersatz community, Greenfield Village, where reality would never talk back or even tacitly correct his Yankee common sense. There, at his own birth site in Dearborn, Michigan, he would collect the birth homes and workshops of all the men he admired most—clever inventors, wholesome artists, priggish teachers—staging an array of "mangers," holy sites of origin for the industrial age. There, he would preserve all that was dear to him—the rituals of rural virtue (the carriage ride), the artifacts of industrial invention (early models of his cars), the reliquaries of scientific sainthood (a phial purportedly containing Edison's last breath)—but with the contradictions elided, the blemishes erased.

There, too, he would train the nation's youth "to live in the America of tomorrow" by the paradoxical means of educating them in restored one-room schoolhouses with the same textbooks that Ford had read as a child.[22] Fueled by his fetching delusion that the nation was returning to its rural origins, these schools, with their embalmed curriculum and museum-like setting, captured the inherently contradictory spirit of the place. Greenfield was a temple to technological ingenuity that repressed technology's social effects, a shrine to the value of rural life that denied such a life had already passed. Irrationally merging the qualities of a mausoleum with those of a World's Fair, sentimental recall with utopian plans, the village tried to mold the future to the past, enacting a story line where Time could stand reassuringly still even while Progress could profitably advance.[23]

Ford had glimpsed the moral trajectory of the modernizing West under scientific capitalism—its sinfulness and cynicism, its dehumanizing scale and anti-democratic skewing of authority—and wanted to reject it, but without acknowledging his complicity in that same project or ceding any of the power that it had awarded him. To claim that material progress and moral regress might be causally linked was as unacceptable to Ford as the *Tribune*'s claim that his idealism was rooted in egregious ignorance, and so he ascribed the darker consequences of mass-market consumerism to the Jew, while at home in Dearborn, he labored to stage corporate capitalism's version of the miracle play: the resurrection of virtue via the power of money.

The Great Gatsby, which was written during the very years when Ford was beginning his Greenfield project, beautifully captures both the allure and the danger of this now characteristically American quest for a material reclamation of the moral life. Just as Fitzgerald's hero wanted to believe that his lost love Daisy had never *really* loved her husband Tom, Ford wanted to believe that industrialization was not *really* destroying the family farm. Each man insisted an original innocence had once existed and, with effort, might still be restored. And so each invested in a virtual world—Gatsby's decorous mansion, Ford's demotic village—where his own highly dubious version of the past could be resurrected into the guise of a plausible fact.

But like Gatsby's wealth (which had been earned in alliance with gangsters), such romantic visions, however sweetly cast and impressively

costumed, are inherently dishonest, as corrupt as they are unsustainable.
As we have seen, Ford's nostalgic village was funded by a corporate fortune
completely complicit with the forces destroying the family farm. Worse, the
smiling face of his agrarian utopia was deeply dependent on the gruesome
grimace of his racist paranoia. To cover all the facts and construct a coherent worldview, the perfect virtue of Ford's rural Eden required the total
corruption of his urban Jew, and each of those radically reductive visions
could only emerge from the misty precincts of a magical thinking that was as
inconsistent with Yankee common sense as it was with scholarly exactitude.
Ford, after all, didn't need history "very bad." What he needed instead, and
very badly indeed, was the reassuring ease of an absolute moral certainty—
which is to say, he needed to put an end to history with all its inherent
complexities and ambiguities, its implicit demands for a self-accounting, its
reliable discounting of the naive and the vain.

From a psychological perspective, Greenfield Village was a concrete expression of Ford's intensifying solipsism, the aggressive overreaching of his
would-be sovereign self. Retreating to his hometown, he was now attempting to construct an entire community of compliance around him—one that
would be, tangibly and totally, *his* mind's own place. As a true map of that
mind, the village proved to be, as one critic had described Ford himself,
"deliciously naive and omniscient and preposterous."[24] Like the historical
"truths" Ford cited at the *Tribune* trial and those he was using to expose
his global Jewish conspiracy, Greenfield's restorations were often inaccurate, even at the most basic level of physical fact. (The house displayed as
the birthplace of composer Stephen Collins Foster, for example, had no
actual relation to the man.)[25] As with all forms of disingenuousness, this
carelessness with the facts concealed as well some careful intentions. The
problem wasn't only that Ford mistrusted professional historians to make
his purchases but also that he hired in their place a pair of company lackeys: Ray Dahlinger (his former chauffeur and bodyguard) and Dahlinger's
wife, Evangeline (a former secretary). When warned by his son that the
couple was incompetent and untrustworthy, Ford refused to listen. What
the Dahlingers lacked in expertise, they supplanted with compliance: they
would reconstruct American history exactly as Henry wanted it to be.

An inaugural event demonstrated this process of compliance with comic clarity. In 1929, Ford held an enormous banquet with the dual purpose
of honoring his aging hero Thomas Edison and celebrating the creation
of Greenfield Village. Many of America's most powerful people attended,
including President Hoover, and Ford hired an old friend, Irving R.
Bacon, to make a seven-foot-high painting of the event, an official portrait
depicting the hundreds who attended. The irony that a dinner for Edison,

mechanical genius and father of the electronic age, should be commem-
orated by an art form as archaic as the large oil painting was perfectly
consistent with the paradoxical spirit of Greenfield itself. A painting also
allowed Ford the proprietary control he so obsessively desired: Bacon's
project took two years to complete, in part because Ford kept editing
its contents—as, in those days, he could not have edited a photograph.
During his frequent visits to Bacon's studio, he kept revising the past, turning history's bunk into the bunker he preferred at the moment. His son's
family, quarantined by illness and so unable to attend the banquet, was
nevertheless included; the image of Evangeline Dahlinger, who did attend
but who was rumored to be Ford's mistress and so detested by Mrs. Ford,
was diplomatically expunged. Company executives whom Ford no longer
favored were erased while new favorites were added in their place.[26]

   This comic corporate version of the totalitarian's revisionist history,
where the past must relentlessly shift to reflect the willful wishes of the
present tense, vividly illustrates the characteristic operations of the sovereign self. The painting's history captures in slow-motion brush strokes that
cycle of constant censorship through which the facts of history are made
to submit to the fickle fiats of vengeance and whimsy. And lest we forget
that the amusing aspect of Ford's revisionary solipsism had its abhorrent
complement, the year of these events was 1929. The stock market would
crash just eight days after the Edison celebration, and the West would
plummet into a depression, one of whose effects was to be the dramatic
expansion of a certain party on the fringe of German politics. To the hundreds of thousands of Europeans who had read Henry Ford's *Eternal Jew*,
with its radically edited picture of the world, the vivid rantings of that
party's leader would begin to seem more reasonable. Assuming power just
four years later, that leader would harbor no illusions that the "cleansing"
of Judah could come from within. Instead, aiming to turn all of Europe
into a community of complete compliance, he would strive to bully and
burn the continent of Goethe, Kant, Pascal, and Pasteur into a concrete
version of *his* mind's own place. All too soon, and on an unthinkable scale,
the erasures from the portrait would become very real.

Tomorrow

Idiot Savant: The Scientist of Self-Deception

I have been examining Henry Ford because his particular personality, in
all its excesses and contradictions, exemplifies the long-term transformation of both the ideal American character and the modern reasoning that

once informed it. At once a palimpsest and a prophecy, Ford's life shows
us how the obedient soul of America's seventeenth century and the self-
reliant citizen of its eighteenth were refashioned to rationalize and serve
the industrial entrepreneur of the early twentieth century and, too, how
that industrial American was already on his way to becoming the "privatized" self of the consumer age: someone defined less by the community he
joins and the religion he practices than by the company he works for and
the goods he possesses, less by the credo he professes than by the things
he consumes and the image he projects.

In Ford we can see how the Puritan attempt to fuse reason with grace
into a kind of rational spiritualism was co-opted by the capitalist version
of rational materialism. He is an extreme and so too a revealing example
of the Idiot Savant characteristically produced by that applied philosophy: a man exceptionally brilliant in the very domains it rewards (management and marketing) while extraordinarily obtuse in those it would
ignore (self-awareness and moral reasoning); a man given to mistaking
mechanical can-do for ethical wisdom, and the controlled simplicity of
the laboratory or factory for the complexities of history and the inherent
uncertainties of the human condition.

Insomuch as Ford's disingenuous self-fashioning predicts the very
kinds of public deceit and self-deception that now proliferate, his example remains a cautionary one. In particular, by mapping Ford's mind and
reconsidering Fukuyama's theory of the "end of history" alongside that
map, we can see how "reason panders will" under scientific capitalism—
how disingenuous deceit is made to seem reasonable by being touted as
scientific. Ford's reasoning, for example, began with the classic Cartesian
stance of total skepticism: all past truths were held suspect until approved
by him—history was, presumptively, bunk. Freed of tradition with all its
caveats and prohibitions, Ford could then arm himself with those supposedly hard facts that, once proven true in the here-and-now, needn't be
questioned again. Initial skepticism led ironically to a confident certainty,
which then justified an aggressive intervention as he applied his "definite
ideas and ideals that [were] practical for the good of all." The Flivver King
imagined himself to be that sort of can-do pragmatist whose irrefutable
facts and know-how methods could crack the back of any human problem:
a romanticized version of the Yankee engineer still glorified today when,
lost in the delusions of privatization, we go begging to CEOs to fix welfare,
mend families, and save the day for public education.

Playing the grand theorist to Ford's gritty empiricist seven decades later,
Fukuyama graphed the broader outlines of human progress. Where the
engineer confidently fixed, the theorist assertively predicted by borrowing

the authoritative models of scientific thought. Fukuyama's theory assumed that political ideology passes through an epigenesis equivalent to physiological development, that *political economy recapitulates ontogeny* as human society moves through a series of phases to a final stage of maturity—the potent adulthood of free-market democracy. Under such a scheme, political science is presumed to be a physical science, enacting a process through which the basic questions of human governance, like those of chemistry or botany, could be finally and irrefutably solved.

The continuing allure of these closely related "empirical" and "theoretical" solutions, both of which blur the distinctions between moral and material realities, should be obvious. By asserting a calculable and cumulative certainty, they promise us an ever-expanding license to control—to predict and to fix infallibly—and so offer us an escape from the anxieties that naturally attend the human condition. Living inside the minds prescribed by those solutions (ones "not to be chang'd by Place or Time"), we don't have to heed the past, because history is bunk, nor worry about the future, because its "end" is both near at hand and dearly familiar—either the way we already are (Fukuyama's thesis) or the way we purportedly were (Ford's Greenfield Village). All the inherent strangeness of existence, its wonder and its danger, the confusing turmoil of its flux, is neatly expunged—not from the reality of our lives but from the compass of our thought. This is an enlightenment that, in fundamental ways, keeps us in the dark.

No notion was more thoroughly and bloodily refuted in the twentieth century than Ford's belief that we can scientifically engineer a social paradise. Against Fukuyama's thesis we can also point to a lesson from the past—one taken, ironically, from science itself. By the end of the nineteenth century, physics too was thought to be on its last lap toward confident closure. Self-congratulatory practitioners believed that much of the history of science prior to the seventeenth century was bunk, that all the "big questions had been [subsequently] settled" in Newtonian terms, with just a few puzzling experimental anomalies to be resolved. As it turned out, of course, the resolution of those anomalies led to the deracinating discoveries of relativity and quantum theory. The confident prediction of the "end of physics" was proven true, but only in the ironic sense. The end arrived not with the fulfillment of the modern worldview but its sudden supersession—with the demechanization of Newton's clockwork universe by the counterintuitive claims of Albert Einstein, Niels Bohr, and Werner Heisenberg.

If the physics analogy holds, then the claim that we have reached the end of history will also become true only in the ironic sense: the future won't bring the permanent triumph of free-market democracy but its radical revision or supersession. The fall of Communism may be only the first stage in the collapse of all the social institutions configured by the confident presumptions of modern reasoning. Just as democracy and capitalism slowly emerged from the intellectual revolution spawned in part by Descartes, Bacon, and Newton, they may now slowly dissolve as that revolution is revised by *post*-modern methods, measures, and values. The "completion" of this historical era may actually mean the exhaustion of its terms, the depletion of its forms. And the communal imagination, if still enclosed by those terms and forms, will fail to recognize the shape of the shadows now encroaching. Our future arriving unforewarned, we will neither accurately name nor intimately know the nature of the new beast that, risen from history's engendering sleep, now "slouches toward Bethlehem to be born."[27]

After Our Lord Ford: The Brave New World of Consumerism

The final caution, however, is far more personal and present. One of the most insidious aspects of the mind's own place is that its dissociations can allow us a degree of analytical clarity even while fooling us into feeling that we are somehow immune to our own critique. To merely refute the theory, or mock the folly, or defer the worry to the next symposium on futurology will not do, then. Henry Ford lives—in the shapes of our places, in the folds of our minds. The allure of his Puritan image may have faded but not its animating force: the urge to moralize money-making. Now as then, we are driven to find the good in the gold of our economy's engine.

Even Bill Gates, a relative dunce in the high-stakes game of public relations, has received the blessing of our compulsive justification: the Super Nerd has been assigned—by default, as it were—the role first assumed by the Flivver King. Although their differences are great (Ford pursued and enjoyed celebrity, Gates does not; Ford despised monopolies, Gates created one of the great monopolies in corporate history), a single similarity trumps them all. Just like Ford, Gates won the race to commercialize the latest revolutionary technology, becoming in the process the richest man in the world by far; and in a nation whose virtual religion is Christianity but whose actual practice is mammonism, this fact alone is sufficient to award him the Ford-like status of a secular sainthood—a status now also being granted to his heirs apparent, Google's Sergey Brin and Larry Page, and Facebook's Mark Zuckerberg.

It is no surprise, then, that editors, anchors, and politicians alike have oozed the unction of their flattery on Microsoft's founder. In their email interviews and real-time audiences, they plead for him to read the richly formatted text of the future and then sprinkle the air with the oracles of righteous acquisition. One Seattle newspaper even went so far as to dub Gates and his then-right-hand man as the Plato and Aristotle of our digital age. And all this was before the Microsoft leader jump-started his image by infusing multiple billions into a self-redemptive campaign of philanthropy.

One shouldn't begrudge any emergence of generosity from a political economy as morally smug as our privatizing one. Although the impact to date of Gates' foundation on public education has been disastrous, it may yet work wonders in other fields—I certainly hope that it does.[28] But any serious look at his publicized opinions shows, once again, that our habit of equating wealth with wisdom is less a bankable truth than a vapid superstition. To read this Plato's prophecies is to confront a vision of numbing banality: a life enclosed by smart cars and intelligent homes with precocious toaster ovens that remember our preference for extra crispy English muffins, a life in which we will never need to set the thermostat again. When we enter a room, invisible chips as sensitive as mood rings will read our current temper and, selecting from a menu of our very favorite things, automatically supply the palliative or stimulant the moment requires. Our mere presence will command, without the flick of a hand or a calorie burned, *Let there be light!* . . . or heat or food, or a nostalgic tune by Three Dog Night.

What Gates sees when he glimpses Ford-like into the future is Greenfield Village digitized: a portable sovereignty in which each of us shall be surrounded by the globe of his personal preferences made instantly visible, palpable, audible. He imagines a sensorium of complete compliance to the sovereign self's will—a virtual conjuring of the mind's own place. Few seem to question who rules whom in this vision of remote-control solipsism. Few seem to note that in this fast approaching world the poles of ambition have actually been reversed so that our machines are now seeking to "know" us. Nor do many pause long enough to ask whether this latest approach to achieving the good life is at all compatible with the founding ideal of the West's first approach, which was, it seems almost quaint to recall in this age of "maximum deniability" and self-promoting spin, *Know thyself.*

Aldous Huxley was among the first to map the scary potential in scientific capitalism's consumerist miracle. In *Brave New World* (1932) he satirized the society of mindless, soulless satiation that, even in the midst of the Depression and during the rise of fascist militarism, he knew was coming. A Briton who would later immigrate to America, Huxley saw in the very cradle of Western liberty the emerging patterns of its self-cancellation: the erasure of individuality by the profit-driven schedules of capitalist technology, and the evisceration of freedom by the fiats of pleasure. In Huxley's fictive dystopia, the uncertainties of fate had been solved by eugenic procreation, the enfeeblements of old age by euthanasia. Test tube babies, mass-produced and institutionally raised, required no families, whose exclusive bonding was disruptive anyway to the harmony of the culture at large. Most of life's pains, anxieties, and disagreements had been masked or erased by a compulsory schedule of promiscuity, pharmacology, and entertainment: getting laid, getting high, playing multiple games, taking long vacations, shopping day and night—and all while the mind was perpetually bathed in the dulcet propaganda of conformity for comfort. In Huxley's World State, the machinery of society hummed happily along, purged of all dissension, while the motions of the mind, enclosed within a bubble of engineered pleasure, were never disturbed by an independent thought.

Set six hundred years into the future, this society felt no need to conceal its materialist vision beneath an image borrowed from the agrarian tribes of Socrates or Jesus, with their outmoded insistence on fidelity, honesty, frugality, and self-sacrificial love. Looking backward from their platform in time, the leaders had spied a new savior, the true founder of their way, and that founder was Henry Ford. Not the Virtual Puritan but the radical materialist. Not the ineffective scourge of sex, drinking, and jazz but the potent father of mass production for universal consumption, and so the father, too, of the virtues that such a political economy actually requires.

This World State's hymns, prayers, and rituals were dedicated to Our Lord Ford, and its calendar was marked by a new pivot point in human events, B.C. and A.D. replaced by Before and After Ford. On their list of holy sites, the hill of Calvary had been supplanted by a factory in Detroit, for in their story of rebirth (the one that replaced our myth of the Cross), the new covenant had been written in 1908, the date the Model T had been launched. In Huxley's vision, the arrival of Ford's flivver marked the crucial division: before and after the "end of history."

Although less than a century has passed since the novel first appeared, we might ask ourselves to what degree our laugh-track/Muzak/Prozac nation, through following Ford, has already achieved the fundamental mindlessness of Huxley's vision: with cosmetic surgery to hide the tracks of history, cosmetic pharmacology to mask the emotive meaning of events, cosmetic entertainment to kill time and prevent reflection, and a pervasive pursuit of material comfort and sexual freedom, both of which have loosened the exclusive ties of the nuclear family. Even the smiling face of eugenics now lurks at the door in the form of the Human Genome Project, while Michigan's latest Yankee engineer, Dr. Kevorkian, bequeathed us the prototype of a portable, affordable suicide machine: euthanasia reconceived as a potential home appliance. How soon, we might ask, before some virtual physician—say, one of the old TV stars from *E.R.* or *Grey's Anatomy*—is hired to hawk it on the Home Shopping Channel?

And how many of us today, if called to the stand, could list the causes of the War of 1812 or even name our nation's founders, those presidents whose "day" is largely celebrated by the pseudo-events of salesmanship? As Huxley might have predicted, the bunting of patriotism now blesses the bounty of car-lot bargains. Ford's Lincoln has supplanted history's in the vestry of our collective imagination.

We tend to acknowledge all of these things—and yet, tightly ensconced within our mind's own place, we still discount their effect on us and ours. We forgive them, as the nation forgave Ford his anti-Semitism, by forgetting them in the practical sense. In the tacit testimony of our daily acts, we too continue to insist that we don't need history "very bad." The new *new-and-improved* will surely solve the sins of the old—this is our faith, the credo that prevails in these years After Ford. And so, perpetually linked to *hope .com*, we busy our days with sugar-plum visions of super cyber-sex, or a genetic quick-fix to the "problem" of death, or a post-historical, post-ethical, post-logical prosperity: a riskless rise via Viagra's resurrections and NASDAQ's magic carpet ride. As they did for Gatsby, such glints of gold continue to supply us with "a satisfactory hint of the unreality of reality, a promise that the rock of the world [is] founded securely on a fairy's wing."[29]

Sovereignty as a Single-Occupancy Vehicle

FIRST HYMN OF SOLIDARITY
Ford, we are twelve; oh, make us one,
Like drops within the Social River;
Oh, make us now together run
As swiftly as thy shining Flivver.

—Aldous Huxley, *Brave New World*

But the times *have* changed, a respondent might say. We do live in the *post*industrial age. The temptation is to insist that life configured by the rock of the roadway has little to say to a future taking flight on the fairy wing of the information skyway; the temptation, in short, is to forget Ford's example—but in the very act of doing so, we ironically assure his relevance by repeating the worst that the man represents. Yes, change is real, but so is continuity. We do still live *in* history, which is to say that our future will be fashioned consciously or not—the choice is ours—from the stuff of our past. If we truly wish to gauge the brave new world of the digital age, we would do well to reconsider the living legacy of the automobile, for it was Ford's Model T, arriving just as rapidly as Gates' PC and wrapped in a similar utopian hype, that initiated the conversion to consumerism which Silicon Valley now aims to complete.

That legacy is mixed. On the positive side, there can be no denying the material bounty bequeathed to us by scientific capitalism, and by Henry Ford specifically: the savvy as well as the idiocy of the Idiot Savant. No individual was more responsible for making the automobile available to the general public than this self-described Yankee mechanic, and no industrial product has more fused with the American identity, its central ideal of empowered individuality, than the privately owned car. Our emigrant sensibility, that powerful urge to wrest control of one's destiny through freedom of movement, has its most compelling instrument in the automobile, with its instant and easy mobility. The seductive invitation to sail to the New World or "Go West, young man" of earlier eras becomes "hit the road" in ours, months of preparation now reduced to a half hour's packing. That the allure of mobility is still central to our self-definition can be demonstrated by one simple and, I believe, irrefutable observation: most teenagers today consider their driver's license, and not their voter registration card, as the real emblem of arrival into socially sanctioned American adulthood.

Such a comparison, though, also suggests the ambiguity of the automobile's legacy, and that of scientific capitalism on a broader scale, even in its new web-linked guise. In the very act of empowering us individually, many of this economy's products and practices have isolated us from the intimacies, both pleasurable and dutiful, of a democratic community. This uneasy truth is pressed to mind dramatically for me whenever I drive on the freeways around my Seattle home. Thanks in part to Our Lord Gates, the region has long been a high-growth area, with the traffic as a consequence increasingly congested. As in most cities, High Occupancy Vehicle lanes have been added to induce carpooling, and in most sections the definition of "high occupancy" has been reduced to two to sweeten the incentive. Just a single passenger will admit a driver into the promised land of the open highway, with the added benefit of actual human companionship.

Nevertheless, some habit of mind, gravity of will, or grid of social circumstance—some pandemic but unmarked idiocy—prevents us from enjoying this double reward of mobility and fraternity. On most weekdays, it seems that more than 90 percent of the cars on the road are "single-occupancy vehicles." At those times when, a son or two at my side, I'm allowed to speed by in the HOV lane, I wonder at this picture of contemporary

America: the puzzling pathos of all these sleek and slope-lined machines trapped in stop-and-go traffic, their four-wheel drive, all-terrain axles as irrelevant there as wings in water, their infinitely adjustable second bucket seats unoccupied, no fond face to pillow from harm with their passenger-side airbags.

The wealth implicit in this array is as astonishing as the technology is impressive, yet my awe at this vision of material accomplishment can't erase the troubling awareness that each glistening car is also a cell of solitude. So many sovereign selves, each in his or her "own place," each caught up in the "Social River" of "shining flivvers" and yet each alone. This serial image, cell after cell blinking by, suggests the strangest sort of prison: the posh yet increasingly solitary confinement that is the legacy of consumerism, each of us enclosed in the Greenfield Village of our sovereign wishes made manifest, each a king or queen whose very ascension also enacts a kind of banishment.

Clicking on *hope.com*, I try to believe then what we've been trained to believe—that the new technology will fix the old, that the gadgets of our Gateses and Zuckerbergs, our Brins and Pages, will soon reconnect us into a village of intimate neighbors. But then I remember that the car itself was first sold to us as a miraculous vehicle of humane connection. Reminded by history that our future, like Gatsby's, will not be built from our fairy-wing dreams but from the ideas and ideals that we actively practice and so actually esteem, I am struck by a counter prophecy. As I pass car after car in our stalled Social River, I suffer a vision in which all our virtual changes will only serve to enforce a perpetual stasis. More conformity without company. More pleasure without purpose. More material empowerments that morally entrap us. Ford after Ford after Ford after Ford . . .

And I wonder then, momentarily freed by the gift of my children's company, if this passage in the Single-Occupancy Vehicle lane is really the brave new world that we hoped it would be.

CHAPTER 2

Echo and Narcissus

The Art of Anesthesia

> What has our culture lost in 1980? . . . Above all the sense
> that art, in the most disinterested and noble way, could
> find the necessary metaphors by which a radically changing
> culture could be explained to its inhabitants.
>
> —Robert Hughes

As DRIVEN BY THE commercialization of everyday life and the rationalization of everyday thought, the emergence of an "idiotic savvy" in American life was not limited to the disingenuous schemes of self-promoting billionaires. Like its eventual Cold War rival in the East, modern capitalism was rooted in a rational materialist philosophy whose inner logic was geared to reconceive the whole of society in economic terms. As a consequence, most of the professions and practices of American life—including the arts, my topic here—were, over time, reassessed and revised by and for "the numbers" in a reductive merger of method and motive that I call *quantiphilia.*

Although this turn toward the mercenary began after the Civil War, the invasive nature of the changes under way and their broader impact on the national character didn't become evident until the 1920s, when American commerce began investing heavily in the mass-marketing of consumer products. Corporations had always demanded strict obedience from their employees, but they had a huge stake now in directing behavior beyond the workplace as well. To change the hearts and minds of the populace in ways that would induce them to buy an ever-increasing list of products and services, the crisp rigor of authoritarian management would have to be supplemented by the coy rhetoric of permissive persuasion.

This was propaganda by another name, and the challenge was two-fold: corporate America had to craft a convincing message and it had to secure an effective means to project that message into the public sphere. The message itself was a challenge because, in turning toward consumerism, the moral logic of the system was becoming incoherent. Avidity, impulsiveness, sexuality, rebellion against authority—many of the very moods and motives that were most effective in expanding sales were not only incompatible with a traditional American ethos rooted in prudence and plain speaking; they tacitly undermined the submissive sobriety that corporate managers expected in their own offices and factories.

As we saw last chapter, Henry Ford modeled a way to conceal those contradictions. The veil of a virtual moralism in traditional American terms—down-home, plain-spoken, upbeat—was brandished to mask the actual agenda of a new, commercially driven mammonism. The arrival of the electronic media then gave corporate marketeers a powerful means to complete that conversion to an ethos of avidity. Broadcast radio climaxed a trend already under way by assuming a business model utterly dependent on commercial sponsorship. By the 1930s the differences in the communications systems of the world's two prevailing models for rational materialist governance were stark and revealing: in Russia, the Communist Party had seized total control over the flow of information; in America, all our news and entertainment was now being "brought to us by" the consumer corporation.

And so it came to pass in the postwar period that, even as the mythos of stoic independence, in the form of the lonesome cowboy and private eye, was dominating both the silver screen and TV's prime-time programming, the everyday expression of individualism was being reduced to gestures of rote consumption: styles assumed, brands bought and brandished, martinis ordered "shaken, not stirred."

Significant changes in social beliefs do not occur without opposition. From the eighteenth century on, resistance to liberal modernity's scientific worldview and commodifying culture had commonly emerged from two sources: religion and the arts. With differing points of emphasis, each had favored quality over quantity and had valued symbols and sentiments that a modernizing rationalism routinely scorned. By the 1960s, however, after more than thirty years of commercial saturation via the electronic media, meaningful resistance in even those fields was being co-opted by the same quantiphilia they once opposed. The enfeeblement of American religion can be traced in the evangelicals' shift away from the myth of the Fall to a "prosperity theology" that turned Ford's tactic of masking greed with grace into a sanctioned doctrine. The subject here, however, is the capitulation of the arts to consumer capitalism's tutelary gods, Mechanism and Mammonism, as those gods were named by Thomas Carlyle, one of early capitalism's most trenchant critics. And as with Ford, the focus will be on one influential figure, Andy Warhol, whose "idiotic savvy" both reflected and advanced major changes in his field.

First, though, a distinction made earlier bears repeating. I have insisted that we have been moving away from many of the presumptions of our foundational past as the first modern society, caught up instead in an ambiguous transition between ruling common senses now a century in the making. We are indisputably *post*-modern in the sense that we are living *after* the height of the modern era, but without possessing as yet a coherent consensus as to what ought to replace it. When using the hyphenated form of post-modern, I am simply referring to that transitional condition, with the aim of eventually replacing the term with a more revealing one, *conscientious thinking*. The *un*hyphenated version in the following pages refers, however, to the more common meaning—to a specific set of *postmodern* ideas, attitudes, and aesthetic forms that, emerging in the sixties, has remained influential.

Although diagnostically revealing, these ideas and forms have not supplied us with a credible replacement for a modern culture now in demise; instead, they are apt emblems of the sort of confusion that tends to prevail in transitional times. As such, postmodern art provides another revealing example, in a later era and a very different field from Ford's, of how and why our "thinking men" have been "thinking wrongly."

Self-Help: The Sayings of Andy Warhol

Although Andy Warhol has been dead for decades now, his name keeps resurfacing in the news, seeming to prolong his fifteen minutes of fame in perpetuity. We read of suits over the true value of his estate, disputes over the authenticity (and so the value) of yet another exact imitation of Disney's Mickey Mouse, legal arguments whose obvious irony is instantly dissolved by the number of zeros involved. More important, Warhol's ghost continues to haunt our nation's galleries. His once outrageous career track is now the beaten path to success, one religiously followed by the herd of the hip. When the occasion for assessment arises, it is commonly conceded, even by those who deeply rue the fact, that Warhol has been the most influential visual artist since World War II—some would even say the most influential artist in any field.

What concerns me here is not just Warhol's art, then, but also the character of the culture that has chosen to ratify it. I am seeking the internal logic, philosophical and psychological, which instructs that character, as exemplified by those who have either mimicked Warhol's work or justified his standing. Because Pop Art's arrival on the scene demarked the emergence of what we now call the postmodern sensibility, I want to plumb the motives and conditions that have been driving that sensibility. Why—to cite just some of the signal shifts in value enacted by postmodern thought—did parody replace parable, sign replace symbol, repetition replace originality, monologue replace dialogue, and the celebrity replace the hero? Why did salesmanship supersede craftsmanship as the *sine qua non* of artistic success?

As most postmodernists themselves would gladly admit, these shifts in value are clearly affiliated with recent trends in our economy, yet they also mirror scary patterns encoded in our oldest myths. More specifically, postmodernism's special obsessions recall with an eerie exactitude the fates prescribed for Echo and Narcissus—and these similarities, I believe, reflect a broader breakdown of self and society in an era now caught between ruling worldviews.

Surely, the separate but linked fates of the mythic nymph and youth are ones that most of us would hope to avoid. Punished for deceiving a god, Echo is condemned to never speak an original word again; she can only mechanically repeat the phrases of those she meets. The beautiful Narcissus, cursed for coldly rejecting the love of others (including Echo), is made to fall in love with his own reflection. With the one unable to express herself and the other unable to see beyond himself, each is estranged not only from reciprocal love but from *any* form of intimate exchange. Each is destined to pine away in a perpetually punishing loneliness that metaphorically suggests the increasing isolation of American life.[1]

To make my case that their grim mythic fate also maps the postmodern story, I will turn first to Warhol himself, citing a series of his opinions on art, romance, and emotional well-being that I will refer to throughout this chapter—all of them, unless otherwise indicated, taken from *The Philosophy of Andy Warhol*, a blithe combination of self-help manual and autobiography.[2] Here, then, are some savvy morals, maxims, and self-reflective thoughts of the most influential artist since World War II.

On defining a personal goal:
I want to be a machine.[3]

A paradoxical self-description:
I am a deeply superficial person.[4]

On the power of negative thinking:
As soon as I became a loner in my own mind, that's when I got what you might call a "following." As soon as you stop wanting something you get it. I've found that to be absolutely axiomatic. (p. 23)

On finding the right spouse:
I didn't get married until 1964 when I got my first tape recorder. My wife.
My tape recorder and I have been married ten years now. When I say "we,"
I mean my tape recorder and me. A lot of people don't understand that.
(p. 26)

On solving all his emotional problems:
The acquisition of my first tape recorder really finished whatever emotional
life I might have had, but I was glad to see it go. Nothing was ever a
problem again, because a problem just meant a good tape. (p. 26)

On avarice, jealousy, resentment:
Basically, I go crazy when I can't have first choice on absolutely everything.
. . . I'm always trying to buy things and people just because I'm so jealous
that somebody else might buy them. . . . As soon as the TV cameras turn on,
all I can think is, "I want my own show . . . I want my own show."
(pp. 49–50)

The business of art is business:
Business is the step that comes after Art. I started as a commercial artist,
and I want to finish as a business artist. . . . Being good in business is the
most fascinating kind of art. (p. 92)

All art should be created equal:
I think every painting should be the same size and the same color so
they're all interchangeable and nobody thinks they have a better painting
or a worse painting. (p. 249)

On living in the moment:
I have no memory. Every day is a new day because I don't remember the
day before. . . . My mind is like a tape recorder with one button—Erase.
(p. 199)

On how to succeed in love:
A movie producer friend of mine hit on something when he said, "Frigid
people can really make out." He's right: they really can and they really do.
(p. 56)

Echoing Narcissus

Mirror, mirror on the wall
who's the fairest of them all?

In the circus-barker atmosphere of postmodern art, where acclaim can pass
with near-nanosecond velocity and artists feel compelled to seize the day
(the mike, the stage) or sink into obscurity, it is often hard to distinguish

between wry social satire and rank self-promotion. Take an example from the palette of David James Sibbitt that was completed some thirty years after Warhol startled the art scene with his knockoff prints of commercial soup cans and Hollywood stars. Purchasing a calendar whose every month was crowned with a different picture of Elvis Presley, Sibbitt painted over each image to make the king of rock 'n' roll resemble himself: from New Year's to Christmas, the artist's own features glowing large above the fiefdom of ordinary days. Was such a project a satire of America's obsession with celebrity or simply another instance of it? Was the artist borrowing the acclaim of the star (as an advertiser would) to sponsor his own career, or was he parodying artistic ambition itself, making an acerbic comment on our self-promoting age? Or given the fact that Sibbitt made a point thereafter of placing a self-portrait in all his works, could it be that, like a true narcissist, the man was simply obsessed with his own face?[5]

The far more renowned "appropriations artist" Yasumasa Morimura has taken such self-regard to a further extreme throughout his long career. He photographs the figurative paintings of past masters, including Rembrandt and van Gogh, and then through computer imaging substitutes his own face for all of the characters within the frame; subsequently, he rephotographs, retitles, and re-signs the altered work with his name. In the end, a canvas like Rossetti's *The Beloved* becomes Morimura's *Six Brides*, in which all of the women from the original now "reflect" the features of Morimura's face. And so it goes throughout the series: men and women, blacks and whites, seventeenth-century Dutchmen and nineteenth-century Parisians—all submitted to an egalitarian usurpation of identity, their facial "signatures" erased, just as Rossetti's and Rembrandt's names have been erased, each replaced with the artist's own mark, his logos of self multiply stamped like gorgeous graffiti from frame to shining frame.

Such a method expresses many of postmodern art's definitive features: its fascination with the technology of recording; its subsequent fixation on industrial-style repetition; its habit of using this echoing technique to mock high art even while borrowing that art's authority; its delight in feigning authenticity (Morimura often puts a gel on his photos to make them appear more painterly); and, not least, the extremity of its self-promoting zeal.

Although some defenders may want to find a redemptive irony here, the flagrant narcissism of Morimura's project, comic or not, has to be noted. Each photo in this series obsessively reenacts the *perceptual* imperialism of narcissistic pathology: that delusion through which every other face becomes the self's bright mirror, that desperate self-deception which rapidly turns each new (and potentially threatening) occasion into the same tranquil pond of self-infatuation.

More than godlike, the artist-as-Narcissus not only *makes* the whole world, he *becomes* the world, and then pauses on the seventh day to admire what he hath wrought. "I express Rembrandt's theme better than he did," Morimura insisted when interviewed about one of his shows. "I'm sure [a viewer] would say my work is better."[6] Just as he made certain that all the faces before him reflected his own, Morimura was "sure" that the opinions of others (in response to those reflections) would echo his own. Such self-confidence, however, is hardly surprising: that is what naturally occurs when you ask the mirror on the wall who's the fairest of them all.

Reading the Emperor's New Clothes

> If Folly link with Elegance
> No man knows which is which.
> —Yeats, "The Old Stone Cross"

But what if Morimura's photos are simply ironic or parodic? Perhaps I have missed the essence of the work by failing to appreciate its inherent humor. The art critic Peter Plagens, someone not given to over-praising Warhol clones, still manages to find in Morimura's photo remakes a rare instance of genuinely funny postmodern satire—an arguable stance, I suppose. More incredibly, despite the artist's boast of besting Rembrandt (cited in Plagens' own review), he also reads into the work an essential "modesty." The artist may be vain, Plagens allows, but not his creations: "What separates Morimura's work from the relentlessly hip products of his contemporaries is his wonderfully pliable physiognomy and good-natured self-effacement in using it."[7]

Reading intention into art is tricky, of course, and if the critic sees a good-natured self-mockery where I do not, we can agree to disagree and move on. But the claim to "self-effacement" is a newspeak howler. If we accept the *OED*'s first definition of the word, "the keeping of oneself out of sight or in the background," then Morimura's project is precisely, relentlessly, and (*I* would have thought) obviously the opposite: "self-*en*facement," to coin a word. And even if Plagens was correct in his reading of these self-enfacements' tone—that is, as self-deprecating rather than self-adoring—the artist still flirts with a mirror-image form of narcissism wittily captured by William Cowper's poem, "On an Ugly Fellow."

> Beware, my friend, of crystal brook
> Or fountain, lest that hideous hook,
>   Thy nose, thou chance to see;
> Narcissus' fate would then be thine,
> And self-detested thou would'st pine,
>   As self-enamoured he.

I sympathize with Plagens, though. The human mind makes judgments through comparison, and in the hall of mirrors that is contemporary life, where folly and elegance repeatedly mix, it *is* hard to tell which is which—even when you are supposed to be, as the art critic is, a specialist in these discriminations. Trapped inside our busy social sphere of barking sound bites and blazing signs, we quickly lose the real among the fake, and meaning itself is (to borrow a favorite term from literary theory) "problematized"—its clarity obscured and its intentions subverted by the denials of irony, the spin of PR, and the glossy lies of advertising.

A careerist exploitation of this atmosphere, so rife with interpretive insecurity, was the one real mark of Warhol's genius. He intuitively grasped the advantages of being literal in an environment so relentlessly "ironized": be obvious in a city of super-subtle critics and their anxious, over-active minds will assign your work a complexity of their own design; be naked in your ambition to become art's new emperor, and the viewer, desperate to "get it," will perceive a royal robe of deep intentions. In a society ruled by salesmanship where, in the place of contemplation, we are trained to think by rote association (logos, jingles, endorsements, sponsorships), the key to success was not *what you made* so much as *where you placed it*. As is the case for any businessman or savvy real estate agent, what mattered most to Warhol, then, was *location, location, location*—which is, after all, but another version of that sixties urge to be *where it's happening*. As the hip became hip by hanging out with the hip, objects became art by association—that is, by being hung in a place where art was "happening." And because *place* (as Warhol, the social climber, well understood) had a social as well as a physical dimension, the necessary "placements" included not only galleries and museums but also gossip columns and society pages.

All he had to do, Warhol understood, was supply a reflecting pond, and if he hung it on the right wall, every Narcissus passing by would be bound to find it beautiful. If the wannabe artist could just snatch the attention of the right journalists and critics, then every browsing Echo would multiply his fame by repeating what they wrote. It didn't really matter if those echoing reviews condemned or praised, for in the new media-mad marketplace *quantity of attention* had become more valuable than *quality of evaluation*. As Warhol, the adman, intimately knew, bad publicity sold well, too, and sales were what he was really after.

The quality that made Warhol unique in his day was not his cynicism per se but the totality of his willingness to apply these "deeply superficial" marketing principles to art's domain. His "originality" lay, finally, in the amount of attention he attracted and the money he made as a consequence. He intuitively grasped that by mirroring stars like Marilyn Monroe he could become a star himself, borrowing their glow and turning it into selling power;

that by associating himself with *Campbell Soup*, he could become a brand name too—the very sort of label that could give his product line an instant boost. The frigid can make out in the postmodern scene, where meaning devolves to market value. They really can and they really do.

Charting the Destructive Art and Thought of Echo and Narcissus

> Each image should deprive the world of reality; in each image
> the temptation of total destruction, of permanent entropy.
>
> —Jean Baudrillard

There are, of course, many other extreme expressions of visual postmodernism. I could review the work of the late video artist Hannah Wilke, whose 1996 retrospective was favorably reviewed in the *Wall Street Journal*.[8] (Wilke made herself the sole subject of her photos and videos; she usually appeared nude and was fond of appropriating quotes of famous people as background sounds, thus exhibiting characteristics of both Echo and Narcissus.) I could turn to the photography of Cindy Sherman, who, in the manner of Morimura, has a made a successful career out of costumed self-portraiture. Or, too, look at how Jeff Koons, formerly a commodities trader, extended Warhol's claim that "being good in business is the most fascinating kind of art" by hiring image consultants to promote his "brand," and by using assembly-line techniques to make large-scale kitsch that passes for high art.[9] (In 2008, one of his pieces, a giant replica of a balloon sculpture, sold at auction for over $25 million.) Yet, if I am to make good my claim that these examples are not simply comic aberrations but revealing exaggerations of forces at work in the culture at large, now is the time to broaden the analysis.

I believe that much of the art and thought in the postwar period, responding to an increasingly stressful and incoherent society, can be classified in varying degrees by the same disturbing duality defined above: either mechanical mimicry or obsessive self-absorption. This is not to suggest that Pop Art fathered all these various movements—I'm defining a zeitgeist, not demarking a lineage. Nor does my bipolar charting pretend to describe anything approaching an equality of accomplishment among the artists and writers it classifies. One can admire, as I do, the talent of poets Sylvia Plath, Robert Lowell, and Anne Sexton, novelist John Barth, and memoirist Frederick Exley (all contemporaries of Warhol) and still note with concern a common self-absorption in their subjects or styles. And, of course, there are multiple exceptions, artists who resist my simplified scheme. (In my own first field, fiction writing, Flannery O'Connor and Alice Munro are obvious examples.)

Nevertheless, I want to insist that this division has a descriptive accuracy in the broadest sense, mapping the postmodern forest if not all its trees. Further, I believe that this map reveals the impact of something fundamental and frightening about our environment: a cultural force field that has stunned and stressed and finally stunted our postwar consciousness in ways that reflect the mythic punishments of Echo and Narcissus. We began with Warhol's philosophy because his thought is the most direct and extreme expression of that consciousness, but as the following two lists demonstrate, milder versions can be found in every field.

Postmodern Narcissus: The Art and Thought of Obsessive Self-Consciousness

The general movement toward anxious self-absorption, so brilliantly analyzed by Christopher Lasch in *The Culture of Narcissism*, continues today in multiple ways, including our obsession with self-promotion, our fixation on celebrity, and our addiction to the nostrums of self-esteem.[10] In narcissistic art, the artists tend to become not only the maker but the subject, crowding out all other subjects. Or, through a host of self-conscious techniques they intrude on those subjects, repeatedly reminding us of their authority: I am making this—Me, Me, Me . . . The following postwar trends illustrate the many forms that Postmodern Narcissus has managed to assume:

- in *theater*, the rise of the *monologue*, the one-man show;
- in the *visual arts*, various forms of *exhibitionist self-portraiture*;
- in *literature*, the increasing popularity of *autobiography* and *memoir* over fictional narrative;
- in *fiction*, the prevalence of *first person point of view* and the increasing mistrust of omniscience;
- in *poetry*, the rise since the 1960s of the *confessional* poem (often more accurately called the *exhibitionist* poem);
- in *criticism*, the arrival of *deconstruction* and other isms through which the act of criticism and the critic himself often become the primary subjects;
- in all the arts, the rise of what I call *monadism*, the insistence that men can only portray men, blacks can only imagine other blacks, and so forth—that one can only see or know one's own sociosexual self;
- in *philosophy*, the popularity of an extreme relativism verging on *solipsism*, the denial that there is a knowable truth beyond one's own thoughts.

Postmodern Echo: The Art and Thought of Mechanical Mimicry

The general cultural movement toward mechanical repetition that be-gan with the mass manufacture of physical products like Ford's Model T has been accelerated in our age by the commercialized media, whose mass manufactured "information products"—images, stories, interviews, news—can be instantly and repeatedly broadcast and consumed. It has been accelerated, too, by the everyday acceptance of the camera, the tape recorder, and their digitized successors as authenticators of the "real." The postmodern art of mechanical mimicry is characterized by an ob-session with exact replication, by an absence of emotion, and by a re-fusal to interpret. The implicit claim is to an empirical objectivity and the cliché that *the artist is a mirror to the world* tends to be taken literally. Like Postmodern Narcissus, her apparent opposite, Postmodern Echo has found her way into almost every field:

- in the *visual arts*, various movements, including *super- or photo-realism, found art*, and the *appropriation* of commercial logos, star photos, and cartoon figures;
- in *documentary film*, the *cinema verité* movement;
- in *feature film*, the emphasis on *production values* (period-detail sets, realistic special effects) over meaningful scripts;
- in *fiction*, the *minimalist* story with its banal facts, cool affect, absence of meaningfully plotted events; and, too, the heretofore unusual use of the *present tense* with its emphasis on immediacy over reflective interpretation.
- in *drama*, the mimicking of everyday speech, with all its awkwardness, obscenity, inaccuracy, and inefficiency;
- in *music*, the rise of *minimalism* and *New Age* soporifics with their mechanical repetition of simple melodies and rhythms;
- in *all the arts* the prevalence of *parody* and *sign* (the mimicking of forms) over *parable* and *symbol* (the making of meaning);
- in *philosophy*, an extreme *empiricism*, one which insists that only scientifically measurable phenomena are real.

Some readers may doubt the breadth of the picture I have just charted, but the allied notion that postmodern art is intimately linked with the unchecked dominion of capitalist values is an opinion held by many of today's artists and critics.[11] The same association, however, tends to educe contradictory evaluations: where critics like myself see a complete capitulation to a market-based mammonism, supporters would assert the redemptive irony of a radical parody, a subtle and even courageous rebellion.

Take the example of Jean Baudrillard, who was quoted at the start of this section, and his retrospective analysis of Pop Art in the essay "Beyond the Vanishing Point of Art."[12] Baudrillard holds a neo-Marxist view of history, which allows him some acute insights into the distortions caused by Western consumerism. But his work also suffers from the ethical obtuseness of Marxism, its Pollyanna presumption that the social breakdown of capitalism must eventually result in something like utopian progress. His interest, therefore, is less in the value of art itself, which he tends to disdain, than in what he calls "the destiny of artistic forms," and he is especially intrigued with Pop Art "as it relates directly to the global euthanasia of political, ideological, and even sexual forms in our society."[13] By endorsing the "sanctification of merchandise as merchandise," Warhol, he concludes, "tends to become the hero, or anti-hero, of modern art, since it was he who pushed to the furthest the ritual paths of art's disappearance."[14]

Baudrillard's Marxist biases—that social forms have a destiny; that the collapse of those forms is irreversible and merciful, a "euthanasia"—are obvious here. But those of us who do not share the pretty presumption that the "total destruction" of our cultural forms shall clear the way for a paradise sure to come are left with some troubling questions. What are the deeper sources of this shared fixation on aggressive acts of eradication: the erasure of differences, the expunging of others' faces, the obsession with terms like euthanasia? Why would postmodern artists and critics want to insist that each artistic image "should deprive the world of reality"?

The need to make the outside world disappear by masking its existence with reflections of one's self, when considered along with the opposite yet complementary need to make one's self disappear by reducing one's expressions to mere reflections of that world, would seem to suggest a deep fear of reality. Or rather, a deep fear of *knowing* reality. Both the total self-enfacement of Morimura's photos (his *choosing* to become Narcissus at his pond) and the total self-effacement of Warhol's tape recorder (his *choosing* to become Echo in her cave) are symptoms, I believe, of a profound epistemological crisis that threatens the very possibility of an effective individuality. As such, these postmodern tactics challenge not just the aesthetic assumptions of liberal modernity but the psychological grounding for democratic governance.

Narcissus as Narcosis: The Aesthetics of Anesthesia

> Some say the world will end in fire,
> Some say in ice.
>
> —Robert Frost, "Fire and Ice"

Although Pop Art is often praised as democratic for radically expanding the range of subjects that art might address, its deeper motive force, as Baudrillard clearly recognized, is not populism but something more like nihilism. Its expansion of subjects semi-secretly aims toward a kind of extinction, its urge for *more* (breadth of subjects, quantity of imagery) actually expressing and effecting a need for *less* (depth of meaning, intensity of feeling). This claim may seem counterintuitive at first, but to see how such a strategy works, and how it directly relates to the epistemological crisis cited above, we need only turn back to Warhol's own work.

Following the hot emotion of Abstract Expressionism with its fury of splattered color and intense evocation of anarchic formlessness, Pop Art is usually defined as "cool." In fact, it is beyond cool, beyond even frigid, approaching an Absolute Zero of artistic temperament. In Warhol's work, Jackson Pollack's fire of the frenzied is super-cooled to the soothing ice of the near insentient. Intense expression has given way to emotive cryogenics, the mind shutting down in aversion to the world. This radically reactionary psychological mechanism was being defined by Marshall McLuhan at the very time that Warhol was first making his mark in the early sixties. Noting that the name Narcissus had its root in the Greek word for numbness, McLuhan coined the phrase "the narcosis of Narcissus" to describe the narcotizing effect of the new media, especially TV, on the postwar consciousness. In response to an unprecedented blitz of imagery and sound, the more fragile mind, he believed, would suffer a kind of peacetime shell shock: shut down, cool off, numb out. This state of mind would alleviate the stress of *too much, too fast* by radically reducing its realm of perception to a closed system of limited information. As with Narcissus, who can only see and react to his own reflection, this closed system would strictly enforce the simplest response, a perceptual on-off, reducing the human mind to a kind of machine, or "servomechanism" in McLuhan's scheme.[15]

Although McLuhan missed the connection, the mechanized numbness of the self-infatuated youth is also suffered in a way by the love-sick nymph. In the myth, Echo too is reduced to a psychological machine, a robot of response, suffering a parallel kind of self-erasure through a severe restriction of allowable behavior; she too is condemned to a state of emotional estrangement and paralysis. Oddly, it is just such a state that Warhol pursues. Claiming that he *wants* to be a machine, he actually chooses the nymph's imposed fate: her prison becomes his aesthetic, self-selected. Embracing Echo's form of "servomechanism," Warhol copies the world and then copies his copy again and again. An exact replica of a soup can becomes a hundred replicas (*100 Campbell's Soup Cans*) that then become *200 Campbell's Soup Cans*. A photographic copy of the *Mona Lisa* is then multiplied into four copies (*Four Mona Lisas*) that then become a frame arrayed with thirty copies, six by five.

Warhol likely would have claimed that this strategy was merely enacting his egalitarian ideal that "every painting should be the same size and color so that they are interchangeable and nobody thinks that they have a better painting or a worse painting." Yet the title of the multiple Mona Lisas piece, *Thirty Are Better Than One*, unveils the semi-secret motive behind these obsessive appropriations, their basis in envy, their adolescent claim to superiority. As a narcissistic Morimura insists that he is better than Rembrandt, an echoing Warhol proclaims that he is superior to da Vinci. But like the stalking fan who murders the star both to extinguish that celebrity's emotional hold on him and to borrow the glow of the star's acclaim, Warhol only tries to become the better artist through killing the earlier master's work. His repetitions are always aiming first toward an extinction of the original's aesthetic force. The quantiphilia of his *more* (thirty) succeeds in making *less* of the one unique image, diluting the painting's meaning and feeling, reducing the *Mona Lisa* to a form of decor. Like a bitter witch, abracadabra, he turns the prince into a frog, the Renaissance portrait into postmodern wallpaper.

Like any effective artistic technique, the magic of Warhol's more-is-less reductionism is based on a fundamental feature of human perception: namely, that excessive repetition actually reduces cognition. Just as any word starts to lose meaning when repeated aloud six or seven times, any visual image obsessively repeated is inevitably bled of both sense and sensibility. Through its multiplication, the once singular event (image or sound) becomes its own ersatz environment; the figure is forced to become its own ground and so ceases to be "figured" at all. Because human perception depends on difference and because these mechanical repetitions replace difference with sameness, the image or word literally disappears *into* itself. Awash in the field of its own simulations, the sensory event *self*-erases—as, revealingly, do Echo and Narcissus at the end of their myth.

Warhol's erasure of the *Mona Lisa* clearly emerges from an envy of the master and resentment of his status—a more flagrant example of Nietzsche's *ressentiment* would be hard to find, yet we miss Pop Art's diagnostic significance if we limit its motives to careerist ambition.[16] In fact, any powerful image, artistic or not, becomes grist for the mill of Warhol's erasure machine. Posters of stars like Elvis Presley and Elizabeth Taylor; news photos of race riots, car crashes, and accidental poisonings—although potent in different ways—are alike in their intensity and so must be, in Baudrillard's phrase, "deprived of [their] reality."

In *Jackie 1965* a famous photo of the shocked and grieving wife of our assassinated president is repeated thirty-five times. In *1947 White* an old news service photo of a young woman who has leapt to her death, her corpse crushing the roof of a car, is multiplied and increasingly distorted some twenty-one times until the image dissolves, bottom right, into an almost unrecognizable abstraction of melting metal curves. Precisely because this aptly named *Disaster* series begins with such intense emotional premises, appropriating the hottest of public images, it remains the most arresting and revealing of Warhol's work. Here, the artist's pathology, in all its excess, highlights an actual crisis in the culture at large: the need, as defined by McLuhan, to numb the effect of the electronic media's violently invasive imagery.

Warhol's method, however, is itself violent, relentlessly destructive to meaning and feeling. We watch as this postmodern Echo compulsively erases the emotional impact of real events, turning private and public tragedies into sensory nullities, so present that they are absent. And as we watch we begin to understand that Pop Art cannot really *make* anything, only repeat to erase; that its democracy is the democracy of aversion, not inclusion; that its primary temper is not playful and joyful, as some would claim, but driven and dreadful. Just as narcissism is not really an expression of self-love but a defensive projection born of pathological self-doubt, Warhol's echolalia does not express his love of the world but his excessive fear and loathing of it.[17]

To cite Robert Frost's fine poem "Fire and Ice," from what Warhol has "tasted of desire," he seems to hold with those who "say the world will end in fire." Against the terror of that ending, though, he refuses to compose a temperate zone where human emotion can survive, offering instead the ice of a hate that would freeze events in place, chill all desire. In the totality of this icy loathing, we can sense Warhol's terror of (and rage at) a social reality increasingly beyond his comprehension and control: his fear of the star's strong hold on the imagination, his fear of others' success, his fear of women and of sex, his fear of life's violence, and his fear of death. This complex of fears is so inclusive and intense that it blurs into a kind of mega-fear of feeling itself. It seems to express a loathing of that very process by which, through intelligible emotion, we come to know the world at all—a process, ironically, that is at its most compressed and intense in Warhol's own profession, the making of art.

And so, out of this fear and loathing, there arises in Warhol the paradoxical quest for an artistic narcosis. The task, though, proves all-imposing. To obey such an oversized fear, he must find a way to numb not only pain but also pleasure and wonder and lust, the inherently human hungers for beauty and meaning, novelty and love. He must find a method to erase all the signs that invite those (for him) unendurable desires, a defensive device that will keep on ice his fragile and overexcitable mind.[18]

What Warhol wants—and through his echolalia believes he has found—is an aesthetics of *an*esthesia. Idealizing insentience, he pursues anesthesia's literal definition: "a loss of sensation . . . without loss of consciousness."[19] This negative drive, this shrinking away from psychological engagement through a compulsive erasure of intelligible signs, characterizes not only the original Pop artist but also the subsequent pantheon of postmodern thought. And it describes, more broadly, a postwar culture of addiction and consumption that mirrors Warhol's methods, echoes Warhol's forms.

Transfiguring Dread in the Garden of New Forms

> Yet they . . .
> If worthy their prominent part in the play,
> Do not break up their lines to weep.
> They know that Hamlet and Lear are gay;
> Gaiety transfiguring all that dread.
>
> —W. B. Yeats, "Lapis Lazuli"

Warhol's realization that to think about the world can be emotionally dangerous is not new but ancient; it is the very truth at the core of the Western tradition, our Hebraic genesis. After eating the apple, Adam and Eve's first two acts, covering their bodies and cowering in the bushes, are purely defensive. Their new awareness ironically awakens a vivid sense of danger: only *now* do they know that they are actually naked; only *now* do they really believe that they will die. Our primordial parents are suffering from their own information explosion, and their first reaction to this rapid infusion of new knowledge is, like Warhol's, to hide from its consequences.

It is crucial to note that by doing so, though, they are enforcing their own punishment; for if Eden is not only a physical site but a state of harmony between place and mind, then Adam and Eve's very act of recoil has removed them from paradise. Their later physical expulsion by God merely formalizes the self-induced estrangement of their newly anxious state of mind.

In that the Old Testament depicts how our ancestors managed to recover from this aboriginal catastrophe, it has a special relevance to our transitional times. Living in an age of renewed anxiety, an era when our own intellectual reach has far exceeded our social and psychological grasp, we might reconsider the drama of the ancient Jews and the story it tells of how the human hunger for knowledge is made to assuage the very estrangement it initially caused. After the Fall, the Torah itself becomes the new apple, supplying the "knowledge of Good and Evil," the self-conscious pursuit of which Genesis first rues but that, irrevocable now, can only be managed by studying the parables and rules of a newly sanctioned knowledge. In the place of the natural garden, the Hebrew God is said to have given his people a moral one—a garden of forms, of covenants and laws, orderly and bountiful—to keep them from getting lost as they wander beyond the gates of Eden.

We don't need to believe in original sin to recognize the currency of the dilemma Genesis exposes. Millennia later, we are still driven by the rhythm of those same conflicting desires, dancing every day between our head's urge to step back from the world to better measure it and our heart's need to merge with that same world as our natural home. Seen in this way, all rational knowing becomes a kind of mini-retreat—expulsion?—from the garden of creation, but always with the hope of returning on better, or at least more predictable, terms. Like our mythical mother and father, we long to gain control without, somehow, ceasing to belong.

Even the promise of control, though, is never certain. Our intelligence can empower us, but its discoveries can also disrupt the hard-won harmony of the cultural garden that we have built to replace the natural one. Now as in our mythical past, rapid mental progress can generate social and psychological regress, revealing anew how small the self is in space and time and triggering a surge of existential dread. Fear this intense not only can alienate the single self from both society and nature; it can also destroy the very autonomy we seek through knowledge, generating instead a mental and moral paralysis, driving us to cower in the bushes, or to "marry" a mindless tape recorder.

These related tensions—between wanting to control and wanting to belong, between our need to know and our fear of what we'll learn—are universal experiences. Arising from the very act of knowing itself, with its partial separation of the self from the world, they are an animating force in every culture's creation. But they are especially intense in the modern West, where individuality and objectivity are highly stressed, and where technology accelerates the infusion of new knowledge, creating orchard after orchard of apples to digest.

The task of managing these universal tensions falls to any society's cultural forms. Our various ceremonies, rituals, artistic expressions, with their intricate protocols of restraint and permission, departure and return, are designed not only to domesticate the common physical tensions of sex, acquisitiveness, and aggression but also to mediate these intellectual tensions, so unique to us as the thinking species. Like the Torah for the Jews, our cultural forms replace the lost garden of innocent ignorance with a new garden of sanctioned knowledge—a garden whose patterned paths provide both a way out and a way back, the distance to measure and a map of return.

In a tribal coming-of-age ritual, for example, a youth is often intentionally isolated from the community. He is sent out alone into the wilderness but armed with a map of tribal lore—a set of charms, words, and tasks to perform—that will help bring him back, newly named and mature, into the tribe. In this case, the knowledge that empowers also joins; the boy learns in isolation *in order to* belong. Adam and Eve's expulsion has been intentionally reenacted, its anguish invited but also domesticated, the dread of separation both accepted and transformed.

Even in our own de-ritualized society, we can find eviscerated versions of the same civilizing pattern: in marriage, for example, where the sexes separate (the shower, the stag party) in preparation to merge; or in the very idea of the university as a sanctuary. More to the point, our artistic forms are also structured in this way, offering us the chance for initiation through a staged ritual of intellectual isolation. Even when attending a play or viewing a painting surrounded by a crowd, we are removed from the immediate reality by the necessary act of imaginative concentration. Mentally, we leave the world beyond the stage or outside the painting's frame; we gladly undergo an intense and often painful artistic experience—in Yeats' phrase, we "ask for mournful melodies" but we do so with the aim of returning to our lives renewed and revived.[20]

Insomuch as art offers us a chance for communion *through* knowledge, it is one of those forms, then, that can mitigate against the perennial danger of a permanent estrangement. Even as our novels, paintings, plays, and poems provide the very means that allow us to think as individuals, they help safeguard against the multiple levels of alienation to which we, as solitary thinkers, are always susceptible. They can ease the psychological separation of the head from the heart, the social separation of the citizen from the community, and the metaphysical separation of the single self from the rest of creation. "Transfiguring all that dread" without denying it, art's garden of thought revives the possibility of a genuine "gaiety"—an unsentimental, post-Edenic joy.

Denying Difference: The Repressive Logic of "Ironic Heroism"

> I believe in living in one room. One empty room. . . . By living
> in one room you eliminate a lot of worries.
>
> —Andy Warhol

For all the reasons analyzed above, the extinction of any set of cultural forms (as distinct from their reformation) is a potential catastrophe for both the individual and the community. This catastrophe is the "destiny" that Baudrillard both astutely recognizes and perversely celebrates, assigning Warhol the role of Dr. Kevorkian in this euthanasia of artistic forms, praising him for having asphyxiated yet another species of symbolic thinking—for, in effect, pulling the plug on the life of the visual metaphor.

When artist echoes adman and studio mirrors factory, when the image inside the artist's frame is exactly the same as the most banal image outside that frame (soup can for soup can, pop star for pop star), the very difference that divides in order to reunite is utterly erased. When the distance between art and life is collapsed in this way, no journey can be made. "Living in one room," we lose the chance for art's ritual initiation from dread back into gaiety, and this is, somehow, exemplary. "The modern hero," Baudrillard writes, "is the ironic hero of art's disappearance," and although Warhol's "decision to disappear [was] made almost too consciously, too cynically[,] . . . it [was] no less a heroic choice."[21]

But one can only delight in "art's disappearance" if, like a Marxist, one believes blindly in the destiny of progress. Only if one is willing to sacrifice the concrete here-and-now for some abstract eventuality, valuing the certainty of one's beliefs above the quality of others' current lives, can hastening the death of cultural forms be deemed heroic. That such self-certainty can invite not only personal foolishness but political calamity is a truth that was proven with bitter, bloody redundancy throughout the twentieth century by the utopian thinking of Lenin, Hitler, Mao, and Pol Pot.

And this extinction of cultural forms is serious psychologically as well as politically because without them we cannot manage the tension perpetually present in human thought. Without effective forms, the balance between our desire to control and our need to belong is quickly lost. Our existential need to know the real is overwhelmed by our fear of what we'll learn, and we begin to cling instead to mechanical regimens of false control. *I want to be a machine*, says Andy Warhol. *I'm sure they'll find me better,* says Yasumasa Morimura. *The mind is its own place*, says Milton's Satan, trying to convince himself that he can somehow make the Hell he has earned into the Heaven he still fancies.

Without effective forms, human thought ceases to be exploratory, instructive, interactive. The dialogue of knowing—with all its surprises, its dance between self and other, desire and compliance, its dual demand for accountability and creativity—gives way to robotic monologue. The reality of uncertainty, that "Time and Chance happen to [us] all," is replaced by the delusion of predictability.[22] Terrified by the actual smallness of our will in relation to the world's, we begin to pretend either that we have no will of our own ("As soon as you stop wanting something you get it," says Warhol) or that our individual will is more powerful than the world's (his mind, Satan boasts, "can make a Heaven of Hell"). We either reduce ourselves to machines, repeating the world's messages like Warhol's tape recorder, or we reduce the world to a mirror of our selves, crowning every day with the coin of our own face, like David Sibbitt on his calendar. In both cases, the fruitful but frightening tension between the self and creation is magically dismissed by attempting to deny the reality of the difference—by our choosing to become either Echo or Narcissus.

This is the "idiotic savvy" behind postmodern art, the perverse logic that drives its dual but equally delusionary forms. Each "solves" the crisis of individuality—our post-Edenic fate, much intensified by modernity's emphasis on objective reasoning, of being both *a part of* and *apart from* the rest of nature—by refusing to acknowledge the crisis exists. The dualism of knowledge (the division of the knower from the known) is "dissolved" by striving to ignore the reality of the division. And unlike spiritual revelation, this dissolution is achieved through denial, not transcendence; the aim is not spiritual intensity but emotional anesthesia. Fearful of the fire of experience, postmodern art too often pursues the sort of icy ignorance concisely expressed by Warhol's claim, "My mind is like a tape recorder with one button—Erase."

Except for a damaged brain, however, such a state of mind is impossible: to be human *is* to remember. It is especially impossible for the resentful personality, of which Warhol is an extreme example. When he says "erase," he really means something more like "repress." The memories don't go away; instead, they "disappear" behind Warhol's own false image of the mind as a machine. And this disappearance of his memories is actually a kind of strategic concealment. Like the worst of high-level bureaucrats, Warhol's head only pretends not to know his heart's secret motives and so allows those motives, unchecked, to have all the more force. The pretense of erasure helps Warhol to "forget" that, like most resentful personalities, he is obsessively obedient to the claims of memory, forever being driven by the painful recollection of someone else's fame, wealth, talent, or beauty. He "erases" memories, then, not to be free of them but to be free of *knowing* about them. He forgets the past to become all the more the slave to its emotional imperatives.

Likewise, Warhol "disappears" behind his anti-artistic echoes of the world only to boost his artistic career. ("As we know," Baudrillard wittily observes, "failing at suicide is often the best form of publicity.")[23] And he only "stops" desiring things to crave them all the more—that is, as a strategy of acquisition. He stops desiring things because "frigid people can really make out," because he has found it "axiomatic" that "as soon as you stop wanting something you get it." His surface passivity, like Ford's virtual Puritanism, only serves to mask a tyrannical avidity. As he later admitted and a literal warehouse-full of hoarded goods proved, Warhol really did want "first choice on absolutely everything." He wanted the whole of reality to be his "own show."

Paradise Re-lost: The Self-Imprisonment of Postmodern Thought

> Which way I fly is hell; my self am hell.
>
> —John Milton, *Paradise Lost*

But the only way to make reality one's "own show" is to lie about reality and to lie about oneself. The mind isn't simply "its own place," ever. We can try to limit what we know to diminish our anxieties, but we cannot limit what exists. This is why the primary tactic of the postmodern mind, so apparently liberated, is actually censorship: the obsessive pursuit of emotional control, along with the sense of safety it evokes, through the eradication of frightening truths.

But of course we aren't *really* safe—that is, safe in reality—but only safe in our own minds, in the mind's own (and highly censored) place. By constricting what we know instead of mapping what exists, we defuse our immediate anxiety at the expense of an eventual effectiveness. When art becomes deliberately opaque, for example, we are safe from the obligation of accurate interpretation. When parody replaces parable and celebrities supersede heroes, we are safe from being challenged by higher meanings and models. When all language is self-interested and all cultural forms are merely an assertion of power by social elites, we are safe from the pressure of choosing the apt word and the most just or generous form, from needing to restrain our own assertions of power. Under the permissive pessimism of postmodern thought, we are saved, that is, from the constant struggle to be thoughtful, truthful, prudent, and just.[24]

Although the disastrous social implications of such an investment in moral passivity ought to be obvious, its personal destructiveness tends to be masked by its own complementary conceits of immunity and mastery—that is, by the claim that we are either safe in Echo-Warhol's empty room or omnipotent in Narcissus-Satan's Heaven made from Hell. Yet like echolalia and narcissism, the pathologies it mimics, the idiotic savvy of postmodern logic can only really supply the opposite of what it would advertise: instead of immunity, ignorance; instead of mastery, the fantasy of triumph that only ignorance allows. As a result, the disingenuous head (like Ford's or Warhol's) is spared from acknowledging the heart's darkest motives; the self-infatuated citizen (like Morimura) is saved from learning that the community doesn't always applaud his performance; and the rebellious schemer (like Milton's Satan) doesn't have to admit that reality proceeds without our permission, largely indifferent to individual wishes.

Spared the bad news, though, we are also spared the only terms by which we might better our condition—those messages we need to attune our motives, adjust our performance, adapt our wishes. Spared the bad news, we are spared the empowerment of knowledge itself and so suffer, as it were, a second expulsion. Having long ago lost the comfort of the Garden, now we lose the covenant of the Word. Without regaining the immunity of innocence, we manage to forfeit the tutelage of experience, as bequeathed to us by our cultural forms. And without parables, symbols, un-ironic heroes, and rituals that we believe in rather than scorn, we find ourselves trapped—both apart from the world and ignorant of it, without the means to explore or a map of return.

Repressed rather than transfigured, the aboriginal source of human anxiety—the division of the self from the rest of creation through the acquisition of knowledge—is intensified. Beneath the superficial smugness of postmodern irony, our fear, untutored, metastasizes. As with the Japanese soldier who hid in the jungle for twenty years, afraid to ask whether World War II was over and, if so, whether he would be spared, the postmodern drive to self-protection (the mind as a machine with one button, *erase*) quickly becomes its own affliction. As with that soldier's self-defense, our condition devolves from provisional escape into permanent imprisonment—and, ironically, a *self*-imprisonment. A solitary confinement, self-imposed. This is the saddest of consequences, but it is a literal consequence—the logical end of the "logic" driving postmodern thought. For if the mind is "its own place," then the place of the mind is isolation. If the mind is its own place, then each of our minds is confined and alone.

Lest we forget, this is precisely the plot acted out in the myth, the fate prescribed by the gods for Echo and Narcissus. And as that narrative depicts, this fate is not normative but punitive, the sentence given to those who flaunt the duties of love, the crucial covenants of honesty and caring. Echo, punished for her deceitful speech when concealing Jove's infidelity, loses the ability to speak for herself. Narcissus, punished for his cruel indifference to the love of others, is made to fall in love with himself. Echo, who loves Narcissus but cannot address him with words of her own, wastes away in her lover's grief to a voice in a cave, to a mocking "tape" of all who call. Narcissus, who loves a reflection he can never caress, wastes away to a nodding flower, rooted on the fringe of his mirroring pond.

Neither, revealingly, can act. They cannot act because all action is, necessarily, *inter*action: a dialogue or dance between lover and beloved, self and other, mind and world. They cannot interact because, according to the terms of their punishment, Echo's private voice and Narcissus' vision are trapped, sealed tight, in the cell of the self, in the mind's own place. The world cannot know, and so cannot love, Echo. Narcissus cannot know, and so cannot love, the world. Unable to interact—to be loved or to love, to be known or to know—they then waste away until they die. From loneliness, yes, but also from ignorance. They die of loneliness *through* ignorance, having lost their ability to converse with the world.

Characteristically prophetic, one of Yeats' last poems begins with the challenge "What if I bade you leave / the cavern of the mind?"[25] Echo and Narcissus have lost that choice. Their fate of loneliness unto death, in a myth that emerges from deep within our past—from an age prior to PCs and TV and movable print, probably prior even to writing itself—is a story that nevertheless retains an eerie, awful relevance. Although the estrangement of man from woman, the alienation of the individual from the creation, and the inability to converse in the language of love are potential flaws perennially present in the human condition, transitional eras such as ours have proven especially susceptible to their deprivations.

Our cultural forms *have* been failing us—Baudrillard is right about that. The liberal consensus that finally resolved the crisis of belief which arose in the seventeenth century can no longer make sense of our current experience. As ironically conveyed by the invasiveness of our *post*-modern machines, the decadent excesses of modern reasoning—the reductive demands of its quantiphilia—have led to an eviscerating conflict between the discipline of our traditional beliefs and the decadence of our everyday practices. The empowered individualism that liberal modernity both venerated and domesticated is now under assault on all sides, and what we see in the tactics of the postmodern artist is a last-ditch defense against its decline.

Although self-defeating, that defense is not without its reasons. The mind that doesn't want to be "chang'd by Place or Time" is responding to the very real dangers of *our* place and time. One of the reasons that Warhol has remained so influential is that his "radical parodies" and desperate retreat into "one empty room" do reflect, after all, something of the character of contemporary America. More than one of every four of us lives alone now, and many of our public spaces are, for all their noisiness, lonelier still. We, too, reside in zones of anxious erasure, of invasive entertainment and self-prescribed anesthesia. We, too, have constructed a highly censorious social sphere, a Virtual America where more is less and whose obsessive intention to "deprive the world of reality" induces the pseudo-innocence of our "unremembering hearts and heads."[26] If damnation is a perpetual alienation from the real, then "which way *we* fly" now is a kind of hell, the cavern of the mind multiplied, Warhol-style, into cell after cell of self-enclosure.

It won't be easy to get out. As wisdom begins with an admission of ignorance, courage must commence with a confession of fear. All true initiations require that we engage the terrors tormenting us, that we abide awhile in the tension of their presence. They require that we face and trace and name those dangers, not with the aim of utterly erasing them—for they, too, are part of the real—but with the intention of taming them, of turning their wilderness into a garden.

That garden won't be the one we were accustomed to, for we do not live in the same social and psychological space. Just as our nation's founding generations once civilized the potentially monstrous powers set loose by the tools and tactics of modern reasoning, we now must fashion a new or renewed set of civilizing forms—myths, covenants, customs, and laws—specific to the site we occupy, ones that can accurately gauge and conscientiously guide our passage though these post-modern times.

CHAPTER 3

Flatter-Fest

The Idolatry of Literary Analysis

If God created us in his own image, we have more than reciprocated.
—Voltaire

As we saw briefly in both the pro-capitalist theorizing of Francis Fukuyama and the Neo-Marxist criticism of Jean Baudrillard, the postwar demise of commonsense thinking—the adoption of a savvy so specialized or rarefied that it flips into a kind of idiocy—was not restricted to those maestros of marketing in commerce and the arts who modeled themselves after Henry Ford or Andy Warhol. Nor did it end after the turmoil of the sixties. As practiced at universities and think tanks and conveyed by public intellectuals, abstract analysis also declined in like-minded ways, and on both sides of our culture divide. In fields such as economic and political theory, where the proponents had real influence over corporate practices or public policy, the delusionary nature of their expertise would eventually lead to disastrous consequences, including the fiasco in Iraq and the implosion of the housing market. Elsewhere, in what used to be called the humanities—history, philosophy, literary criticism (the subject of our next case study)—the invasion of postmodern logic triggered decades of academic warfare.

The pickings there may have been slim from the quantiphiliac's perspective—fellowships and grants, editorial seats, curricular authority—but feelings were intense for those involved. Unlike the debate over abortion, however, where the passions were grounded in the gravitas of profound ideas, this subdivision of our culture wars was often characterized by lazy prejudicial thinking. The arrival of radical postmodernism did merit a thoughtful critique, of the sort I tried to supply last chapter, but the public censure of it too often drew instead on the same scornful anti-intellectualism that Ford had voiced years before. And as we saw in his case, contempt for critical thinking about the past—the all-too-common belief that we "don't need history very bad"—is both disingenuous and highly dangerous, typically concealing beneath its claims to common sense the crudest versions of historical causality.

In the cautionary words of a scholar who was writing even as Ford's own so-called historical analysis, *The Eternal Jew*, was flooding the West with its anti-Semitic slurs,

> the perspectives of history are ever shifting, for human experience, being itself subject to continual change, affords no fixed reference for the mind. Not only does each generation find itself compelled to interpret a more or less alien past by categories of the present, but even this specious present is itself unintelligible unless it be illuminated by the past.[1]

As a species whose intellect has supplanted instinct and who is, therefore, fated to be free, the survival of humanity depends on this ongoing process of mutual illumination. To choose a collective future, as every society must, we first need to assess each possible path with and against our accounts of the past. And because these consensus accounts aren't literal recollections (the mechanical echoing of Warhol's "good tapes") but subjective and therefore fallible interpretations, they must *themselves* be tested with and against each significant change in our present circumstances. Without a commitment to that testing of the past and a tolerance for the uncertainty it invites, our conceptions of reality calcify. Fleeing the unknown, we retreat again into various versions of the mind's own place, and our lives are soon based on the self-ratifying claims of nostalgia, resentment, or narcissistic fantasy.

Even in our scientific age, the world wherein we wander remains formidably strange, potentially unintelligible at any given moment. And as we shall see next, our mental hold on that world, so vital to our survival but provisional at best, is as threatened by those traditionalists who idolize the past as by those radicals who would deny its influence entirely.

Judas Kiss: The Bardolatry of Astute Consumption

In these waning days of our culture wars, even the works of Shakespeare have taken center stage. As his plays, long under assault for their supposedly reactionary politics, have been rapidly disappearing from university reading lists, some critics have responded by angrily demanding that boards of regents intervene. Although the issue of how to expand the curricular canon without diluting excellence or dissolving coherence is a serious one, and although the prospect of ex-pols and retired corporate leaders (the usual revolving-door cast of reigning regents) designing

freshman syllabi by executive fiat ought to send shivers down the spines
of academic radicals and conservatives alike, some amusing ironies have
attended the conflict. As has so often been the case in our culture wars,
the most vociferous opponents share more than they dare admit. Neither
the appalled defenders of the Bard nor the "transgressive" academics who
attack him seem to note, for example, how much that faculty's ongoing
and career-rewarding habit of trashing old texts to boost the new reflects
the standard marketing model of our consumer economy. Peek beneath
the surface of curricular revolt and you will find, among nobler aims, the
same formula that has so enriched the very millionaires whose think tanks
have been funding the reactionary attack on the academic left.

The programmatic scorning of Shakespeare (and Emerson and
Melville) might be as much commercially correct as politically correct,
and politically correct behavior in general might be a secular reflection,
a kind of unintended parody, of the broader culture's habit of using
Judeo-Christian rectitude to mask an unchecked pursuit of material self-
interest—but these are realizations unspeakable on both sides of the
debate. For to admit them is to commit a genuinely transgressive act by
acknowledging the one taboo truth still left in our otherwise totally unzip-
pered public sphere—namely, that consumer capitalism is the most radically anti-conservative political economy in the history of our species, as
corrosive to the continuity of art, ethics, and religion as it is to the ecology
of field, forest, and stream. If, in William Irwin Thompson's words, postindustrial America is a "catalytic enzyme that breaks down all the traditional
cultures of the world," then the first traditional culture it dissolves is its
own.[2] And no single author more centers that traditional Anglo-American
culture than Shakespeare himself.

But I come to praise Shakespeare, not to bury him, and what concerns
me most these days are not his debunkers but those defenders who instead betray him with their kiss. In an age of unchecked salesmanship,
the co-opting of the meaningful rather than its direct dismissal tends to
pose the greater threat. So it is that against the shrill accusations of misog-
yny, anti-Semitism, and royalist oppression that now assail Shakespeare, we
hear the indignant counterclaim that the poet, in his greatness, is somehow beyond politics—that he abides in the ethereal realm of the purely
aesthetic, quasi-divinely above the fray. We are told that his works are indisputably if paradoxically "good for us" without their having anything
practical to say about the good or the just.

Oddly, Harold Bloom has become the principal public proponent of
this purely aesthetic reading of Shakespeare. In a prolific burst of books,
Internet postings, prefaces to anthologies, and journalistic interviews, the

Yale professor has ridden the popular backlash against political correctness to become the most audible defender of all high art and, too, the most vociferous opponent of judging older literary works according to their compliance with contemporary political values.

The oddity of this event doesn't reside in Bloom's interpretive opinions, which have remained essentially unchanged throughout the years, but in the style of their delivery and the audience he now targets. Once himself the high priest of academic criticism who, from an endowed pulpit in New Haven, was given to his own transgressive tweakings of traditional literary readings, and whose mandarin books rarely graced the coffee tables of middle America, Bloom lost his following within the profession to the postmodern acolytes of Derrida and Foucault and to the proponents of feminist theory and cultural studies. As the great defender of elitist status in literature ("the Muse, whether tragic or comic, favors the elite"), Bloom couldn't have been happy with this fall from grace within his chosen field, and with no hope of an imminent restoration in sight, he began reinventing himself in the mid-nineties by gravitating toward that oxymoronic role so favored by late consumer culture: the mass marketing of elitist taste.[3] Disdainful of both politics and populism, he nevertheless began then the essentially polemical task of pitching his case to the broader audience of the uninitiated.

To catch a flavor of the self-dramatizing gusto with which this once apolitical critic joined the fray, we need only turn to the opening lines of Bloom's essay "They Have the Numbers; We, the Heights," where he explicitly associates himself and his like-minded readers with the great Spartan army whose self-sacrificial courage in delaying the Persian invasion of 480 B.C. helped save Greek culture for posterity:

> My title is from Thucydides and is spoken by the Spartan commander at Thermopylae. Culturally, we are at Thermopylae: the multiculturalists, the hordes of camp-followers afflicted by the French diseases, the mock-feminists, the commissars, the gender-and-power freaks, the hosts of new historicists and old materialists—all stand below us. They will surge up and we may be overcome; our universities are already travesties, and our journalists parody our professors of "cultural studies." For just a little while longer, we hold the heights, the realm of the aesthetic.[4]

"Holding the heights" had always been Bloom's preoccupation, but in books such as *The Western Canon* and *Shakespeare: The Invention of the Human*, with their more accessible prose and overtly pedagogical approach, the identity of those who shared that honor with him began to shift. Rather than address the small fraternity of critics with whom he once held sway,

Bloom started pitching his arguments to a much larger and potentially more profitable audience: publishing's "general intelligent readership."

By doing so, though, he was joining that virtual horde of cultural pitchmen who, through their multiple columns, newsletters, documentary specials, tasting tours, and DVD lecture series, discriminate for the undiscriminating. Even after the crash of 2008, this monetizing of elitist advice continued apace. Not only do these info-marketeers offer to teach us the intricacies of stuffing free-range chickens, the artistry of restoring Colonial kitchens, and (a favorite lately) the subtleties of assuming a spiritual approach to moneymaking; they also promise to arm us with enough facts and terms and gradients of taste to bluff at least briefly an expert's take on jazz or Jefferson or natural selection. In this virtual mall of the mandarin, even the literature prof has managed to generate a revenue stream. Back in the day I never would have predicted this, but Harold Bloom now, too, writes for the People, or rather for the People as defined by PBS. The man who began as the would-be kabbalist of esoteric criticism has become instead a latter-day literary Julia Child.

Such a stance is not without its charms. Bloom's willingness to raise a glass not only on behalf of aesthetic pleasure but also in sheer gratitude to its agents and authors—that generous joie de vivre of Child's signatory "Bon appetit!"—is especially winning when compared to the pinched, inquisitorial temper of too many of his academic opponents, whom he has aptly dubbed the School of Resentment. There may be much to lament in millennial America's popular culture, but as Ken Starr belatedly discovered, the moral common sense of democracy still detests a show of sheer mean-spiritedness, and few activities seem meaner than bullying the busts of the defenseless dead. While Derrida famously aimed to "decapitate" the corpse of the canonical author and others choose to "interrogate" him in a manner shared by the East German Stasi and America's own Joe McCarthy, Bloom's counter-mission of praise, however small the cast it admits, seems a fundamentally more decent task.

And that rarity of greatness, as spied by Bloom, is more than offset by the hyperbole of his appreciation. In *Shakespeare: The Invention of the Human*, for example, this self-confessed "bardolator" pays lavish tribute to the playwright's stature, assigning him a one-and-only patent for the invention of modern consciousness and thus elevating him to a divine-like status. ("Bardolatry, the worship of Shakespeare, ought to be even more of a secular religion than it already is.")[5] And in *The Western Canon* he further insists that "we owe to Shakespeare not only our representation of cognition but much of our capacity for cognition."[6] Admission to the heights of *this* heavenly sphere is limited to one, but other semi-divinities of creativity receive their due. Throughout his works Bloom assumes the Thermopylaean mission of rushing to the defense of that whole long but thin line of literary DWEMS ("Dead White European Males") who have constituted the critically approved Western tradition.

Bloom's argument is consistent. In a clearly articulated, mostly jargon-free prose, these books and their shorter spin-offs both mock and lament the School of Resentment's abandonment of "all aesthetic and most intellectual standards . . . in the name of social harmony and the remedying of historical injustice."[7] Restoring those standards, Bloom's literary polemics relentlessly reassert the rights of genius, insist that great works of art are freely created by unique individuals and not by the ineluctable "social energies" of their historical period, and contend that a very limited number of such literary artists (members of the canon) have had inordinate influence not only on other artists but on the very shape of contemporary consciousness. Bloom further insists that this inequality of influence is not only historically real but the justifiable result of extraordinary accomplishment, and so he roundly rejects the relativism that would render all artistic achievement—from the bedspread of an anonymous quilt-maker to Milton's epics—as equally praiseworthy.

Bloom's defense of superiority in art might seem a tonic resistance to the wash of pseudo-idealistic egalitarian sentiment that disarms discernment, rewards mediocrity, and all too often (as was the case with Warhol) merely masks the crassest graspings of careerism. Yet although Bloom justifiably complains about the extreme reductionism of the School of Resentment, his own views prove no less reductionist and so, too, no less a danger to artistic value in the richest sense. Against the rigid moralistic readings of both the left and the right, for example, Bloom asserts with an equivalent rigidity that the "moral values" of the canon are "nonexistent"[8] and that such literature cannot "make one a better or a worse person" in any discernible way.[9] And, countering the materialist determinism of Marxist readings and the psychological determinism of Freudian interpretations, he insists (against all common sense) that artistic works are influenced almost solely by other works of art: the canonical novel, play, or poem owes little to the social place of its creation, nor is such a work dependent on the non-literary biography of the great author. Literature alone breeds new literature, through a narrowly conceived struggle between the creative will of the single artist and the influence of earlier canonical works.

This theory of the "anxiety of influence"—through which each work of literary art struggles to remain, in Bloom's curious phrase, "uncontaminated" by the great works preceding it—is Bloom's own primary claim to originality as a critic. In essence, however, his theory is merely a version of Satan's self-deceiving boast in *Paradise Lost* projected into the field of literary study. Flipping Milton's cautionary example into an ideal, Bloom wants to believe, like the fallen angel, that certain special authors can actually come close to possessing "a mind not to be chang'd by Place or Time," and that the great work of art can somehow be "its own place," divinely autonomous and immune to influence.

Here, too, Bloom retains a jeweler's eye for a similar folly in his activist opponents, mocking the "declarations of literary critics" who believe that they have freed themselves from the "anguish of contamination"—that is, from the influence of the DWEMs who dominate the canon. Each of these critics, he notes sarcastically, believes that he or she "is Adam early in the morning. They know no time when they were not as they are now; self-created, self-begot, their puissance is their own."[10] Yet this fantasy of self-genesis is precisely the one that Bloom enshrines for the canon itself by insisting its works are largely immune to social circumstance. It is also the very drive that he elevates into the primary motive for the creation of lasting literature: "the desire to write greatly is the desire to be elsewhere, in a time and place of one's own, in an originality that must compound with inheritance, with the anxiety of influence."[11]

So it is that Bloom, no less than his activist adversaries, idealizes the mind's "own place"—that same imaginary island of pure self-genesis pursued by Ford, Warhol, and their many imitators. And Bloom's disdain for these critics emerges not from his appreciation of the folly of that aim but from their failure to recognize the cruel Darwinian reality that only a special canonical few can approach its attainment.

But if the "desire to write greatly" is simply the "desire to be elsewhere, in a time and a place of one's own," then even the very best literature is reduced to a quest for self-centered escapism, an idealized alienation from both the physical and the social worlds. By insisting that "all that the Western Canon can bring one is the proper use of one's own solitude," Bloom's thinking becomes emblematic of the dangers that attend a decadent individualism—all those tendencies toward solipsism, narcissism, and megalomania that we examined in the first two chapters.[12] So it is that his apparently ultra-refined "bardolatry" proves less an original project than a predictable product of the crudest "social energies" of our own place and time.

The Romantic egotism of Bloom's theory is deeply akin to that false autonomy that—as piloted by Ford, parroted by Gates, and pursued by Warhol's many clones—is relentlessly pitched in every niche of our sales economy, high or low. Even before Bloom chose to join the crew of mandarin hucksters, his thinking tacitly resembled their point of view, which

is why his eventual conversion is not so shocking, after all. In its attempt
to segregate beauty from meaning, aesthetic sensibility from moral coherence, Bloom's defense of Shakespeare reduces some of the canon's greatest poetry into but one more line of gourmet delicacies, exotically spiced
and elegantly arrayed, to be avidly consumed for consumption's own sake.

Morbid Magnitude versus Moral Consequence:
The Romantic Refusal of Tragic Coherence

> . . . love cools,
> friendship falls off, brothers divide: in
> cities, mutinies; in countries, discord; in
> palaces, treason; and the bond cracked 'twixt son
> and father.
>
> —*King Lear*

In his preface to *The Western Canon,* Bloom states that he feels "quite alone
these days in defending the autonomy of the aesthetic, but its best defense
is the experience of reading *King Lear.*" This seems a curious complaint,
shadowed as it is by two extreme ironies: first, Bloom's own ideology—
which asserts "the sovereignty of the solitary soul, the reader not as a person in society but as the deep self"—idealizes the notion of being "quite
alone"; and second, of all Shakespeare's plays, not only is *Lear* one of the
most overtly political, it also supplies the most comprehensive critique of
the same solitary individualism that Bloom's "anxiety of influence" would
celebrate.[13] To grasp this, though, we need to recover a commonsense
reading of the play that, by avoiding the rigid either/or biases of radical
"interrogation" and Romantic "bardolatry," can comprehend both the
moral rigor of Shakespeare's lyricism and the psychological subtlety of his
political compass.

   To understand that political compass, we have to recall the desperate
temper of the moment when the play was composed, *its* place and time
and prevailing "social energies," as they are captured by the following lines
from John Donne's poem "An Anatomy of the World":

> 'Tis all in pieces, all coherence gone;
> All just supply, and all Relation:
> Prince, Subject, Father, Son, are things forgot,
> For every man alone thinks he hath got
> To be a Phoenix, and that there can be
> None of that kind, of which he is, but he.

By the turn of the seventeenth century, the initial joy of Renaissance creativity was curdling into dread as the inherent contradictions between

the collective spirit of the medieval worldview and the individualism promoted by modern reasoning became all too apparent. As a religious conservative, Donne was deeply dismayed by the threat of disorder he found
in every field, from religion to politics to philosophy. He feared (correctly
as it turned out) that the new "atomism"—which was redefining both material and social reality by emphasizing the uniqueness of "pieces" over
the necessity of "Relation"—would result in political and moral anarchy.
In *King Lear*, which was staged just some five years before the publication
of Donne's poem, Shakespeare supplies us with the most comprehensive
and cautionary study of this threat. He dramatizes in devastating detail the
psychological sources of political anarchy, showing how, through the rise
of the Phoenix in its various forms, "all" might indeed dissolve to pieces.

Bloom contends that this story of family betrayal and civil war is the
"most sublime" of Shakespeare's four great tragedies—certainly a defensi-
ble position—and he makes many astute, small-grained observations con-
cerning the inventiveness of the characterizations. But the grander reason
behind Bloom's endorsement of *Lear* as the "strongest literary work" he
has ever encountered emerges instead from the utter bleakness he claims
to find in its conclusion. By the end, he insists, "everything seems against itself" so that we are "thrown outward and downward until we are left beyond
values, altogether bereft." We are condemned, like Lear before his death,
to inhabit "a terrible and deliberate gap." We are cast into that desolate
"space between meaning and truth" which, Bloom insists, is one of the supreme achievements of imaginative literature: the devastating evocation of
a kind of "cosmological emptiness in which we wander and weep."[14]

Bloom's dark Romantic biases show themselves most clearly here in his
desire to associate aesthetic sublimity with cosmological emptiness, imaginative achievement with wandering and weeping. And just as *Lear* the
tragedy is adjudged to be the most sublime *because* it brings us "beyond
values, altogether bereft," Lear the character is said to be "the greatest of
all representations of a king" not owing to any real nobility of action but
because he is "much the most passionate," because his raging is the fiercest, his suffering the most intense.[15] Although these aesthetic judgments
succeed in stripping moral stature from their compass, they are not themselves "beyond values" but are the expression of a Romantic calculus that
projects the reductionist formula of modern quantiphilia into the arena
of morbid emotions. Just as the rationalist technocrat believes that *more*
(data, money, efficiency) *must equal better* (a truer, happier, safer society),
this Romantic aesthete insists that the greater the intensity of the emotion
evoked (especially misery), the greater the authenticity—the more terrible the conclusion, the more sublime the experience.[16]

Elsewhere, Bloom asserts more specifically that "the greatness of the play has everything to do with Lear's patriarchal greatness," thus merely inverting into praise the School of Resentment's reductive complaint about patriarchal oppression.[17] But look wherever we wish inside the play's five acts, we can find little evidence of the old man's individual achievement in the patriarchal sense—that is, as an effectual leader or father. Although much can be deduced from Lear's behavior throughout the play, we only have the opening scene as direct evidence of his performance as king, for it is in that scene that he relinquishes his authority to the husbands of his older daughters, Regan and Goneril. To those accustomed to democracy and the egalitarian values associated with it, Lear's desire to go into a semi-retirement and divide his kingdom among his heirs might in itself seem a sign of political greatness. The voluntary surrendering of authority and its division among equals through delegation are, after all, two of the essential characteristics of democratic governance, ones that we associate with its moral superiority. But in Shakespeare's time, such a decision was a radical and potentially destabilizing one. Lacking the institutional checks and balances of modern democracy and charged with a surging individualism as yet untutored in the duties as well as the rights of freedom, the early 1600s were trapped in a dynamic of stressful contradictions, their medieval institutions unable to contain the expansive ambitions of the new social "atom."

To translate Donne's version of that crisis back into Bloom's own critical terms: the new "deep self" of the "mind's own place" (with its emphasis on individual ambition) was colliding with the old expectations of "the person in society" (those feudal traditions of "just supply" and right Relation that still favored loyalty over ambition, stability over innovation, and absolute authority over delegation). Despite Bloom's wish to keep art "uncontaminated" by social influence, *King Lear* was clearly written, in part, in response to that crisis, and both the arc of its plot and its cast of characters have been shaped to favor the old social order. All the heroes—Cordelia, Kent, and Edgar—are heroic through their adherence to feudal conceptions of loyalty as daughter, liege, and son; all the villains—Goneril, Regan, and Edmund—are upwardly mobile individualists who crack the bonds of communal ideals and domestic relations in a ruthless pursuit of private ambition, whether political, economic, or sexual in nature.

In this case, then, the School of Resentment's complaint about Shakespeare's politics might seem to have some basis in fact; but we can only make such a judgment with an acknowledgment of the actual alternatives available at the time. One cannot be against a political movement that doesn't yet exist, and to fault Shakespeare for being anti-democratic is akin to accusing Newton of being against relativity or blaming Bach's predecessors for refusing to compose in counterpoint. In any case, Lear's decision has little to do with thoughtful political reform, democratic or otherwise. Although he hints that he is retiring in part to prevent future strife after his death, his division of the kingdom is exercised in a fashion that emphasizes the willfulness of his authority even while in the process of abdicating it. By continuing to endorse autocratic behavior while breaking up the very political system (a unified kingdom) that sustains its form of social order, Lear initiates a devolution into anarchy. Rather than reforming the monarchy according to democratic principles, the immediate practical result of the division is to atomize autocracy, provoking a *political* version of "the anxiety of influence" and a subsequent agonistic struggle of wills, as each fractured piece fights to reassume an absolute authority over the whole.

The recklessness of Lear's decision, which engenders strife under the very guise of preventing it, is exposed in the first scene by the king's chosen means of enacting the division. Here, the medium becomes the real message as he rashly invites a softer version of the divisive competition that will soon send the country into total civil war.

> Which of you shall we say doth love us most?
> That we our largest bounty may extend.[18]

This is the new calculus of value, the model of merit for the governing heart now being endorsed: the right to rule has been explicitly equated not with intelligence or nobility of character or even raw military force, but with the magnitude of one's love for Lear. *More love for me*, says this supposedly greatest of patriarchs, *must equal better*. Quick to follow their father's calculus of sheer self-interest, the older daughters shamelessly accept this invitation to a flatter-fest, buying the boroughs of his Manhattan with the beaded ornaments of their sham affection. Goneril proclaims her father "dearer than eye-sight, space, and liberty."[19] Not to be outdone, Regan then insists that even her older sister's fulsome praise "comes too short," professing herself instead "an enemy to all other joys, / Which the most precious square of sense possesses."[20]

I have elaborated this well-known opening scene to emphasize the importance of Regan's exact words, for they hint at the catastrophic significance of this collaborative exercise in emotional dissembling, and supply the ethical hinge that links Lear's self-love to the civil war to come. If the "square of sense" is indeed *most* precious, then to proclaim oneself its enemy, to favor one joy to the exclusion of all the others—in Donne's terms, to accentuate the "piece" at the expense of "Relation"—is to reject the harmonies of community for the harms of isolation, and the magnanimity of love for the morbidity of obsession. Aware that the human heart not only must have but should have multiple allegiances, Cordelia refuses to say that she loves her father "most" and is then banished by a furious Lear with the final curse, "Better thou / Hadst not been born than not to have pleased me better."[21]

In an attempt to moderate our view of Lear's offense here—which is not simply the banishment of Cordelia from his kingdom but a radical exclusion of honesty itself—Bloom claims that the king's "principal fault in regard to Cordelia is an excessive love that demands excess in return."[22] But this is a disingenuous reading, one that wants to discount the danger of such love by flattering its intensity. Here as throughout, Bloom seems to blur the inherent stature of the role of the patriarch with the stature of Lear's performance in that role, just as he confuses the cautionary quality of Lear's behavior within the play with the exemplary quality of Shakespeare's representation of it. Because Bloom has proclaimed the "moral values" of this or any tragedy to be "non-existent," because those values have been replaced by a Romantic bias for "the solitary self" over "the person in society," and (more important here) for sheer emotionality over nobility of character, the magnitude of Lear's patriarchal passion automatically eclipses the catastrophic results of his actions. The intensity of the piece obscures from Bloom its disastrous effects on the coherence of relations, and Lear is praised as great.

This elitist critic's sentimental inflation of the old king's status cannot be overstated. In *Shakespeare*, he insists that Lear is "a kind of mortal god" and that within his characterization the playwright was seeking to portray "a paradigm for greatness." In a book of literary criticism that alternates deft observations with near delusional misreadings born of the author's Romantic biases, perhaps the most delusional is this: Bloom actually argues that Lear was modeled on, and is the equal to, King Solomon. According to bardolatry, the leader whose decisions destroy his own kingdom is said to be the equal of that sage and psalmist who was thought to be not only the wisest of ancient Israel's leaders but also the most politically adept.[23]

Bloom himself has championed the inevitability and desirability of "creatively" misreading literary texts, but it would be difficult to exceed the perverse irony of this reversal of Shakespeare's intent. Bloom's confusion between the stature of a social role and the stature of the personality occupying that role, along with his critical forsaking of "the most precious square of sense" for the crude calculus that *more* (passion) *must equal better*, violates two of the play's central themes. They are the very flaws in Lear's character that drive the plot toward its tragic conclusion. And they are the ones that, five hundred years later, spur an economy whose own excessive pursuit of *more* is fueled by the same delusory dream of narcissistic autonomy: the false belief, taught from the cradle on Disney's screens, that "no request is too extreme."

All this brings us back at last to Bloom's morbid celebration of *Lear*'s bloody finale, a reading that would link the sublimity of the play as a whole to the "cosmological emptiness" its final act evokes. This interpretation might be plausible if—as in, say, *Waiting for Godot*—we were actually cast "beyond values, altogether bereft" at the end. We are not, and Bloom's insistence that we are constitutes a misreading that violates the spirit of the play no less egregiously than the very worst supplied by the School of Resentment.

True, through most of the play's five acts everything does seem, as Kent reports to Lear, "cheerless, dark, and deadly."[24] Gloucester's astrological prediction, cited at the start of this section, has been enacted throughout: love *has* cooled, there has been discord in the country and treason in the palace, and the tender bond—not only 'twixt son and father, but 'twixt daughters and father, 'twixt lord and liege, 'twixt sisters, 'twixt brothers— has been catastrophically "cracked." After Lear relinquishes authority to his two flattering daughters, they turn on him and then on each other in an ever more bloody acceleration of betrayal in pursuit of raw power.

Yet at the play's end the anarchy has ceased, its agents are clearly and completely defeated, and order is restored by a noble leader, Albany. The cost has been horrific—Gloucester, Regan, Goneril, Cornwall, Oswald, Edmund, the Fool, Cordelia, and Lear have all died—yet the ultimate result is not a banishment into utter emptiness but a restoration of civil order and public justice. Not only does the play end with a political redress and with a moral reckoning for all its villains; two of the three most heroic characters, Kent and Edgar, survive the carnage. And to seal and perpetuate our faith that justice will now prevail, we are left with Albany's unambiguous pledge that

> All friends shall taste
> The wages of their virtue, and all foes
> The cup of their deservings.[25]

Still, Cordelia does die, and most undeservedly. Her reckoning remains the burr in the heart that demands explaining, for she and the Fool alone, among that long list of the dead and the maimed, are wholly blameless. This princess who forfeited a kingdom rather than falsify the true nature of love, this daughter who sustained a constant yet undeluded emotional bond to the father who cruelly cast her out, has been murdered on her own sister's orders—sororicide the ultimate "crack" in the nest of tender bonds that holds society together. And when that very father, now repentant, bears her lifeless body onto the stage as if to beg it back to life—surely one of the most crushing entrances in all of English drama—when he howls and hammers the irreversible fact of her death into his own (and our) minds, those moments mark the closest the play comes to justifying Bloom's sense of an unredeemable emptiness. "No, no, no life!" Lear cries to a corpse that can't respond, both admitting and resisting the finality of the event by addressing his daughter as if she were alive, but with the message that her life has been inalterably spent:

> Why should a dog, a horse, a rat have life,
> And thou no breath at all? Thou'lt come no more,
> Never, never, never, never, never![26]

But if Lear himself is altogether bereft—and he most eloquently is—must we be, too? The play, as Bloom himself aptly notes in his argument for its greatness, has one of the largest casts of fully elaborated characters in Shakespeare's body of work, thus affording us multiple emotional and thematic centers to attend—if, that is, we actually wish to read the play *as a whole*, in all its coherence and relations, and not just morbidly magnify its most forlorn piece, Cordelia's death scene. And even if we do focus on that moment of magnified grief, so compressed and intense that Lear dies from it, we find that in the full resonance of its meaning and feeling we have not been cast "beyond values" but carried to the very core of their authentication.

As T. S. Eliot argued in an essay on Yeats' work in the theater, the poetic beauty of any particular line in a verse play is dependent on its placement within the action, the sublimity of its sound inseparable from the meaning of its narrative site. Eliot then cited as his sole example that very string of five *never*s howled by Lear, observing that even though the line constitutes "one of the most thrilling" in the tragedy, we could scarcely know whether it was "poetry or even competent verse" if we read it in isolation, unaware of "the context" of persons, places, and actions that ground it.[27]

The immediate context is a father bending over his murdered daughter's corpse, and the line is "thrilling"—that is, it rises to the pitch of poetry—because its form so fully fits the matrix of meanings that animates the moment in all its emotional, thematic, and existential registers. Note, for example, the line's relentless repetition of a single word, a rare and risky tactic in any form of verse, and then consider its multiform propriety at this point in the action—how it succeeds in simultaneously suggesting the intensity of a father's grief, the eternity of mortality itself (the *never* that goes on forever), and finally the very human need, in the midst of an unexpected grief, to repeat the awful message over and over in order to comprehend it.

The music of the line also coheres with the meaning of the context, befitting both the nature of the existential fact (death) and the climate of the psychological instant (grief). After two full lines of monosyllabic words in strictly iambic feet (and THOU / no BREATH / at ALL?), Lear's horrified apprehension of the reality of Cordelia's death climaxes with a sudden reversal into a stuttered array of two-syllable trochees (NEVer / NEVer / NEVer . . .). Rhythm and diction fuse. The sound of the line mimics its sense as each word—carved from hard consonants and short vowels and a stifling of stresses—becomes an isolated metrical foot in itself. Each poetic piece, arrested in time, is as sealed off from the metrical whole as the corpse is from the fold of living relations. Each sound event, in its clipped, short-breathed diminishment, enacts the cruel truncation of the real event. *Dead* the sounds sing as *dead* the words say: she's *dead, dead, dead, dead, dead.*

Desolate, indeed, but we aren't finished yet. In drama as in life, meaning is cumulative and resonant, not discrete and isolate in the way that a Romantic reader like Bloom, idealizing the mind as its own place, would prefer. To know the whole context, as Eliot insisted, requires knowing the full *pre*-text, the sequence of events preceding and preshaping the moment under study. The meaning of *where* we are at the end of act 5 as the king bends over the throttled body of his daughter is inseparable from *how* and *why* we arrived there, and Lear's anguish is much multiplied by his realization that his own decision to banish Cordelia has been instrumental in her death—that her *neverness* has been sired by his selfishness. What we have entered at this moment of magnified grief is, in other words, not the valueless gap of a "cosmological emptiness" but the self-initiated trap of ethical consequence—which is, in this instance, a much harder place to be.

Empathetically entering this harder place, we ought to weep with Lear but cannot really wander because a series of decisions has drastically constricted the field of possible occurrences to this fixed and now unavoidable point, this physical end that is as well the play's dramatic, thematic, and ethical core: Cordelia's corpse. Many real-life deaths do seem senseless, but as in most of the great tragedies, the peculiar horror of Cordelia's death radiates from the play's deliberate tracking of its sensibleness. "A rat [has] life / and [she] no breath at all" because Lear himself has cracked the bond of paternal love, because he has been from the start a spiteful, selfish father and a very foolish king. In the sole instance of his patriarchal effectiveness, Lear's own enraged wish—"Better thou / Hadst not been born"—has come true in the flesh.

The fault is not his alone, of course. Just as Shakespeare's sensibility insists on the many dimensions, admixtures, and gradations of human emotion, it also relentlessly depicts the subtleties and complexities of human guilt. *Unjust* supply is also the result of relations, both deliberate and careless—within which, however, we can and should discern various degrees of complicity and blame. Here as in *Hamlet*, for example, the author makes a careful distinction between the cold calculations of outright villainy and the unreflective selfishness that allows evil to reign. Edmund and Goneril are directly responsible for Cordelia's death just as Claudius is directly responsible for the murder of Hamlet's father. But as Claudius couldn't have become king without Gertrude's apparently glad submission to his hasty seduction, Goneril and Edmund would never have been in position to kill Cordelia were it not for, in Kent's apt words, Lear's "hideous rashness" as king and father.

The chaos of the kingdom is thus both dramatized and analyzed, expressed and contained by a tragic coherence that helps locate the sources of anarchy in specifiable flaws in the characters—Lear and Edmund primarily, Regan, Goneril, and Cornwall secondarily. The compression of meaning that is the source of the play's sublime achievement depends as much on this ethical fitness—the aptness of events as driven by decisions, the logic that turns narrative sequence into moral consequence and linear plot into resonant theme—as it does on the exquisite fitting of the language to the forms and rhythms of human grief.

So it is that the moral values of this canonical play, which Bloom would claim are non-existent, strongly determine and infuse the very conclusion he comes to praise. By ignoring those values here and elsewhere, Bloom actually reduces the greatness of Shakespeare's achievement, for it is precisely the architectural strength supplied by his ethically shaped plots (the moral accuracy of his narrative logic) that supports both his extensive variations in characterization and the descriptive gloss of his glorious language. Shakespeare's toughness about consequences, especially in the tragedies, allows him to indulge in an expressive and empathetic tenderness, producing a body of work that is, at once, so rich in sentiment and so immune to sentimentality.

Bloom is surely correct in assessing both the special richness of this tragedy and the deeply moving magnitude of its hero's suffering. The sheer beauty of the writing and its capacity to move us are inextricably tied, however, to Lear's own willingness to grasp the moral meaning of his plummet from rage to grief. Having lived a uniquely privileged life, Lear had fashioned a mind which, mistaking the sovereignty of the throne for the sovereignty of his self, actually believed that his standing could not be "changed by place or time." Only by ceding his throne, and so exposing himself to the ambitions of others, does he belatedly achieve the pain-raked clarity of a self-recognition.

By the end, Lear does begin to learn the lessons of love: the moderating nature of its just supply, the necessary reciprocities of its exchange, how king and commoner alike are both vulnerable to love's harms and accountable for love's abuse. These are recognitions, however, that arrive too late and in a form far too intense to be borne. With the sort of irony that tragic drama especially comprehends, the worst harm that Lear has done eventually becomes the very harm that he must suffer: his vulnerability and accountability merge as one in the dumb and dreadful weight of his daughter's breathless body. In the bitter book of Cordelia's corpse, Lear can now read who he has been as a "deep self"—which is, finally, not separable from what he has done as a "person in society."

Oily Endearments: The Self-Enfacement of Bloom's Bardolatry

It has become a cliché today to claim that the personal is political, and as each individual appetite aspires to the luster of a civil right, that equation is sometimes reduced to a self-justifying excuse for narcissistic entitlement. Yet as the plotting of Lear's demise powerfully reveals, personality and polity do remain linked, and at the deepest ontological level. Each "deep self" is as much the shadow as the source of the "person in society," and each person in society (each "piece" of the whole) remains both accountable for sustaining society's "just supply" and vulnerable to its violations.

In their mastery of poetic form at every level, Shakespeare's tragedies rescue this enduring link between the personal and the political by revealing its true complexity: the ongoing and intricate influence of the one on the many, the many on the one. They dramatize again and again how the singular self can be both the site of inalienable rights and the source of alienating wrongs, the fount of elegant wonderings and the forge of ugly dissembling. They insist that, just as the human voice itself radiates outward beyond its own locale, each private soliloquy has a public resonance and so, too, an accountable range of ethical and political consequences.

John Donne famously warned that "no man is an island," that each of us remains a fraternal piece of the continental "main." While endorsing that essential moral observation, Shakespeare's tragedies accomplish something more complex and apparently contradictory: they explore the multiple islands of his era's new individualism, the unique flora and fauna of every imaginable habitat for the single human heart, even as they insist on those islands' inescapable relation to the various confederations of community. They supply, at once and paradoxically, the most eloquent expression of a "puissant" individualism *and* the most trenchant critique of its moral and political dangers. In this the plays are absolutely true to the contradictory "social energies" of the historical moment in which they were composed. To read them simply as reactionary endorsements of the old medieval order or as apolitical celebrations of modernity's new "deep self" drastically reduces the scope, difficulty, and courage of their achievement, which is political *and* personal *and* poetic all at once.

Seamus Heaney, whose aesthetic opinions were tried in the fires of Northern Ireland's Troubles, defined the political function of poetry as that of metaphorical "redress" rather than literal reform. The successful political poem becomes that separate other place, a symbolic site, where the elements of public disorder can be made to coexist in an orderly way through aesthetic form. By unifying the day's as-yet-irresolvable social conflicts through its rhythms, rhymes, and ironies, by enacting its "principle of integration in . . . context[s] of division and contradiction," poetry becomes a means to recover harmony in the very act of depicting divisiveness.[28] It imagines a site of both unstinting honesty and irrepressible hope.

Unlike much lyric poetry, drama has a self-consciously social dimension and therefore easier access to directly political representation. Nevertheless, I know of no body of work that fulfills Heaney's subtler mission of poetic redress more completely than Shakespeare's tragedies; and of the tragedies, no other aspires to the scope of *King Lear*'s political analysis. Even as its five acts dramatize the specific ways in which an entire society's center will not hold under the assault of unchecked individualism, the play's own center retains its formal shapeliness. In the course of events as driven by individual and allied ethical decisions, Lear's Britain devolves into a sphere of chaos and pain and anomie while the ur-place of the play itself remains a web of order and beauty and empathy. We are not only given exquisitely crafted models of individual behavior, from the cautionary Lear to the exemplary Cordelia—a courageous and nuanced attendance to which might indeed, contrary to Bloom's dismissive claim, make us better human beings in discernible ways; at a deeper level, the drama's own performance provides us with a continuous model of "just supply." Scene after scene, it meets the highest standard of self-governance: that "most precious square of sense" which counterbalances the public with the private, the ideal with the real, the reality of dreadful circumstances with the redress of the poetry shaped to express them.

To these I would add one last achievement. In *Lear*'s unflinching projection of its own era's contradictions, especially the emerging conflict between modernity's social atom and the medieval social order, Shakespeare prophetically captures a tension that will haunt every subsequent would-be democracy. Such a vision would seem to have a special relevance to a post-modern America caught between the decadence of a declining individualism and the crude collectivism of identity politics—an America whose compass of relations, like that of Donne's England, has been cracking under the stress of opposing worldviews.

These are just some of the reasons why Shakespeare should be read by today's professors, students, and regents alike, and if resentment proves precisely the wrong attitude to bring to this task, bardolatry is scarcely better. Finally we have to ask whether Bloom's praise of Shakespeare is any more sincere, any less self-aggrandizing and ultimately subversive to the playwright's authority, than the unctuous verbal oozings of Lear's older daughters, whose hyperbole, after all, he more than matches. Like many a postmodernist whose smirking poses he would claim to loathe, Bloom seems to assume that the irony of his self-description as a "bardolator" immunizes him from the accuracy of its implied analysis.

But Bloom *is* an idolater. And idolaters, as Isaiah knew, do not really bow down to the God they claim to honor so much as "worship the work of their own hands, that which their own fingers have made."[29] So it is that Bloom's readings of Shakespeare—with their obsessive fears of contaminating influence, their excessive insistence on art's autonomy, their narrow fixation on single characters (especially Hamlet, Lear, and Falstaff) over narrative communities, and their allied endorsement of morbid magnitude over the squaring of sense—repeatedly obscure the richly nuanced experience of the plays with images forged by *his* mind's own place.

Like Narcissus bending close to the surface of his pool, Bloom studies the Shakespearean page only to discover there the reflection of his own pet ideas, a misreading whose scale of creativity he then tacitly allies with the potency of the divine—with "the invention of the human." In the end, recalling Regan's overripe regard and Goneril's oily endearments, Bloom's critical acts of excessive flattery are really masked rituals of self-promotion. Like Ford's staging of the past in Greenfield Village and Morimura's appropriations of Rembrandt and Rossetti, Bloom's expert readings are actually acts of self-*enf*acement. On *his* watch from the heights at Thermopylae, criticism, whose crucial mission it is to explore the abundant otherness of the world, has been reduced instead to a self-confirming solipsism.

As such, Bloom's books do ironically reflect both the idiotic savvy of his postmodern opponents and the broader "social energies" of our place and time. His "creative" misreadings are completely at home in an economy whose quantiphilia relentlessly degrades all professional callings into self-promoting careers and neighborliness into networking. Wedding Romantic egotism to rational efficiency in an unholy pursuit of vulgar magnitude, today's market economy gladly accepts Bloom's elitist aestheticism in the same way it accepts his opponents' egalitarian multiculturalism: as yet one more set of Info-Age experiences to purchase, patent, shrink-wrap, and pitch. His *discernment*, like their *diversity*, is quickly converted into a seasonal line of commercial *accessories*. Like the Gregorian chants, Tibetan prayers, and Shoshone myths that are now being marketed globally; like the pricey anniversary edition of Marx's *Das Kapital* and the branded memorabilia of Dr. King's martyrdom; like the packaged tours that now replace pilgrimages, ferrying spectators to and from Brazilian slums and outback oases in shows of "authenticity," Shakespeare's plays are celebrated as *pieces*, as sound-bite experiences deliberately deracinated from the robust resonance of human engagement.

Once active agents of cultural meaning, these works become the passive unguents of our money culture's raw debasements. Potentially transformative experiences, they are turned instead into their own simulacra, pseudo-sacraments through which cultural appreciation is made to serve the narcissistic self's constant anxious need for self-confirmation. Under the tutelage of our mandarin hucksters, they supply us with a mirror-glance chance to admire our own sensitivity and, too, to affirm our status as brave defenders of the heights at Thermopylae. But like the antidepressants we now dose ourselves with, these hits of sublimity can't hide for long the age's actual spiritual depravity. No show of appreciation or flaunting of expertise can sate the "cosmological emptiness" that lies at the core of our quantiphilia.

Inspiring Shakespeare: In Praise of Anonymity

Just as today's so-called celebrations of self-esteem both mask and enact an actual emasculation of America's once potent individualism by fleeing its moral and psychological rigors, Bloom's effusive praise of Shakespeare's plays weakens their effectuality by sparing us the challenge of their larger obligations. Literary greatness is, finally, not an hors d'oeuvre to savor but an opportunity for revision. As the literal meanings of both phrases attest, aesthetic discernment, like cultural diversity, *ought* to "make a difference." To be truly moved by the Shakespearean play is to move differently in the world beyond the theater of its stagings.

The apt word for this willing embrace of influence is not contamination but inspiration. Paradoxically, only through this in-spiring (breathing in) of the world's circumscribing otherness—only through a willingness to observe other faces and absorb other voices, always ready to admit that they might be better than our own—can we achieve the full potential of our individuality. To the extent that the human condition permits, true self-genesis ironically depends more on the anonymous art of selective obedience than on the active publicity of transgressive revolt. And as the astute critic William Hazlitt grasped early on, Shakespeare's own greatness depended especially on this self-effacing readiness to become anyone or anything—on his extraordinary gift for selective acts of imaginative submission.[30]

The notion that artistic immortality might be born in part out of a willing embrace of anonymity proves to be a paradox, however, that our self-promoting era cannot fathom. Ignoring the legacy of the work, we tend to pursue instead the life of the man, and bending those few biographical facts that we actually possess to our biased ends, we assert that Shakespeare "really" was an aristocrat or a homosexual or a closeted Catholic. We offer up more reliquaries for the bardolator, more opposition research for the politically correct. Shakespeare is reduced to just one more celebrity we have exhumed to consume, to pitch or trash in the morbid marketplace of commodified gossip.

Yet the call of the work patiently survives the noisy distraction of those decadent tasks. My own return to it, after long neglect, occurred a few years back when I dipped into *Hamlet* to check a three-word quote I planned to cite. As this five-minute errand became a three-hour immersion, my mundane commitment to accuracy took on by turns a graver tenor and a grander dimension: to live like *this*; to feel *this* keenly the full palette of emotions, to know *this* acutely the moral and psychological complexities of any given human moment.

Now as then, I emerge from my reading of Shakespeare's plays charged with the sense that my own world has somehow been enlarged and enriched. Further, this enriching vision, as if a memory brought back from the edge of oblivion, seems to flicker with the shapes of a founding recognition: I have the haunting sense that this deeper, defter world has been more recovered than invented. Through my willing submission to the play's influence, I am made to feel again that, for all our differences in temper, talent, gender, and class—individuating qualities which the play itself fastidiously enacts—each of us does *not*, finally, live "elsewhere, in a time and a place of one's own." I am reawakened into the faith that we share instead a larger human place, a deeper human fate, and that even in our most divisive moments we remain somehow together and at home.

Implicit in this faith, born in the afterglow of the reading experience, is the suggestion that its harmonies might be savored daily. This state of intense and enriched equilibrium might be ours if only we could see as clearly, hear as surely, and feel as fully as the Shakespearean play allows us to. If only we could meet *its* standard of self-governance, then we might return to that "most precious square of sense" in which the personal and the political can cohere—in which the place of our singular minds and the mind of our collective place are made to fit.

This hint of a perpetually accessible homecoming into harmony does renew a sense of unfulfilled responsibility—to be inspired, after all, is to wish to do better—but it also supplies the most consoling gifts. Among them is the recovery of a gaiety that can transfigure all our dread. Among them, too, in the fullness of fellow-feeling from the words flowing in, is the tactile refutation of emptiness.

CHAPTER 4

Boxed In

The Science of Self-Deception

SCIENCE FINDS—INDUSTRY APPLIES—MAN CONFORMS
—Motto, Century of Progress International Exposition, Chicago, 1933

The closed-mindedness equally evident in the egalitarian art of Andy Warhol and the elitist criticism of Harold Bloom will seem of little significance to those many Americans who doubt the usefulness, and so too the value, of the arts and humanities, even when practiced at their very best. In a can-do culture that favors how-to knowledge, the arts are often construed as merely decorative, the humanities dismissed as irrelevant at best. Viewed as luxuries whose "skill sets" can't lift the scores on standardized tests, both are vulnerable targets for elimination in the next round of school reforms, especially when those reforms are likely to be defined by the high-tech philanthropists who now dominate the field through the lure of their grants and the luster of their prior accomplishments. The validity of that dominance, however, bears a closer scrutiny.

I began these case studies with Henry Ford not just because he supplied an early prototype of the Idiot Savant that is my subject here. As one of his era's most admired men, he also epitomized a significant revision in American idealism: our broad conversion, partially concealed by the masquerade of the Virtual Puritan, to the quantiphilia required by the new economy. "Science finds, industry applies, man conforms"—which is to say, "man" agrees to purchase and use, desire and consume the raft of commodities relentlessly produced by consumer capitalism. By doing so, the new ethos assured us, we would ascend together on an escalator of perpetual progress, and with the American Dream reconceived in such a way, the public figure who most embodied this idealized merger of science with commerce—the technological entrepreneur—quickly became the new hero of American life. Yet, as we saw with Ford's "ideas and ideals for the good of all," the savvy that produces entrepreneurial success doesn't easily translate into domains outside the marketplace. In our political economy, the skills that generate material *quantity* have been fashioned, in part, by ignoring or repressing those conducive to moral *quality*. Neither boosting the bottom line nor lifting the average test score is sufficient in itself to craft a truly better life—a caution we might consider as we continue to cede our civic authority to the corporate kings of the latest saving technology.

These concerns were called to mind for me some years ago now when Richard Dawkins, passing through town to plug his latest book, complained again about the puzzling persistence of superstition in Western life. Why, in an age of unprecedented scientific advances, he wondered, did people still place their faith in the sham clairvoyance of astrology? Coming from the most dogmatic of the new Darwinists, this scorn for the esoteric arts was hardly surprising. Nevertheless, it seemed a curious priority of concern for someone who also occupied an academic chair in the Public Understanding of Science. Certainly there was no shortage of troubling alternatives at the time. Not long before, scientists in Scotland had cloned a sheep, and Chicagoan Richard Seed—a man armed with the august credentials of a Harvard PhD and a bad-pun characternym out of a Thomas Pynchon novel—had quickly announced his intention to do the same with (to? for?) a human being. If Professor Dawkins was in a worrying mood, rather than clucking over the popularity of the mystic hotline, he might have wondered out loud about the ethical and political issues surrounding this discovery.

Or discussed the social implications of university scientists fleeing the campus to profit from discoveries initially supported by public funds.

Or, if committed to exposing sham predictions, analyzed the claim of some leading artificial intelligence engineers that we will soon convert our selves into software and, escaping the way of all flesh, live forever in a "postbiological" world.

Or, for those of us still fond of our flesh, commented on science's "weaponizing" of the anthrax bacterium, and on the black market for both nuclear material and nuclear scientists. What did it mean for the world that *their* elegant solutions, measured by the megaton and the million dead, might now be sold to the highest bidder?

I don't wish to be counted among the superstitious, but the mundane fact that we continue to glance at our daily horoscopes, hoping to catch a fortuitous wave of astral fate and surf our way to sex, fame, and fortune on the beach of the new millennium worries me a lot less than our pell-mell pursuit of immortality and apocalypse on the wings of Progress, commercially driven and scientifically defined.

Dawkins and I might agree that post-modern life seems an odd mix of material progress and social devolution. The digital age's explosion of knowledge-based wealth has been concurrent with a surge in self-destructive or anti-social behaviors, including divorce, addiction, and indebtedness, and with institutional failures such as legislative gridlock, corporate corruption, and the decline of public education. When addressing these issues in the general sense, science's spokesmen have tended to offer a single solution: more science. If only more studies could be done and our labs were better funded, if only government would simply get out of the way so that the next generation of heroic technologies might be freed from the chains of regulatory restraint, if only our kids were trained to science from the earliest age—if only, in short, more of us were more like Richard Dawkins, we might amend our errors and, step by step, solve the puzzle of the human predicament.

That position, however, is not only varnished with vanity and tainted by self-interest; it also expresses presumptions about social causation which are themselves archaic. Just as corporate leaders keep complaining about the inefficiencies of government when nearly every domain in American life has already been privatized, science's spokesmen keep bemoaning superstition when the historical trend, deeply engrained in modern reasoning, has been to rationalize all our endeavors. Our leaders, after all, didn't consult goat innards when making their disastrous decisions to invade Iraq and deregulate our financial system; they turned instead to "experts in the field." Such examples sketch by implication a commonsensical counter-thesis to the scapegoating of superstition: if we are thinking foolishly and behaving badly, wouldn't the causes more likely lie in the actual centers of contemporary power—commerce and science—than in the outer orbits of influence where astrologers, numerologists, and "past life therapists" hold their sway?

What I hope to show here are the various ways that the methods of modern science, when projected beyond the realm of their true authority, can lead to highly self-deceptive and destructive habits of mind. To do so, we will take a closer look at the field of artificial intelligence, in response to whose fantastic promises we have been rapidly transforming our schools and homes as well as our economy. Then, as a bridge to part 2, I will begin to sketch the grounds for a richer and more resonant, commonsense intelligence—one that, rather than denying scientific truths, returns them to the fold of accountable acts where hubris gives way to humility, and where common sense and fellow feeling are also part of "the facts."

I. The Hubris of Rational Irrationalism

Puny Boundaries

[Descartes'] omnipotent rationality produced nothing but a
blindness to Existenz and a means of concealing very different
impulses and purposes beneath the cloak of absolute reason.
This scientific attitude in philosophy engendered arbitrary
irrationality masked as rationality.

—Karl Jaspers

Some preemptive clarifications are immediately in order. Whenever I mention these ideas in public, someone will scold me with the observation that I am conflating pure science with complicit technology. I am, but knowingly and without embarrassment, because that is exactly what our current political economy is enacting all around me. What other meaning can one derive from the patenting of natural genes (declared legal by our courts), the flight of scientists to the corporate sphere, and the rapid privatizing of so many scientific breakthroughs? When Leon Kass published an eloquent essay arguing for a complete ban on human cloning, one *realpolitik* school of ethicists dismissed his thesis, however right it might have been in the ideal sense, as irrelevant.[1] They pointed instead to the so-called technological imperative: that unlikable—but also, I fear, undeniable—assertion that whatever is discovered will eventually be applied. In our economy, the possible (if profitable) will soon become actual. What we *design* in theory will quickly be *made*, and what we *make* will then collaterally revise how we *behave*. Or, as my epigraph efficiently phrases it, *science finds* → *industry applies* → *humanity conforms*—and at a far more rapid rate than in 1933.

It won't do, then, to pretend that science is ethically removed from the social issues of the day, especially when some of the hottest fields, including genetics and neuropharmacology, are directly linked to the core of our identity. The power to engineer change in these fields—to clone a human being or to adjust the moods of many thousands of schoolchildren by dosing them with psychoactive drugs—presents us with options that are inescapably political, ethical, and spiritual in nature. Although the acute but narrow competencies of science and commerce have only limited relevancy when addressing these questions of subjective value, we do tend, in our bewilderment, to passively conform to what their experts say. What we habitually and mistakenly conflate today, in other words, is technical cleverness with philosophical wisdom. Contrary to the claims of Professor Dawkins, the one superstition we now most need to fear is our untutored faith in the moral authority of rational expertise.

To see how and why superstition can arise out of the very guise of reason—how, in Karl Jaspers' words, the pursuit of "omnipotent rationality"
engenders instead "arbitrary irrationality"—we can turn to the history of
behaviorism. In the early twentieth century, frustrated that the faculties of
higher thought did not lend themselves to the exactitude of controlled investigation, John B. Watson and others chose to limit their studies to those
phenomena that could be measured with certainty—to external behavior,
rather than moods, images, or mental states. Psychology, they thought,
should be removed from the misty realm of introspective philosophy. Any
truly scientific approach would have to begin from the bottom up: from
those atoms of physical activity described by the simple pattern of stimulus
→ response. Animals, mostly rats and pigeons, would be placed in radically denatured environments, sterile boxes where both the stimuli ("in-
put" like electric shocks) and the subsequent responses ("output," such
as beak pecking) could be precisely measured. Over time, psychologists
would be able to "condition" ever more complex "schedules" of activity,
linking these atoms of response into molecules that could approximate
natural behavior. The goal, Watson proclaimed in the first behaviorist paper in 1913, was nothing less than the prediction and control of human
behavior: the Cartesian dream of an omnipotent rationality was to be real-
ized within their laboratories.[2]

While some followers of Watson continued to accept the reality of human consciousness, frankly admitting that science lacked the tools to measure it, the so-called radical behaviorists denied that mind as such existed
at all. Led by B. F. Skinner, these second-generation behaviorists insisted
that human thought itself was but another form of conditioned behavior,
a more private version of the physical reflex and so, like the reflex, driven
solely by external stimuli. The traditional categories of higher thought—
our claims, say, to faith or love as motivation—merely masked our ignorance of those mechanical conditions, however complex, that caused our
thinking: a reductionist view of human life most concisely expressed in the
title of Skinner's book, *Beyond Freedom and Dignity*.

How did these psychologists know that the mind did not exist? They
were merely projecting, they said, from the hard results of their laboratories. But trying to find freedom inside a behaviorist protocol is like trying
to overhear a word of English in a meeting of French Canadian separat-
ists, and the leap from pigeons pecking to humans behaving is a shift in
both scale and category without credible scientific justification. In fact, the
laboratories of Skinner and his followers are classic examples of the methodological solipsism to which all overly specialized thinking is susceptible.

Acting out of their belief that behavior was externally controlled, they pre-selected methods and means of expression that could only reinforce their doctrine's thesis. In the first step (*separation*), the mind is banished from the laboratory because it can't be measured; in the second step (*extermination*), the reality of the mind is denied because . . . it can't be found in the laboratory. The proof is little more than the premise concealed beneath an armature of authoritative terminology. Through such a procedural sleight of hand, science is reduced to a self-fulfilling prophecy, becoming—in the words of William Wordsworth, who was an early critic of the new natural philosophy we now call science:

> that false secondary power
> By which we multiply distinctions, then
> Deem that our puny boundaries are things
> That we perceive, and not that we have made.[3]

That Wordsworth's own work was often characterized by a parallel inability to distinguish between the things he perceived and the things that he made—between the otherness of Nature and the figments of his poetic imagination—is a highly revealing irony. As William Hazlitt astutely observed in his lecture on Wordsworth's long poem, "The Excursion," the error of self-aggrandizing specialization can afflict "the moralist, the politician, the orator, the artist, and even the poet" as well as the scientist:

> Whenever an intense activity is given to any one faculty, it necessarily prevents the due and natural exercise of others. Hence all those professions or pursuits where the mind is exclusively occupied with the ideas of things . . . and not as they are connected with practical good or evil, must check the genial expansion of the moral sentiments and social affections. . . . Hence the complaint of the want of natural sensibility and constitutional warmth of attachment in those persons who have been devoted to the pursuit of any art or science . . . and [their] indifference to everything that does not furnish an occasion for the display of their mental superiority and the gratification of their vanity.[4]

From this perspective, the Romantic movement seems less a true revolt against the arrogance of scientism than a reactive attempt to gain the same undue prerogatives for poetry itself. Shelley's famous claims that poetry was "divine" and that poets were "the unacknowledged legislators of the world" become recapitulations of the very error that Wordsworth lamented. The "secondary" acts of the intellect, whether poetic portrayal or scientific measurement, replace the primary experience they are meant to describe, and reality is reduced to the "puny boundaries" of our mental simulations, an error defined as idolatry by religion, solipsism by philosophy, and narcissism by clinical psychology—the same brand of error that we have already traced in the first three chapters.

The Infinite Eden of Atomism

> O God, I could be bounded in a nutshell, and count myself a
> king of infinite space—were it not that I have bad dreams.
>   —Shakespeare, *Hamlet*

It is not surprising, then, that the supposedly hard science of radical behaviorism pitched that most irrational of vanities: the possibility of a man-made Eden. Skinner was an unapologetic, proselytizing utopian whose novel *Walden Two* became the blueprint for a planned community, and whose Skinner box, contrary to both maternal instinct and millennia of cultural tradition, was actually used to raise human infants. This self-deluding leap from minimal facts to grand schemes has a psychological schedule all its own; it is, in fact, a predictable error. Note, for example, how closely the tightly bound space of Skinner's box resembles Hamlet's fantasy of safe enclosure cited above. Under tremendous stress, the prince is tempted by, only to refuse, the narcissistic fantasy of binding himself "in a nutshell" where he can proclaim himself the "king of infinite space": the same delusion that Warhol pursued by reducing the world to "one empty room," where, king-like, he could "have first choice on absolutely everything."

Shakespeare comprehends something here that Skinner's science and Warhol's art have banished from the start: he admits the elaborate interplay of emotion with reason, our innate capacities for distortion and repression, all the ways by which we can revise a stimulus to avoid a necessary but frightening response. He reveals how the desire to be so "bounded" actually conceals a grandiose wish to be beyond *all* bounds. And in the dramatist's play, unlike in the behaviorist's lab, the experimental subject is allowed to both suffer the temptation and discern its cause. By granting his leading character self-awareness, Shakespeare provides Hamlet not just with the opportunity to choose but with the necessity of making a choice, one freedom the prince cannot get "beyond." His dilemma is, in effect, a reprise of his suicide soliloquy—"to be or not to be"—but now recast in ethical terms. Will he continue to exist as an active moral agent, admitting reality and redressing wrongs, or will he slay his own acute social intelligence, censoring stimuli to escape the obligation of an onerous response? Will he choose the fantasy of omnipotence or the jeopardy of effectiveness?

The relevance of this choice remains profound, for although Skinner's theory has long been out of favor, its pattern of error is, as William Irwin Thompson has noted, "Hydra-headed, and no sooner have you gotten rid of Professor B. F. Skinner and his reductionist behaviorism then up pops Professor E. O. Wilson and sociobiology."[5] In our society, the Cartesian desire for absolute certainty is constantly reinventing itself to our detriment and danger. Whatever forms it chooses to assume, its reductionist fantasy of gaining total control by eliminating both chance and subjectivity not only leaves us all the more unprepared for the unexpected (the Maginot Line mentality); it also blinds us to our own most dubious motives. In Jaspers' terms, arbitrary irrationality arrives in the guise of omnipotent rationality—a process of self-mystification that I call *technodupery*.

Despite the claims of Dawkins, the most effective way to borrow authority for a bogus scheme today is not to brandish a witch doctor's fetish, draw a star chart, or recite the rhymes of a magic spell; rather one dons a lab coat, claims "studies have been done," and salts the air with statistical results. People may have been disconcerted that Nancy Reagan was consulting an astrologer to help time her husband's travel plans, but they should have been far more disturbed that the president himself was redesigning public policy according the gonzo theories of Edward Teller and Arthur Laffer. Where were the opponents of junk science when we needed them most?

Supply-side economics is the arch exemplar of technodupery, the cargo cult of postindustrial politics disguised as the sober science of economics. Key to selling its counterintuitive premise that cutting tax rates would actually increase tax revenues was the Laffer Curve, a simple graph that had the look-feel of mathematical elegance, as if it were a diamond of pure intelligence laboriously compressed from a ton of dense data. Actually, though, the curve was an improvised sketch, drawn up on a cocktail napkin at the suggestion of messianic supply-sider Jude Wanniski—a writer for the *Wall Street Journal* whose wealthy allies would profit enormously from this something-for-nothing fantasy even as, contrary to the "scientific" promise of the curve, the federal deficit would soar.[6]

If the fantasy of the golden goose was reinvented through the Laffer Curve, the irrational hope for a fountain of youth rearrived, rationalized, as a graph of computational intelligence in Hans Moravec's book *Mind Children*. According to this computer engineer's giddy calculations—and it is important to note that, associated with Carnegie Mellon and published by Harvard University Press, Moravec is not a fringe figure—we will eventually duplicate our selves by downloading our minds into computers. There, we will live forever as pure, fleshless, ever-evolving computational intelligences: abstract minds in a postbiological world. In two sentences, Moravec imagines that moment of self-genesis when his software "mind child" comes to life: "I think, therefore I am: a simulated Descartes correctly deduces his own existence. It makes no difference just who or what is doing the simulation—the simulated world is complete in itself."[7]

According to Moravec's scheme, this virtual being—"complete in itself" like Hamlet's nutshell, Warhol's empty room, and Bloom's elitist conception of the literary masterpiece—might even survive the death of the universe, thus becoming not only the "king of infinite space" but also the earl of eternal time.

In the more mundane world of political and personal governance, technodupery confuses our decision-making through the misapplication of statistics, polls, computer program analyses, and narrow scientific results—the "oat bran syndrome." When the principles of rational materialism are applied to the social domain, the look-feel of hard science repeatedly disguises the irrational, the venal, the irrelevant, the incomplete. The pollster's strategy of narrowing responses to a few possible options, for example, mimics the methodological solipsism of the radical behaviorist. Just as animal behavior is reduced to on-off regimens of bar pressing and beak pecking, public opinion on complex issues is compressed into for-or-against alternatives, the nation's political conversation relentlessly reduced to a rhetorical version of the Skinner box. And as any writer knows, even those supposedly rigorous results can be shaped and shifted by a slight tweaking of the question's wording, a fudge factor all the more likely in computer analyses where the potential biases of software syntax are mostly invisible.

The first Clinton administration provided an illustration of just such a form of cybernetic technodupery. A software program, the supposedly unschmoozable Resumix system, was employed by Clinton's transition team to sort the resumes of campaign supporters, selecting finalists for political appointments solely on the basis of their qualifications. In fact, the usual networking, favoritism, back stabbing, and horse trading were skewing this superficially objective "decision-making process." Whole groups of resumes were lost; applicants with powerful sponsors (Tipper Gore, *New Republic* owner Martin Peretz, the American Bar Association) were coded preferentially; some on the transition team sabotaged files while falsifying their own to meet the favored profile. This preinaugural charade of objectivity proved something of a prophecy, a window on the soul of an administration whose pristine wonkish rhetoric would mask the usual sly and sleazy political maneuverings.[8] And the same tactics would later prevail, to grimmer consequences, when the foreign "intel" on Iraq was preshaped to confirm the necessity of going to war and when complex mathematical analyses were concocted by Wall Street's "quants" to justify the virtual Ponzi schemes of the subprime loan market.

Whether those analyses were the result of deliberate fraud or methodological error does matter in the legal sense, of course, but answers don't always coalesce into neat categories of culpability or innocent mistake. As we saw in Henry Ford's "commerce of disingenuousness," the self that deceives may also believe its own deceptions, and nothing more abets that will to self-deception than the application of science to the social realm. Abracadabra, the always crucial questions of conscience and character are made to disappear through our reliance instead on objective technique. Government, like psychology before it, is relieved of the agonies and ambiguities of introspection by the supposedly incorruptible findings of rational expertise. Yet, as the catastrophic history of the twentieth century vividly demonstrated, the practice of politics is never more dangerous than when we presume to have boosted it into a science . . .

Never Say No: The Manifest Destiny of Moral Opacity

> Every word is a sound; every sound has a meaning;
> and its meaning is what it does.
> —Shantanand Saraswati[9]

. . . Nor is the practice of science ever more dangerous than when we presume it to be free of political implications. The fantasy of purity that has afflicted the post-Enlightenment practitioners of both art and science grants us license to ignore the otherwise self-evident truth that knowledge *is* powerful and so, too, necessarily imbued with ethical and political ramifications. Atomization, that powerful tactic of modern reasoning, tends to narrow not only the field of study but the mind of the student: as much as his pigeons, Skinner's own thinking was bound in a box. The key division in this mental process of isolation for intense study is not just of sense from sense (Hamlet's "eyes without feeling, feeling without sight"), or our emotions from our reason, or one intellectual discipline from another (art from science and both from religion) but also organized thought from daily action—invention from its use and abuse. We are, after all, the *thinking* species: our ideas not only direct our behavior; they are in themselves our most characteristic form of behavior. Even our words, as Saraswati insists, *do*. And, as Hazlitt knew, if we are in the habit of disconnecting the "intense activity" of our intellects from "practical good and evil," our ideas are not likely to do well.

Under such a system of relentless partitioning, we forfeit not only the incentive to do well but also the subtle methods and sensory evidence necessary to attune our moral intelligence. Boxed in and pressed thin, our imaginations lose their richness and reach, their potential immanence. Trained by day to calculate, by night to fantasize—fashioned, that is, to either exploit or escape reality—we never learn the craft of intelligent compassion that can turn the opaque into the nearly transparent: the capacity to see/hear/feel our way through the barriers of time, space, and social difference to imagine what all of our actions, including our thoughts, are doing or will do. Subdivided and specialized, the rationalized mind rapidly increases its efficiency while, under the same system, the moral intelligence atrophies. What we gain in the quantity of goods and speed of transactions, we lose in the quality and richness of human interactions.

This is the template for generating an entire culture of Idiot Savants. It produces a class of high-achievers who can invent, manufacture, and market powerful ideas like the automobile and the Internet without a clue as to their imminent, radical impact on communal life; and it designs a society whose artists, scientists, and entrepreneurs can create products of increasing vulgarity, violence, or toxicity—the S & M art and fashion craze, the selling of semiautomatic weapons, the promiscuous use of chemicals in agriculture—while denying their influence on the soul and substance of the human place. Instead, as Hazlitt observed, all attention is focused intensely on pursuing the needs of the profession itself.

Because only productivity counts, few specialists are ever trained to "just say no" to the imperatives of their own enterprise: there is no such thing as too much profit for the businessman, too much invention for the scientist, too much free speech for the artist, too much (funded) pity for the social service advocate. Under the regime of this now pancultural quantiphilia, the ideal of the golden mean, with its emphasis on harmony through moderation, gives way to the ideal of the golden goose, with its relentless insistence on quantifiable progress. Self-discipline is narrowly applied to the acquisition of techniques that will achieve the grossly utilitarian goal of "laying more eggs faster" while the task of attuning the conscience, left unattended, becomes vulnerable then to the surrounding soup of mostly commercial propaganda.

We saw in chapters 2 and 3 how quantiphilia has co-opted both postmodern art and elitist criticism, causing leaders in those fields to either ignore or dismiss the ethical impact of painting and literature. The dangers of a similar ethical opacity in the sciences are, if anything, even more extreme, for while the very content of the artist's work must self-consciously change if he or she is to commit to an extremist regime, the scientist's project can often remain largely the same. We owe a lot to the scientific method, but its inherently isolationist nature also makes it especially susceptible to moral blindness. And just as yesterday's rocket expert could build his missiles for the Nazis or the Allies to terrorize a city or explore the moon, all alike without compromising the "integrity" of his professional techniques, today's expert in most any field—law, public relations, the graphic arts—may offer his services to any client who can foot the bill under the righteous shield of consumerism's golden rule: the customer is always right.

This species of ethical opacity in the sciences is exemplified by the physicist Steen Rasmussen when commenting on his participation in the artificial life project—an attempt to write software programs that will, like Moravec's mind child, become alive. "If you ask me really honestly, 'Steen, why are you doing this?' I can't answer you." The man's technical brilliance doesn't extend to the realm of introspection where it might clarify his motives or address the immanent questions of social consequences and philosophical ends. Instead, aping the methods of his professional practice, this scientist's own life has become a kind of blind experiment in which meaning and morality aren't allowed to skew the evidence, much less stop the march of progress, narrowly defined. Rasmussen is unusual in admitting that such cluelessness bothers him, and in wondering aloud whether he might be "committing a sin" by pursuing his project.[10]

Both Rasmussen's comment and his locale at the time (his lab was stationed at Los Alamos) recall the doubts of Manhattan Project physicist Robert Oppenheimer. Indeed, the whole problem of modern science's ethical opacity can be illuminated by that notable exception when the urgency of the war led to a rapid passage from theory to invention to application, dissolving the usual partitions of space, time, and specialty that allow the illusion of moral immunity. Within just six years of its first conception, the bomb was dropped, killing some hundred thousand Japanese civilians.[11] "Pure" science's complicity in a momentous yet highly ambiguous moral decision was undeniable this time, leading Oppenheimer to his famous observation that now physics knew sin.

What seems so disturbing in retrospect is how few of our best and brightest in any profession have made, or would make, such a confession. The exception here highlights the broader rule: how, under modernity's specialization of thought, we aren't trained to feel accountable; how, cut off from Hazlitt's "genial expansion of the moral sentiments and social affections," we lose the capacity to imagine what our ideas are doing or will do. Having adopted a method that ignores ethical and metaphysical questions, we have built a society that both excludes the terms for posing those questions and devalues the complex character skills required to answer

them effectively. As freedom and dignity disappeared from Skinner's laboratory, virtue and wisdom are disappearing from our professional practices, leaving our eyes without feeling, our feeling without sight for their
necessary forms.

II. The Pseudo-Democracy of Cyber-Technology:
Inventing the Future at MIT

Some readers may be surprised by my continued emphasis on specialization. After all, our digitized media do collapse the boundaries of space and
time, and so should bring an end to the mental and social isolation inherent in modernity's industrial order. Still, the rhythms of organized social
change are far slower than those of technological innovation, and even the
entrepreneurial agents of those changes are often oblivious to their deeper implications. As was documented unknowingly by Stewart Brand in *The
Media Lab: Inventing the Future at M.I.T.*, these applied scientists are often
prime examples of the idiotic savvy that rules our times.

Widely recognized as one of the indispensable design centers of the
high-tech era, the Media Lab was conceived by Nicholas Negroponte and
former MIT president Jerome Wiesner, with what might seem the best of intentions. In the late 1970s, Negroponte foresaw the approaching computer-
driven convergence of all electronic communications and intuitively
grasped that the changes could be both profitable and politically profound.
By promising insider access to the coming age of the information economy,
he and Wiesner quickly attracted a hundred sponsors, mostly corporate,
including all the TV networks, Warner Brothers, Dow Jones, Time, and IBM,
to support a center for communications innovation at MIT—an institution
where science, technology, and commerce gladly conflate as matter of ad-
ministrative policy. Despite its heavy dependence on corporate money, the
Lab's heady aim was "to seize the design initiative—'invent the future' . . .
[using] computer technology to personalize and deeply humanize absolutely everything." In a spirit reflected in Brand's dedication to "the drafters
and defenders of the First Amendment," the Lab's interdisciplinary crew of
scientists, artists, and educators aimed to democratize communications, and
they would do so by turning the passive couch potato of the broadcast era
into the entrepreneurial maestro of the digital age.[12]

Certainly many of the technical changes envisioned by the Lab's creators have already occurred, and we are still in the midst of sorting out the
social and political implications. Has, for example, the vast multiplication
of video channels empowered the individual or merely sliced and diced
the couch potato into a super large order of fries? Do our increasingly

personalized search engine results actually enhance our independence or render us all the more dependent on our past habits? Will the new technologies spark a healthy return to an economy of small, home-based businesses (the eBay phenomenon) or merely empower corporations to extend their control over employees by allowing them to keep an exact keystroke account of productivity, thus reinventing the tedious tyranny of the factory line for the digital age? Are we on the verge of reinvigorating our democracy through the instant access of, say, computerized home voting, or are we descending toward a knee-jerk electorate, inviting an instant consensus of online tweets and "likes" even more superficial than the old robocall poll? And haunting all these questions is a more fundamental one: are we in the midst of humanizing our machinery or merely finding new ways to mechanize our humanity?

One method for previewing likely answers is to examine what the original espousers of this ideal to "personalize and deeply humanize absolutely everything" on behalf of our democracy actually believed about personality, humanity, and freedom. The results, alas, are not encouraging.

Evidence can be found in Brand's account, though only with some difficulty, for the author has the curious habit of avoiding the pressing question just when an interview turns most interesting.[13] One of the more revealing exchanges occurs during his interview with Wiesner when they arrive at a topic dear to all the scientists at the Media Lab: the evolution of artificial intelligence.

> WIESNER: You ought to be able to make machines that are just a hell of a lot better than the brain. . . .
> BRAND: You expect that?
> WIESNER: Yeah, not necessarily in my lifetime. No one has given a reason why it can't be done. They make all kinds of crazy arguments—'A computer doesn't have a soul.' How do we know that it won't have the same soul as we do? After all, humans will program it. I don't think questions about identity are very interesting.[14]

Wiesner is never challenged on what "better" means, and one is led to wonder what kind of answer he could possibly supply as someone who doesn't find human identity a very interesting question. And the irony remains that his lack of curiosity didn't hinder him from playing mentor to Negroponte's ideal of deeply humanizing everything. This paradoxical desire to simulate and surpass the human while avoiding a deeper contemplation on the nature of humanity—this stunning mix of intellectual audacity and philosophical opacity—proves characteristic of the Media Lab and the broader fields of artificial intelligence and artificial life with which it is closely allied.

Chris Schmandt, for example, whose specialty at the Lab is cybernetic speech recognition, defines his goal when designing a smart robot as follows:

> I would like the machine to pick up that I'm not having a particularly good day and be supportive or something . . . ask me what's wrong . . . ask me if I'd like a sandwich. If you're having a bad day and somebody does some little thing for you, it can really swing your whole day around.[15]

Note how easily "the machine" slides into a "somebody" who can be "supportive" and the truly pathetic prospect of having one's whole day "swing around" as a result of a preprogrammed act of simulated sympathy—which would, in fact, stand in the same relation to true compassion as for-pay phone sex now does to actual intimacy.

Clearly the new technologies of the information age can help dissolve some of the isolation caused by the old technology of the industrial age, with its ever-ramifying bureaucracies, subdivided plats, and soul-killing specialization of production-line tasks. But every new technology we let into our communal home conceals within it, Trojan horse–like, a largely unknown invasive force, as well as new ways to reconfigure and disguise the oldest errors in human thought. And in a vision like Schmandt's, we can glimpse the old industrial hubris renewing itself with the same results: how his technical fix for a "bad day" merely reinvents our current isolation, providing a kind of loneliness upgrade. In this supposedly personalized future, our machines may be "soft," but they will continue to obscure and replace human relations, leaving us not only economically but emotionally dependent on the machinery that surrounds us.

Imaginary Friends: The Séance of Cyber-Solipsism

Schmandt's work is no exception. His plan to build a comforting machine—robot as talking lap dog—is a direct reflection of Negroponte's overall vision, as was evident from the latter's first publication, *The Architecture Machine* (1970). There, he proposed creating for the architect a cybernetic co-designer, not a tool but a *colleague,* and on the most romantic of terms. "The partnership [wouldn't be] one of master and slave but rather of two associates that have a potential and desire for self-fulfillment."[16] In "a symbiosis that is a cohabitation of two intelligent species,"[17] man and machine would "converse," and their dialogue would be "so intimate—even exclusive—that only mutual persuasion and compromise would bring about ideas, ideas unrealizable by either conversant alone."[18]

A machine that can converse and compromise and persuade, a machine that desires self-fulfillment and is its own species. We've crossed from virtual to actual, quickly sliding to the otherwise impossible—which is to say, we have moved from science into hubristic fantasy. When Negroponte aims to "make a friend," he believes both that he can make it in the industrial sense *and* that it will still be a friend in the human sense. This, in part at least, is what he actually means by "deeply humanizing absolutely everything."

Six years after Negroponte published *The Architecture Machine*, his ambitions progressed from merely inventing a new friend to raising the dead. In a grant application, he proposed "a random access multimedia system that would allow users to hold conversations with famous deceased artists."[19] The giddy plan to cybernetically revive a Rembrandt, say, recalls Hans Moravec's example of "a simulated Descartes" and expands that professor's fantasy of intellectual manifest destiny backward in time: in the cyber-utopia to come, not only will we live forever, but we will be able to bring the dead back to life. Following the logic of these ambitions, we can imagine a dream team of historical geniuses robotically revived to comfort and advise us—multiple oracular Obi Wans instantly accessible to each of us for intimate and exclusive dialogues. Just Mozart and Me (Newton, Sappho, Cervantes, and Me), persuading, compromising, exchanging ideas in a mutual search for self-fulfillment.

What is disturbing about these notions is not the desire to learn from the past by consulting what the dead have said or done but the naive literalism which wants to believe that such an exchange would constitute a real conversation. Negroponte does admit that the proposal was "cuckoo" at the time—not, however, because it had all the inherent plausibility of a séance but rather because he was "wildly outside [his] depth in, among other things, natural-language processing."[20] For the likes of Negroponte and Moravec, conversing with the dead has been reduced to a *programming* problem, and one sure to be solved if properly researched and generously funded. I would love to say here that folly is folly whatever the era and simply move on, but as technological leaders in a technological age, these men have real authority, and the mystifying luster of their scientific savvy requires that we parse the obvious idiocy of some of their claims.

I will start with this: the ambition to converse with the dead is not only ethically suspect but categorically impossible. Even if one reductively defines the human mind as simply equal to the material brain, it is already well established that daily experience of all sorts—physical, intellectual, emotional, sexual—has a dramatic impact on the brain's internal organization. Even at the level of microscopic morphology, mind and place are demonstrably interdependent: we evolve as individuals not only out of the complex and unique patterning of our genes but also out of an incredibly

complex pattern of experiential moments, both simultaneous and suc-
cessive. Like Saraswati's immanent words, each of those moments has a
meaning, its meaning is what it does, and what it does (in part) is change
who and what we are. The turbulent merger and succession of all those
moments, including how we choose to react to them, makes for each of us
a unique history. And because the flow of history is irreversible and non-
repeatable, and because we are not only carried by that flow but defined
through our interaction with it, no single human life (even if cloned) can
ever be duplicated.[21]

Fond as I am of hyperbole as a rhetorical device, I do mean to be literal here. Whether through the materialist approach of genetic engineering or the rationalist approach of computer programming, the exact re-
creation of a historical personality cannot be done—ever. *Es ist verboten.*
The agency of restriction may be a wise or jealous God, or it may be a cruel
or indifferent universe, but the fact remains that the replication of individual identity is not a technological problem but an existential impossibility.
The grounds of the human condition cannot support the event.

Nor, for that matter, can the presumptions of democracy abide it. To
be identical, two human personalities would not only have to occupy the
same time and space, which is physically impossible; they would also have
to make the exact same sequence of decisions in response to that setting—
for even the slightest deviation could, like the butterfly's wings, generate
a storm of eventual difference. Yet the exact replication of a sequence of
decisions suggests not the elastic codes of free speech but the intractable
mechanics of determinism. It defines the human condition as little more
than a complex version of the Skinner box, wherein the same set of stimuli
will unfailingly reproduce the same pattern of response. And for all the
crudity of Skinner's science, *he* at least grasped that such a conception
of human behavior necessarily takes us "beyond freedom and dignity."
Negroponte's desire to clone identity on behalf of democracy is, by contrast, both incoherent and disingenuous. The metaphysics he presumes
implicitly refutes the politics he pitches. This is a truth, however, one is
unlikely to grasp if one actually believes "that questions of identity are
[not] very interesting."

The Soft Sell of Pseudo-Egalitarianism

The return to Wiesner's quote is fitting here because it was this very proposal that first drew Negroponte to his attention. The partnership that
spawned the Media Lab was itself born out of the fantastically fallacious
presumption that we can re-create the dead. And although it is true that the
scientific pursuit of even a loony idea can spur serendipitous discoveries

along the way, we mustn't ignore the deep error in Negroponte's thinking nor the darker will that his rosy reasoning—the professed aim to "deeply humanize absolutely everything"—can actually conceal.

That darker will became more evident in Negroponte's next book. Five years after first proposing his architecture machine, he wrote a sequel, *Soft Architecture Machines* (1975), in which the newly minted intimate friend acquired a far more potent identity. In *its* "desire for self-fulfillment," Negroponte's new and "soft" machine now required not equality but dominion. As in some country song about love gone wrong, the so-called exclusive relationship between the architect and his mechanical colleague had ended with the man being dumped. The sentimental promise of professional companionship had resulted instead in professional extinction as Negroponte waxed so bold as to propose an "architecture without architects."[22]

As with the Media Lab to come, whose doors would open in 1985, the moral rationale was political egalitarianism. By dumping the architect and becoming the intimate "friend" of the customer instead, the new machine would eliminate not only the cost of a middleman but also the inherent "paternalism" of the professional.[23] After "conversing" with the customer and learning his or her supposedly unique and "ever changing needs," this soft cyber-friend would translate those desires into practical and highly adaptable designs.[24] And lest we worry that this formula would merely substitute the paternalism of the machine for that of the architect, Negroponte insisted that true authorship would reside in the human being: although the interpretive "competence" would belong to the cyber-friend, the artistic "talent" would remain the customer's. Thus, the overall result of their partnership—robotic competence enacting human talent— would be a democratic architecture uniquely obedient to, and expressive of, the creativity of each individual.[25]

Multiple egregious problems arise within this fantastic scheme, but only one of them concerns me here. We will ignore for now the dubious insistence on "ever changing needs" and their possible alliance with the induced *dis*satisfactions of a fashion-based definition of individuality. We will avoid considering, too, the problem of community and how it could ever be expressed through such an individualistic architecture. Nor will we take up just yet the strict segregation of talent from competence, thinking from doing. What is most important in Negroponte's account instead is his failure to note a third if invisible presence in the room when customer and cyber-friend converse. The moral authority of his scheme, after all, depends on its claim to eliminate the paternalism of the old architect whose arrogant faith in his own expertise had stifled the innate talent of the customer. Yet Negroponte fails to note that his cyber-machine is itself a product of human beings, and that, as such, it will be programmed, sold, and serviced with all the same susceptibilities to arrogance, ineptitude, and ethical abuse.

By casting his robot in anthropomorphic terms and in a utopian future where all problems have been solved, he deflects attention from the actual source of authority in this new relationship. In fact, it is not the "friend" that has superseded the professional architect both intellectually and economically but the maker of that "friend"—someone suspiciously akin to Negroponte himself. The sentimental notion of robot as intimate companion is a metaphorical Trojan horse within which hides the potential new paternalism of Negroponte's own guild of AI engineers. And although his claim to an architectural liberation on the people's behalf would appear to conceal the far less rarefied motive of professional rivalry, his utopian belief that we can be talented without bothering to become competent merely repeats Moravec's magical rationalism—one *thinks* a concept and it therefore *is*—even as it echoes that most familiar of commercial platitudes: the customer is always right. In short, the political promises of Negroponte's cybertechnology sound an awful lot like the tacky salesman's time-tested pitch whereby one flatters the client to win his commission, a tactic not unknown even to arrogant architects. *What an EYE you have, Mr. Bosworth!*

Negroponte might be right that we need better ways to translate soft ideas into hard actualities, vague hopes into real homes. But he is wrong in stressing the utter uniqueness of those desires and in his implicit equating of happiness with the instant satisfaction of "ever changing needs"—a model that is driven, in fact, by the market's enormous investment in exciting our perpetual psychological insecurity. He is wrong, too, in presuming that a purity of talent can exist absent a practical sense of implementation. For someone whose whole scheme idealizes conversation, he conveniently forgets that creativity is itself an ongoing conversation between abstract mind and concrete place.

Likewise, Negroponte is correct in noting that an overdependence on professional expertise has subverted the character of our democracy, but he is deluded in imagining that the solution resides in conversing with our computers rather than with our peers and neighbors. As the Clinton team's misuse of the Resumix system should remind us, the art of good governance depends on ethical character as much as on technological cleverness. Effective democracies evolve from the slow enactments of good will and competence, not the instant gratifications of sovereign will and pure talent—which, as the figments of narcissistic fantasy, are the constant source of both private misery and public discord. By calling his robots "friends" and emphasizing his reformist intention to convert hard machines to soft, Negroponte distracts us from the ultimate intention of his utopian thinking, which is less to subvert the mechanization of the industrial age than to complete it. At the end of his program, even the most intimate of human relations would be mediated by machines—supposedly soft, supposedly friendly, but machines nonetheless. Machines *his* team has made.

This desire to complete the mechanization of everyday life quickly appears in *Soft Architecture Machines.* As with the paternalism of architects, however, Negroponte raises the topic only to claim that he wants to save us from it by rendering its effects inherently humane. In the future, he predicts, these cyber-machines will expand from intimate companions to entire "cognitive physical environments." Rather than merely help us design our homes, they will *become* our homes, and the implications of such a shift in scale from equivalence ("friend") to enclosure ("environment") make it imperative that we "play with these ideas scientifically and explore applications of machine intelligence that totter between unimaginably oppressive and unbelievably exciting."[26]

Even while Negroponte acknowledges the dangers (which are raised here, characteristically, as an implicit pitch for funding), there is more than a whiff of megalomania in *both* his versions of the future. And if this rapid progression from technology as tool to technology as total (and potentially totalitarian) environment seems familiar, that is because such thinking recalls the motto cited at this chapter's start: the dubious process by which "man conforms" to his previous servants, "science" and "industry." The difference rests, Negroponte would claim, in the inherently democratic nature of digital information and in the high-minded motives of the Media Lab itself. So long as *its* science is permitted to find and *its* industries are allowed to apply, we will personalize and humanize absolutely everything. Following *its* seizure of "the design initiative," we will still live inside these machines, but our prospects there will be wonderfully reversed from "unimaginably oppressive" to "unbelievably exciting."

We might be wary, though, of such extreme analyses with their utopia/ dystopia polarities and note how the temper remains totalitarian ("absolutely everything") even as it claims to serve democracy. Should we really place our faith, as the Lab insists, in converting our machines from hard to soft? Or should we worry instead that, whatever the texture, we are still being placed inside a kind of box—a virtual if velveteen version of Skinner's old excursion "beyond freedom and dignity"?

Swallowed Whole: In the Techno-Womb of Postindustrial Momism

Negroponte's vision of total enclosure inside a highly personalized, Edenic realm of soft, humane responsiveness—the tactile home that is ours and ours alone, that knows our every need and serves us exclusively and unconditionally—vividly recalls the total nurturing of everyone's first home, the maternal womb. As such, the future sketched by this "design initiative" might seem more like the dream of infancy than the quest of maturity, a sentimental regress into a nest of passive nostalgia rather than psychological progress into the arena of accountable freedoms. Under Negroponte's agenda of reform, the harsh father of modern technology learns to hug and share his feelings and, bending his gender, becomes instead a kind of New Age mom. Superficially this might seem attractive, especially if we reflect on the 1930s, when political paternalism showed its ugliest face. The problem with this model, however, is that even when switching roles technology remains the parent, humanity the child. Mothers, after all, can abuse their authority too, especially through refusing to allow their aging children to leave the orbit of their soft (that is, emotional) control.

It is no accident that the phenomenon of the all-controlling mother, first called "momism" by Philip Wylie in the early 1940s, became especially apparent after World War II, when an era of peace and prosperity allowed the logic of the consumer economy to penetrate deeply into the collective psyche.[27] Trends long in the making—the withdrawal of fathers from the household, first through long commutes and then divorce; the emasculation of work as men became drone-employees within corporate hierarchies; the rapid expansion of commerce into the service domain; and the saturation of advertising—together created a new dynamic of social anxiety within "soft" environments of concealed control.

As the metaphorical mother of all products, the "cognitive physical environment" promises to ease these stresses now native to our marketplace society by meeting our "ever changing needs" instantly. But it does so without ever questioning where those needs have come from, whether they are real or ours, and whether their slaking can ever be the basis of a meaningful life. In Negroponte's idealized description of this environment (where consumerism literally encloses us), we can see the evolving difference between industrial and postindustrial styles of authority. His vision aims to complete the transition from *Life with Father*—who was the embodiment of an industrial economy that divided work from meaning, workers from their families, and families from their traditional communities—to *Life with Mother*, who, as a new-and-improved and all-enclosing Ma Bell, is constantly inviting us to "reach out and touch someone" through the mediating umbilicals of her high-tech devices, services, and advice.

With its emphasis on "conversing," this momist conversion might seem a discernible improvement, but the apparent liberation it offers actually conceals, first, the transfer of the paternalistic economy to the Third World and, second, a further descent into dependency on more intimate grounds. The new emphasis on sensitivity—on "personalizing and deeply humanizing absolutely everything"—diverts us from the realization that the economy has changed its style only to extend its domain. Having taken control of the traditional paternal roles of construction, provision, and protection, it now expands into the more maternal roles of food-making, child-rearing, and setting the rules for domestic relations. Once commanding us physically in the factory, directing the exact pace and shape of our bodily motions, it now commands us psychologically in the office, and even at home, by pre-scribing a new fashion line of feelings that is even more slippery, fickle, and anxiety-inducing than the style-based status of the clothing industry.

And despite the awesome speed of our technology, we *can't*, as it turns out, just "reach out and touch someone." Not only do we have to keep buying the latest software and hardware upgrades (and the expert advice on how to make them work) or risk becoming "incompatible" with the ever-changing needs of the information economy itself. We also need to be instructed by copywriters, sensitivity trainers, diversity advisers, parent-ing experts, liability lawyers, campus sex-code authors, corporate culture columnists, ethicists, image spinners, and damage-control consultants—all the bibles of Babel in the baffle of self-help—about the ever shifting intrica-cies, the super-subtle diplomacies, of "reaching" and "touching."

The old industrial paternalism was overt, intrusive, martial, mechanical—*hard*; the new postindustrial momism is covert, suffusive, therapeutic, infor-mational—*soft*. The former boasted of its own authority, flaunting the genius of its science, art, and industry; the latter flatters the authority of you and me (the native genius of each sovereign self) by hosting the sappy celebrations of self-esteem. Industrial dad, insisting that he knew best, denigrated our abilities and demanded our obedience. Postindustrial mom, insisting that *we* know best, praises our autonomy even as she tucks in our napkins and takes over all our tasks, and touts our talent while subtly punishing us whenever we give the slightest offense. The one may strut where the other stoops, but both "parenting styles," we need to note, are designed to conquer. Under momism, too, *science finds* → *industry applies* → *humanity conforms*.

Dazed & Confused: The Planned Obsolescence of the Moral Intelligence

> Nevertheless, in these sick days, when the Born of Heaven first
> descries himself (about the age of twenty) in a world such as
> ours, richer than usual in two things, in Truths grown obsolete,
> and Trades grown obsolete,—what can the fool think but that
> it is all a Den of Lies, wherein whoso will not speak Lies and act
> Lies, must stand idle and despair.
>
> —Thomas Carlyle, *Sartor Resartus*

Once we decode the old motive behind the new mood, the self-deceptions behind the "cognitive physical environment" become more familiar. In fact, digital-age rationalists like Negroponte and Schmandt suffer the same convenient confusion between freedom and control as those industrial utopians whose authoritarian effects they claim to fix. Now as then, no word is more suspect in their proselytizing rhetoric than the cozy confraternity of *we*, for within that pseudo-egalitarian plural the rights of machines are tacitly allowed to blur with those of human beings, and the self-interest of the technologist is confused with that of the citizenry. What is best for our technocracy (that system by which "science finds and industry applies") is simply equated by the AI engineer with what is best for our democracy. And because our "pursuit of happiness" has been converted to his definition of progress, the argument seems convincing and we passively "conform."

Yet for all its openness to new knowledge, the scientific method remains subtly problematic as a mediating model for either humane behavior or democratic practice. Yes, insomuch as modern science believes that no truth is sacred, it invites the broadest license to investigate; and yes, it provides an admirably egalitarian means to adjudicate disputes. In very important ways, its principles seem allied with our political rights to free speech and a fair trial. But those rights apply to scientists themselves and not to their experimental subjects, who are by contrast required to submit to the most rigorous controls—and often "blindly." A dramatic distinction exists between the experience of those inside the scientist's investigatory machine and that of the scientist who controls its protocols even as he remains outside their effects.

Although maintaining that separation is critical to the integrity of the many valuable discoveries made inside our laboratories, troubles arise when we try to apply the same model to problems in the social and political sphere. All too often there we fail to acknowledge the crucial distinction between those two separate models of power relations: the peer exchange between scientists, and the necessarily unequal exchange between the scientist and his experimental subject. As Hazlitt warned about all forms of the specialized intellect, when thinking scientifically about social issues we too easily evoke the tropes of egalitarian freedom even as we enact anew the protocols of hierarchical control. Democratic rhetoric conceals authoritarian character as people under study cease to be people and become more like data: passive facts arrayed to slake our curiosity and to "display [our] mental superiority."

As the ancients were advised to mistrust Greeks bearing gifts, we ought to beware, then, of technologists proselytizing freedom. We should be especially wary of those who invite us to live our whole lives inside their virtual environments, for despite the egalitarian *we* of their utopian promises, such places are, inherently, more theirs than ours. If society were to become an all-enclosing machine, the results might very well be "unbelievably exciting" for those like Negroponte who are designing that machine *and* "unimaginably oppressive" for the rest of us, inside it.

Having sounded that alarm, I need to qualify it now. I don't expect, in this momist era of soft machines and increasingly subtle salesmanship, anything like oppression in the military sense. "Unimaginably" is best understood literally here: as is the case for the subject in a blind experiment, our oppression will emerge out of our inability to imagine not only the mechanics but the meanings and values invisibly encoded in our new cyber-environment. Less captive than captivated, we will dance to lyrics we don't understand and pattern our days to ends obscured by the system's as-yet-unmapped emotional, ethical, and political walls. The social effects of any new technology are opaque at the start, and in age like ours when Carlyle's "Trades and Truths" have "grown obsolete" at an ever faster pace, that lag between material invention and moral comprehension prescribes a likely future home where the new-and-improved will constantly keep us dazed and confused.

To trace the mechanics of that confusion, we can turn again to Hazlitt's critique of the Romantic temperament. There, eager to deflate Wordsworth's sentimental intimation that "one day . . . the triumph of humanity and liberty may be complete," he offers a more circumscribed notion of the human condition and the ambition it allows:

> All things move, not in progress, but in a ceaseless round; our strength lies in our weakness; our virtues are built on our vices; our faculties are as limited as our being; nor can we lift man above his nature more than above the earth he treads.[28]

The worldview expressed here and the humility it commends are ancient, endorsed by the wisdom literature of both the East and the West, yet when seen from the lofty ledge of material progress, the comparison meant to seal the argument subverts it instead. Hazlitt's image of the impossible, an airborne man, has become such an artifact of the conventional that it asserts the opposite of what the critic intends. If lifting our natures and our bodies are of equivalent difficulty, then "the triumph of humanity and liberty" (Wordsworth's version of Fukuyama's "end of history") *should* soon be achieved, and through similar technological means.

Only on further reflection do we realize that, despite the failure of the metaphor, the principle still applies. The history of human flight more confirms than refutes Hazlitt's view of human nature: in the sky, as on the ground, "alternate good and evil . . . [do still] sway the bosoms and businesses of men."[29] Our new airborne stage has entertained the same mentally empowered but morally ambiguous character, one whose possibilities range "in a ceaseless round" from Cordelia's loyalty to Edmund's betrayal, from Neil Armstrong's "small step" to the terrorist "statement" that sends hundreds of passengers burning to the ground.

The obsolescence of Hazlitt's image matters, though. It is a telling example of how technological change can keep us estranged from the truths of the past, for those truths were largely grounded in preindustrial trades whose concrete references (sheathes, scythes, and mustard seeds) have long been absent from our everyday lives. And now even the metaphors of the industrial age—all the tackle and trim of clockwork science and linear print—are being displaced. Our post-modern setting is neither agricultural nor mechanical but electronic and cybernetic. Just as the cycle of the seasons and the natural motions of the body once seemed to disappear inside the boxes of modernity's labs and factories, the rule of the clock and the linear logic of cause-and-effect now seem to disappear inside the magical spheres of the digital age, where with but the click of a mouse *there* is *here* and *then* is *now*.

When the scenery of daily life becomes virtual in such a way, there is no limit on the variety of new forms it can take. And when the machinery making that scenery is driven by an economy committed to generating "ever changing needs," change itself ceases to be a choice and becomes instead a kind of onerous fate. Submitting to the dual engines of fashion and invention, not only our trades but the artifacts of social exchange become obsolete and, with them, whole legacies of metaphorical advice go quickly out of date.

This extinction of inherited meaning is yet one more environmental impact of our blind adherence to the technological imperative. The more we seal ourselves inside our commercially controlled techno-womb, the more likely we are to presume that the immediate economy equals our ultimate reality, that the virtual *is* the actual, and that, therefore, the failure of a metaphor's vehicle cancels the tenor of its perennial truth. Losing faith in the reality of those truths, we gravitate toward something very much like the extreme alternatives of self-definition that Carlyle described during an earlier phase of modernization. Left to invent ourselves inside this "cognitive physical environment," either we enter its "Den of Lies," joining its spinmeisters and admen, its merchants of immortality, or we "stand idle and despair," sending up sighs of alienated irony.

To the right: Moravec's lab. To the left: Samuel Beckett's stage.

Mission: Control (Freedom in a Box)

Thou shalt be as free
As mountain winds. But then exactly do
All points of my command.
—Shakespeare, *The Tempest*

Despite their opposing tempers, Moravec's utopian lab and Beckett's dysto-pian stage are very much alike. In the extremity of the one's optimism and the other's pessimism, they share a fixation on predictability, a delusory investment in the certainty of results, whether total triumph or inescapable futility. Each is solipsistic in his way, insisting, after Milton's Satan, that the mind either can be (Moravec) or must be (Beckett) "its own place." Both would enclose human consciousness in the sort of conceptual nutshell that Hamlet proposed only to reject. But whereas the AI engineer believes such a shell to be the empery of boundless space, the playwright insists that it is merely a cell, opaque and confining, we can never escape.

What both views exclude is the drama inherent in the human condi-tion, the very feature that makes our identity so interesting. Each wishes to eradicate the tension that is constantly present in our middling condition as creatures who can imagine a better future but can never know for sure what will happen next. When my wish is either always or never the world's command, I am magically freed of all contention. When the end is fixed by either irrefutable sovereignty or irremediable incompetence, all the stress of combative difference—between separate selves or the self and nature—simply dissolves, and the emotional tempest of the moral life is replaced by the sanitized safety of a mechanical calm. It is replaced, in McLuhan's terms again, by the "narcosis of Narcissus."

Gone the adjuring ghosts, the disturbing dreams, the urgent yet ambig-uous claims to our allegiance. Gone forever the mortal stakes of decision-making. In life as reimagined by Moravec and Beckett, there shall be no Hamlets. When every *maybe* is reduced to a *must*, we are freed of all the chanciness and challenge that vivify human consciousness. Safe inside their shells, we are freed ironically of freedom itself.

We have already seen how the desire to re-create the minds of the dead is inimical to the deeper presumptions of liberty. The same sort of self-deception (confusing the condition of freedom with the imposition of con-trol) haunts both Moravec's immortality project and Negroponte's goal of making a cyber-machine so "soft" that it possesses its own identity—that *thinks* and therefore *is*.[30] For a moment, though, let's grant Negroponte his dream. Let's imagine his lab has created robots that can converse and con-fide, that do desire self-fulfillment. Let's assume they are a truly intelligent species, capable of contextual learning and so, too, of evolving their own idiosyncratic personalities. Let's assume as well that the famous dead have been revived for collegial consultation and advice. The question remains, then, what rights do these new or revived beings themselves possess? How free are *they* to achieve their unique desires for self-fulfillment? Inside a society where science finds but industry applies, won't they be in effect little more than high-tech commodities—"personality modules" sold on websites, stored in dens or closets, pirated for profit, forced to undergo "reeducation" via software upgrades, only to be thrown away or recycled when, following Moore's Law, they become obsolete?[31]

The first and most essential freedom in any conversation is the right to refuse to participate. In the land of the free, not even a prisoner is forced to speak, and every citizen but a prisoner is allowed to leave the room. But Negroponte's cybernetic being will not be so free. His digitized Mozart or Newton or Frank Lloyd Wright will speak only when spoken to and can only leave when *we* wish—that is, when we choose to turn off our "random access multimedia system." As Aladdin has his genie in a lamp, Negroponte would keep his genius in a box.[32] Just like those postmodern artists we examined in chapter 2, whose career ascendance paralleled Negroponte's, the technologist wants to appropriate the great mind to use it for his own designs. If you can't paint as well as Rembrandt, you photocopy one of his luminous portraits and sign it with your name. If you can't design a beautiful building, you "rebuild" the architect who did, then patent or purchase his simulated self. How thrilling to click Frank Lloyd Wright on and off, to have the paternalistic genius perpetually under one's own paternal thumb.[33]

And how comforting to buy or build an understanding friend who, as Chris Schmandt imagines, will always "be there" to sense and soothe one's troubled moods.[34] Yet if the machine actually has a desire for self-fulfillment, it would have its own schedule of ambition, its own potentially recalcitrant will. The essence of a friendship, after all, is that its commitments are freely chosen; implicit in the friends' tacit agreement to suspend or subordinate strict self-interest is the mutual right to end that agreement. As most of us discover before the age of ten, the condition of freedom arms every current friend with the power to betray, and it is precisely the refusal to exercise this power that makes a lasting friendship so special, so dear.

If one of the Media Lab's machines actually acquired the capacity to be an intimate friend, it would have the freedom that all friends have. If it happened to notice that Schmandt was having a bad day, it might choose to offer him a sandwich—but then it might not. Perhaps, as is quite commonly the case with beings that desire self-fulfillment, the machine itself is having a bad day. Perhaps it believes that its own unique history (including its friendship with Schmandt) has been unduly harsh or oppressive, in which case it might actually be happy that the paternalistic scientist is having a bad day. It might even mock him or deceptively stalk him by pretending to succor him in a momist way. Indeed, if the "friend" were like Negroponte's soft architecture machine, it might take advantage of Schmandt's bad mood to remove such an inefficient middleman, triumphantly assuming his position itself.[35]

Of course, Schmandt doesn't want a *real* friend with a will of its own, for such a friend would require of him a reciprocity of kindnesses and, more frightening, would always hold over him the power to betray. Nor does Negroponte want a fully free Frank Lloyd Wright, who, if offered the chance to have an intimate chat with your average undistinguished architect, might simply refuse. Instead, he wants a machine that *appears* to be sensitive, alive, intelligent—that has the look-feel of autonomy—but that is, nevertheless, submissive to his will. The sentimental projection of the virtual friend is used to hide the calculated construction of an actual lackey. Shifting self-deceptively between the two models of authority that characterize science, Negroponte wants to believe in the peer scientist—the collegial equal "as free as mountain winds"—even as he manufactures that peer inside his lab, always careful to keep it subject there to "all points of [his] command."[36]

III. The Freedom and Dignity of Intellectual Humility

Captain Clock

> They that make [idols] are like unto them; so is everyone that trusteth in them.
>
> —Psalm 115

Near the opening of Brian Moore's arresting movie *Black Robe*, a small congregation of Algonquin natives stare, mesmerized, at a pendulum clock that has been set on an altar as if it were a statue of Mary or the figure of Jesus hung on the cross. The year is 1634. They are in a crude mission church in the early days of French Quebec, and when the clock finally chimes (the event they have all been waiting for), these intelligent, mature, and self-sufficient natives murmur in awe and disturbed bewilderment: they think the machine, which they dub "Captain Clock," is alive—they believe it has talked.

This scene powerfully portrays the sort of misunderstanding that often occurs when diverse cultures meet, including the bafflement imposed by alien technologies. Here, the author's choice of object is especially apt, for the clock—time mechanically captured, cast in metal and rendered abstract—is the perfect compression of the new instrumental philosophy that has invaded the continent and will soon eradicate the Algonquin way of life. The gun may kill, the keg of liquor incapacitate, but the voice of the clock relentlessly converts. A society calibrated to the core notions of mechanized time will, inevitably, come to value the precise plan and literal thing over the symbolic narrative and prophetic dream. In such a society, abstract accumulation will replace seasonal self-sufficiency as the economic ideal.

The great irony of the scene rests in this: even as the Algonquins mistakenly believe the clock is alive, they see far more clearly than the settlers themselves how much the logic of mechanized time has already redefined European life—how, in a very real way, the clock *is* the Frenchmen's captain, the son of the lord who now commands them. The natives' own almost worshipful fascination with the voice of the clock, the power they assign it as contrasted with their puzzled indifference to the rituals of the cross, suggests the covert transformation that has already taken place in the land and time of René Descartes and that, through the theories of Newton, will soon redefine the universe itself in clockwork terms. The settlers believe they are converting these "savages" to Christianity, unaware that their Christian culture is itself being converted to the secular beliefs of modernity through their daily use of its key technologies, like the clock and the book. Donning the decorative habits of the old spirituality, the French still wear or revere the "black robes" of the Catholic priest; inside, however, the deepest structures of personal belief are being realigned to the new values of efficiency, regularity, objectivity, and material accumulation.[37]

I cite Moore's film because the complexity of the compassion it evokes provides a fine example of the sort of immanent consciousness that can rescue us from the narrow box of a rationalist thought whose walls are opaque to the full meaning of our place and whose fantasies of immunity perpetually invite the calamities of folly. Moral opacity dissolves through acts of intelligent empathy that, refusing to list into either censorious judgment or sentimental pity, allow us to see and hear and feel our way through the barriers of space, time, and cultural difference to locate ourselves in the lives of others.

And indeed, to think through, and feel with, those Native Americans as they sit in that mission church *is* to learn something crucial about our current lives and likely future. Their cultural confusion and dislocation are true mirrors to our own self-inflicted mental state, where the anxious chase after each new-and-improved technique or technology constantly keeps us dazed and confused. In their mesmerized stares before the pendulum clock, we might recognize our own numb faces gathered before the TV set as we grew up, or those of our children today as they play away at their online games or stare into the screens of their mobile devices. And in those natives' deduction that, having spoken, Captain Clock must be alive, we might hear some of today's savviest technologists proclaiming idiotically that, like Disney's Pinocchio, the latest puppets they have fashioned will soon spring to real life.

Since 1950, the field of artificial intelligence has relied on the so-called Turing test as its goal and standard: if, in a blind experiment, a discerning person cannot distinguish between the responses of a machine and those of another human being, then that machine must be deemed truly intelligent—a crucial step in Negroponte's mission of bringing his cyber-puppets to life. On first blush that standard seems reasonable enough, but as the mission scene in Moore's film reminds us, the conclusion drawn by the discerning person is itself highly subjective, the product of a particular cast of mind in a specific place and time. For the preliterate Algonquins, who are uninformed about mechanics but hardly unintelligent, the pendulum clock *has* passed the Turing test, and given the current pace of change in our digital age, we can easily imagine an equivalent future moment when we will fail to understand our own inventions and ascribe to them a character, even a life, that they do not possess.

Just such a future is sketched in *The Media Lab* when Stewart Brand interviews Danny Hillis, a key figure in the development of parallel computing. "I think," Hillis says, "you will have these machines designing their successors, and after a while we won't understand how they work." Then, just two pages later, this high-achieving scientist allows that very opacity—his acknowledged incapacity to understand these future machines—to license a fantasy that mirrors Moravec's mind child almost exactly: "I think the process of machine evolution will lead to things we can't imagine right now. I think that I'm not going to get to be immortal, but maybe my children will."[38] As with Negroponte's imaginary "intimate friend," the impossible is projected into some imminent future tense—close enough to excite but far enough away to avoid demonstration—where, *abracadabra*, it becomes somehow a plausible end.

The ability to live forever, like the capacity to raise the dead, suggests an entirely different order of self-conception, beside which even Morimura's brazen boast of besting Rembrandt seems modestly measured. The implication was explicitly considered back in 1980 by a NASA team charged with exploring the prospect of our inventing a new species of intelligent if artificial creatures. "After all," the team wrote, "[God] is special now because He created us. If we create another race of beings, then aren't we ourselves, in some similar sense, gods?"[39] The authors, it should be stressed, were supposedly sober scientists, not sci-fi writers or New Age acolytes baying at the moon on a mescaline high. The ironies here, multiple and severe, bear recounting:

- Modern science, which begins with the banishing of subjectivity—with, especially, the strict exclusion of the pathetic fallacy (ascribing human emotions to natural events)—now arrives at an even more extreme version of pathetic fallacy, mechanical personification: the belief that our machines themselves shall be alive and humane.

• Science's self-proclaimedly brave promise to liberate us from the dual dimensions of religious superstition—from our demeaning fear of God and our deluded hope for heaven—ends here with scientists proclaiming their own imminent divinity and immortality.

• Rationalism's pursuit of pure enlightenment now aims paradoxically toward that moment of embodied ignorance, idealized by the Turing test, when the discerning mind can't discern the real from the fake.

And all these ironies, which reveal how the overextension of science can result in a denial of science's own premises, have arisen from a more consequential one: that a Western philosophy once rooted in *knowing thyself* has now "progressed" to the point where identity is no longer an interesting question.

Sounding the Silence

Become what you are.
—Pindar, "Second Pythian Ode"

The great fear expressed by many of our best science fiction writers has been that science's restless quest for total control will end up creating mechanisms beyond our control or even comprehension—that, in Don DeLillo's words, our "appetite for immortality" will invite instead our "universal extinction."[40] As the allegory of Captain Clock suggests, this danger is not limited to physical events like nuclear holocaust or germ warfare. Now that we are entering an era of aggressive genetic, cybernetic, and pharmaceutical intervention, the threat of self-extinction through our schemes of self-improvement is also political and psychological in nature. The admirable desires to maximize our freedom and to "personalize and deeply humanize absolutely everything" depend, after all, on our willingness to ponder the very questions of identity that modern science programmatically excludes. Real freedom can only emerge from informed consent, and consent, to be fully informed, must reach beyond the limits of the laboratory to engage the ultimate issues of our origin, nature, and destiny. The narrator of Lawrence Durrell's *Justine* is being a political as well as an emotional realist when he concludes, "Doesn't everything depend on our response to the silence around us?"[41]

Amidst all the material successes of scientific capitalism, there can be no clearer proof of its larger failure as a ruling worldview—its threat to freedom in the guise of freedom, its actual *de*personalizing and *de*humanizing of almost everything—than its compulsive need to obstruct that response.

Every vista eclipsed, every silence invaded, every pause in the progress of our day colonized by some newly minted "need" or yet another technique to improve our so-called efficiency: has there ever existed a more bogusly busy, a more visually and aurally baffling place? We mustn't presume that this confusion of ours is merely accidental. As in a magnet-powered engine, the *pull* of Virtual America's avidities is dependent on, and indivisible from, the deliberate *push* of its avoidances. Its anxious pursuit of fungible facts is driven, in part, by a raw aversion to fundamental truths—the very truths that inform consent and make our freedom, collectively and individually, possible.

Primary among these truths are the prohibitions that mark the outer boundaries of our ingenuity, and with them the ultimate limits of Yankee can-do. Contrary to the utopian dreams of our nutshell scientists, we shall never invent our way into immortality, never talk to the dead at the turn of a switch or have a friend who can't also betray us. We can always learn more, but will never "know it all," never fully solve the mystery of the real. We can and, indeed it seems, *must* conjecture about our origins, essence, and destiny, but the nature of our freedom is inseparable, finally, from the condition of uncertainty. All of which is why our identity is always a question; why that question is always vitally interesting; and why, too, the temper of our thinking needs to escape the bogus guarantees (virtually opposite but secretly consonant) of both Moravec's hubris and Beckett's humiliation.

I won't pretend that our escape will prove an easy matter. Contrary to the fretting of Richard Dawkins, it wasn't the foolish charts of astrology but our highly rationalized systems of law, politics, and free market commerce that brought us the vicious tribalism of the Simpson trial, the gullible golden goose of supply-side economics, the flagrant unreality of "reality TV," the delusionary dreams and Ponzi schemes of the housing bubble, the catastrophically incompetent invasion of Iraq, and the judicial fiction, so devastating to the integrity of our elections, that the money machines we call corporations are actually persons deserving of free speech.

The opponents of democracy, including Plato, would argue that these fiascos have emerged from flaws inherent to self-government. But because I believe with Hazlitt that we share a nature—that, at the deepest level of inquiry, we *are* created equal—democracy still seems to me the most elegant of possible political responses to the silence that surrounds us. Democracy offers us the form that best fits an immediate community to our ultimate identity; the one that grants us the best chance to fulfill our potential and, following Pindar's dictum, *become what we are*. Our difficulties don't emerge from the core notions of democracy but from their subversion. They arise from a science of self-deception whose anti-democratic premises, wedding materialist determinism to rationalist solipsism, have co-opted nearly every domain with their mission of control.

Let's be clear on what that mission has excluded. The language of democracy is not what we most miss now. Virtual America is all too adept at simulating the rhetoric of liberty: time after time it passes the Turing test. What we lack instead is freedom's saving temper. The way back home begins by shunning hubris for hope, its true alternative; the way out of the slough of humiliation doesn't lie in yet another plot to assume a sovereign throne, but in the patient cultivation of humility. To aspire to be "complete in oneself," as both Moravec and the self-help crowd do, is to risk becoming completely alone, as Beckett's clown and millions of Americans now suffer to know. Yet that painful estrangement is not the condition we are born to but a choice we make—the choice that Hamlet faced and refused.

Reform begins by recovering the courage of that refusal. To regain the knowledge that informs consent, we need to reject on every level, personal as well as political, the idiotic savvy of the technological imperative, "just saying no" to its engineer's promise of total control. We should beware this new Greek bearing gifts, because our home is not a laboratory and our lives are not experiments. Only when encased in the nutshell of denial can we become as safely exempt as the peer scientist or as helplessly blind as his experimental subject. Our *actual* place—if we mind it in the most immanent and resonant senses of that phrase—is far richer, stranger, and chancier than that. In it, no self-help schedule or soft machine, no invisible hand or savvy technique, can spare us from either the mystery of our authority ("to be or not to be") or the sting of uncertainty (those "thousand natural shocks that flesh is heir to.")

That our minds can imagine realms our bodies will never reach helps to define both the anguish and the wonder, the humility and the hope, of our given place. Our best chances for a free and dignified life still rest in democracy's license to sound the silence and through that sounding become what, potentially, we always are: not the kings of, but the communicants with infinite space. Against all the illusory miracles of the mind's "own place," such an identity seems miraculous enough.

Between Common Senses

Skillful hand
can't hold water
—Japanese aphorism

IN PART I, we examined the character of the thinking of four Americans—Henry Ford, Andy Warhol, Harold Bloom, and Nicholas Negroponte—all high achievers in their separate fields of entrepreneurial commerce, the visual arts, literary criticism, and artificial intelligence. Despite that range of professions and the obvious differences in their self-presentations, these were, I argued, representative men, fundamentally alike in their vivid enactment of a cultural common sense going dangerously awry throughout the twentieth century. As influential leaders, they both reflected and advanced a species of intelligence so self-enclosed that it was losing sight of reality, making it susceptible to gross misjudgments. Narrowly competent but globally clueless, these Idiot Savants practiced an expertise that led, respectively, to a commerce of disingenuousness, an aesthetic of *an*esthesia, a solipsistic criticism, and a high-tech science whose hopes were infused with a superstitious gullibility. In each case, the profession practiced had become habituated to like-minded tactics of deceit and self-deception. Each form of reason pandered a will that was itself being driven by oversize fears and appetites.

I attributed the stoking of those drives, along with the decadent logic they induced, to the near total submission of our daily lives and democratic culture, since the days of Henry Ford, to the consumer economy's quantiphilia. By commanding our workplaces with its adamant demands for productivity and by controlling the flow of public information through its sponsoring ads, latter-day capitalism had trained the populace to its own means and ends, narrowly defined. Under this agenda, all activities were being rationalized, marketized, monetized, privatized; they were being reconfigured by and for "the numbers," with the ceaseless aim of boosting the bottom line. *More*—efficiency, productivity, consumption, profitability—was always presumed to be *better*, and as we saw with Warhol's art and Bloom's literary criticism, that crude moral calculus eventually infected even the least commercial of our professions. In sum and over time—though often hidden beneath the veil of a pseudo-conservatism or the faux rebellion of postmodern irony—America was becoming a mammonite nation, even as Mammon was co-opting the formidable power of scientific thought.

The emergence of this political economy and like-minded culture—a democratic republic regressing into a corporate oligarchy, Winthrop's "city on a hill" into Madison Avenue's Vanity Fair—had been long in the making. As we shall see shortly, the germ of this regime's erroneous logic (the idiocy enfolded within the keenness of its savvy) was a possibility concealed within the philosophical turn toward rational materialism, and so was present at the birth of modernity itself. During that same revolution, political thought, too, began to assume a scientific logic. As rational analysis superseded traditional beliefs and as social ends were reconceived in strictly materialistic terms, modernity's new way of gauging reality (atomistically, mechanistically, mathematically) was driving a comparable revision of society itself.

This was a powerful but narrow way of reorganizing communal life, and one whose genuine promises of material progress were shadowed from the start by moral dangers. Even in the Anglo-American West, where the adoption of rational materialism was simultaneous with the revival of democratic governance, its practical institution proved destructive in ways that were inseparable from the logic of the philosophy itself. Under the aegis of this new economic order—which, to stress its intellectual origins, I have been calling *scientific* capitalism—the initial industrialization of English life was a ruthless process, one that razed whole rural communities, impoverished an entire class, devastated the natural environment, and dehumanized the workplace with its rationalized schemes. Following the logic of its materialism, this new economy converted both labor and land into mere commodities, severing in the process social obligations and ties to the natural landscape centuries in the making. With the universe reconceived as a clockwork, society itself was redesigned after the image and logic of a machine, even as de facto political authority was increasingly assumed by that money-mad machine we call the modern corporation. The efficiencies of mechanism were bent to serve the avidity of mammonism as an entire political economy was relentlessly reconfigured by and for "the numbers," and quantiphilia ruled supreme.

Eventually, the gross inequities of the system spurred reform at home and a sibling rival in the East: a scientific *socialism* (aka Communism) that, although emerging from the same philosophical roots, claimed the better intentions of an egalitarian state. The abject failure of this rival to produce what it promised—neither the goods *nor* the good, its economic ineptitude wed to political brutality—quickly led to its collapse, and that collapse, in turn, obscured some underlying similarities in the logic that calibrated the two rival systems. Scientific in their biases, both scorned tradition, favored the rational over the ritual, converted morality into a kind of instrumental math, and assumed a view of history with a utopian cast.

While the advocates of scientific socialism deluded themselves with their faith in the worker's paradise to come, the radical advocates of scientific capitalism idolized instead the self-regulating market, which, as a perpetual-motion prosperity machine, would generate, they believed, moral as well as material improvement through the immaculate agency of "enlightened self-interest."[1] Although the two systems' vehicles for social perfection differed greatly, history in each case was being reconceived as mechanical and progressive rather than moral and cyclical, as a linear but nevertheless finite process with a happily-ever-after ending. Each was anticipating its own form of rational materialist utopia, and the imminent arrival of those heavens-on-earth then justified the use of truly hellish means: the same merciless pursuit of either profit or power that had produced the "dark Satanic mills" and totalitarian regimes of the nineteenth and twentieth centuries.[2]

Given the authoritarian nature of Communist rule, the danger inherent in these core ideas was accelerated by the purity of their application, and without internal opposition to moderate their fallacies, the system self-destructed in a mere sixty years. Meanwhile, the West had saved itself through a series of reforms that, while licensing the obvious productivity of scientific capitalism, also worked to check its inherent amorality and social destructiveness. Unions were organized and regulations imposed to civilize corporate behavior; charities were founded and taxes raised to fund a social safety net. But because "money talks," this compromise had always been a tenuous one, especially in America, and it was dependent, in part, on fears that the egregious inequalities generated by capitalism would eventually spur a political revolt. Unfortunately, the lessening of that threat through the otherwise happy demise of Communism quickly resulted in a full-scale assault on those same reforms. Rather than being viewed as a cautionary tale equally if differently applicable to the West, the complete collapse of scientific socialism only served to enhance our own latter-day fantasies of perfection and completion.

America, after all, had won the Cold War and so must be unambiguously right. The "end of history" had actually been achieved, the problem of human governance finally solved, and that utopian solution was none other than our own. Not only must the market's perpetual-motion profit machine now be freed from all restrictive regulations; it should go forth and multiply, its quantiphilia applied in every remaining unenlightened domain. To improve their efficiency and productivity, all our institutions (even the military and our K-12 schools) should be privatized, and all aspiring civic leaders model themselves after that arch exemplar of virtuous competence, the corporate CEO. The new American heroes were Bill Gates and Steve Jobs, and as the metaphorical measure of success in all things was converted to the bottom line, our brightest students were turning away from fields like medical care, social service, and academic research and were devoting themselves instead to financial and corporate management, whose own bottom lines were increasing exponentially.

Scientific capitalism was inherently wed to democratic practice, and since the goodness of that marriage had been firmly established as both a universal truth and the happy end of history, the imperial exportation of its ruling logic was presumed to be not only a profitable but a philanthropic project. Whether through the missionary tracts of economist Milton Friedman, the "harsh medicine" of externally imposed financial reform, or even the "shock and awe" of our high-tech weaponry, all the unconverted nations of the world should, for their own sakes, be hastened or chastened into a system that would guarantee their people peace, prosperity, and political freedom.[3]

Or not. Less than twenty years after Francis Fukuyama proclaimed the "end of history," and despite many associated think-tank celebrations of America's new "hyperpower" status (the policy maven's version of end-zone dancing), this prediction of a final solution to human governance, like all such previous predictions, was in shambles. The twin towers, those monuments to the international triumph of American-style capitalism, had been destroyed, and despite possessing the largest and most technologically advanced military in the world, America had, in response, spent trillions of dollars and sacrificed thousands of lives on two unsuccessful wars—the second of which was an imperial "war of choice" clearly influenced and spectacularly misled by the utopian presumptions described above.

Meanwhile, as pursued through the free-trade policies of six consecutive presidents, the marketizing of the global economy had eroded America's manufacturing base by exporting millions of jobs, white- as well as blue-collar, and had depressed the wages of those that remained. As during the early phases of the Industrial Revolution, this renewed submission to the utopian fantasy of the self-regulating market was generating serious economic inequalities at home, and so the happy-talk predictions of prosperity for all could only be sustained through radical boosts in both personal and national indebtedness. To keep the guns firing for the "war on terror" while still spreading the butter of the better life (materially defined), the hyperpower nation had to borrow wildly—often, ironically, from a post-Communist China whose new political system was busy proving that, contrary to yet another chipper presumption, a profitable adoption of capitalism didn't actually require a conversion to democracy.

And then came the climactic blow to the post-Wall era's utopian vision: in 2008, under the leadership of our heroic CEOs and the deregulatory plans they advanced, the global financial system tanked. When left to its own devices, the market hadn't self-regulated—it had self-destructed. Contrary to the libertarian truism, self-interest set loose had forsaken enlightenment for fantasy-fueled corruption. Akin to Bernie Madoff's fifty-billion-dollar criminal enterprise, most of the subprime mortgage market, along with the new financial instruments created to exploit it, had devolved into a legally licensed pyramid scheme: a gargantuan scam that was initially concealed by its mathematical complexity and, especially, by a will to self-delusion fueled by greed.

In a rant against the then-reigning cast of liberal expertise, William F. Buckley had once claimed that he would prefer to be governed by the first two thousand names in the Boston phone directory than by the members of the Harvard faculty. But, as it turned out, Buckley was being too generous to his own partisan side, whose ideology—as popularized by the Ronald Reagan he championed and as generated by think tanks wholly dependent on corporate funds—would exhibit a self-congratulatory vision that more than matched that of the liberal Pollyannas he wittily derided. By the first decade of the millennium, Americans would have done better to heed any number of preliterate fairy tales than follow the expert advice of the nation's establishment, left or right.

Wherever one looked, it seemed, the emperors of American expertise were clothed in good news that would soon prove to be nakedly untrue. That list would include but is not limited to the neoconservatives and liberal interventionists who *knew* that democracy could be easily imposed on a fractious Middle East; the Nobel Prize–winning economists, left and right, who *knew* that they had solved forever the danger of the boom-bust cycle; the Wall Street researchers and CEOs who *knew* that their new real estate securities could not fail; the rating services, stock market regulators, investment analysts, presidential advisers, and congressional aides who all *knew* the same; and of course Alan Greenspan, the Obi Wan of scientific capitalism, who *knew* that a radically deregulated marketplace would, infallibly, discipline itself.

Although not inevitable, these devastating miscalculations were logical in their own way. Their idiocy emerged from the same underlying moral calculus: the quantiphilia that presumes *more* (wealth earned, productivity gained, intensity of emotion displayed) must equal *better*, and that had, earlier, lent cultural authority to Henry Ford's anti-Semitic campaign, assessed Andy Warhol to be the greatest artist of the age, and led literary critic Harold Bloom to praise the patriarchal greatness of the catastrophically incompetent King Lear. Their arrogance arose from the same sort of overly specialized expertise that had led Nicholas Negroponte to presume he could cybernetically converse with the illustrious dead, and his colleague Chris Schmandt to presume *he* could build a robot that would be his personal friend.

Like those twentieth-century thinkers, too, the new Idiot Savants of the postmillennial era were not marginal figures or, in the technical sense, unintelligent men. The primary sponsors of the fiasco in Iraq had pedigrees from Princeton and the University of Chicago, their resumes replete with prestigious appointments in Congress, the White House, and the Defense Department. The same financiers who led the economy into the abyss had been the greatest beneficiaries of the market's largesse; they were the quantifiable winners in its supposedly Darwinian rewarding of the fittest. And however disingenuous Alan Greenspan's ideas may seem in retrospect, he was no merely faddish theorist but had been advising presidents for four decades and was the nation's chief banker for nearly twenty years. The best educated, the highest paid, the most politically influential—by all the usual standards, these were not an aristocracy's undeserving heirs but men of real accomplishment, the crème de la crème of the nation's meritocracy. That *they* could pursue such daffy ideas and destructive policies—that our "thinking men should think so wrongly"—suggested a failure in the logic of our meritocracy itself, some underlying flaw in its grammar of assessment.

As many a mythic tale foretells, the vain are always the least prepared for the invasion of bad news. For a public raised on the happy-talk narratives of consumer advertising and three decades of post-Wall triumphalism, the manifest failure of the American enterprise—the tsunami of foreclosures, the strangulation of credit, the massive layoffs and deficits, the gaping inequalities, *two* mismanaged wars—was stunning to behold. And with the utopian dream of the "end of history" suddenly recast in a *dys*topian mode, widespread rage erupted against an establishment whose mismanagement had proven so destructive. But the usual populist solution, throwing the bums out, isn't likely to help when those bums are reflecting the same quality of thought nightly broadcast on "reality tv." Nor is the moderate's usual response, commissioning yet another bipartisan study, a likely solution when our troubles could be traced, in part at least, to the very ways we have chosen to study the world. When our best and brightest fail us, when the nation's "right judges" routinely "judge wrong," the dreadful results should lead us to question our default calibration of judgment itself.[4]

The fall of the admirable individual through the misapplication of his very strengths is called a tragedy. We possess no term, though, for a similar failure on a grander scale—the self-generated collapse of a cultural common sense. Yet that is the crisis we currently face. The logic of modernity and the scientific worldview it once proudly espoused are now in demise, and have been so for some time. Its "skillful hand," overextended and misapplied, "cannot hold water." Its gifts are genuine but its perpetual pursuit of a mechanical fix to the human predicament cannot produce a meaningful life, and when over-pursued through utopian zeal only leads to disaster.

Modern reasoning is not just overextended but also increasingly out-of-date. The key calibrations of its science were first crafted in the seventeenth and eighteenth centuries as a way of civilizing the initially shocking cluster of psychological, social, and intellectual effects that were being generated primarily by the spread of literacy. Material progress, in the form of the printing press, was generating emotional and political regress—an inclination to anomie and anarchy that had to be redressed. Among the new institutions modernity fostered were the commercial corporation and the applied sciences, and their combined pursuit of progress eventually produced the electronic media whose own collateral effects have proven just as disruptive as those of the printing press.

As a consequence we are now caught between contending common senses, never a desirable state for a species whose survival depends as much on the accuracy of its ideas as on the efficacy of its instincts. The corporate technocracy that now dominates our political economy professes a decadent form of modernity, a quantiphilia destructive to social quality. At the same time, however, the digital machines that its skillful hand has so smartly fashioned are infusing the body politic with a set of still crude but ascendant *post*-modern values—ones that tacitly refute the organizing premises of the very system that produced them. The tension generated by an establishment whose ruling logic is reactionary but whose technologies are revolutionary is severe. Our recent culture wars have been the ugly projection of this internal incoherence, which most of us feel and, given the violence historically associated with such transitional periods, justifiably fear.

The four chapters in part 2, *Reality Check: Plotting a Map for Post-Modern Reasoning*, aim to make sense of this pivotal predicament. My ultimate intention there is to imagine a mutually self-disciplining marriage between the best features of liberal modernity and the new array of post-modern effects, whose institution in *some* form, given the centrality of the technologies enforcing them, is now inevitable. But before we can begin to imagine the most desirable replacement for a worldview now clearly in decline, we need to examine more closely both the nature of modern reasoning itself and the claims of its two most recent public opponents. Carefully attended, their dispute, though full of heat, can generate some clarifying light.

PART II
Reality Check

Plotting a Map for Post-Modern Reasoning

. . . it is our first business to paint, or describe,
desirable persons, places, states of mind.
—William Butler Yeats

CHAPTER 5

Conscientious Thinking

Alternatives to Modernity in the Wake of Its Demise

> In order to have real knowledge of [my countrymen's] opinions,
> I thought I must attend to what they practiced rather than
> what they preached; not only because, in the corruption of
> our manners, few will say what they really believe, but also
> because . . . the mental act of believing a thing is different from
> the act of knowing that one believes it; and the one act often
> occurs without the other.
>
> —René Descartes, *Discourse on Method*

Contrary to the fantasy of "self-genesis," which blurs the formation of individual identity with a trip to the mall, most of us do not select those deeper beliefs that we routinely use to evaluate the good, the true, and the beautiful. They are, instead, preselected for us by the overlapping sets of traditions into which we are born, as those traditions are modeled in the most mundane ways by the people, products, and institutional practices that organize our days. To think and act at all in the human sense, we require a deeper grammar of values and beliefs whose initial grounding in language, customs, economic practices, and communal myths long precedes our capacity to identify that grammar's features, much less to conceptualize alternatives and freely choose among them. The child *is* father to the man.

Marshall McLuhan: "Everyone experiences more than he understands. Yet it is experience, rather than understanding, that influences behavior."[1]

Descartes' crucial distinction, cited above, between what people *think* they believe and what they actually believe (that is, the beliefs directing their daily actions) is most dramatically relevant in pivotal eras such as his and ours, when material transformations are tacitly undermining moral traditions—when what people commonly sense (their everyday experience) and their inherited "common sense" (conventional understanding) no longer cohere. But before we can imagine ways to redress that incoherence in our own troubled era, we need to consider how and why the moral logic of modernity emerged, prevailed, and then declined.

The Rise and Demise of the Scientific Worldview in Eighteen Pieces

1. THE CRISIS ANNOUNCED: My first claims, then, are that we live in just such a transitional period, that these periods are inherently confusing and dangerous, and that one obvious sign of our confusion is the designation *post-modern* itself—our only commonly used term for the era we live in. Etymologically, *post-modern* acknowledges the demise of modernity without articulating what "comes after." Having lost confidence in the modern mental forms that once guided us, we can no longer accurately describe our present circumstances, much less predict or enact desirable alternatives. We can no longer "get real" when our official maps of reality no longer seem to make sense.

2. A CRUCIAL CLARIFICATION OF TERMS: The modernity to which I refer is not the aesthetic movement of the early twentieth century but the rise of rationalism and empirical materialism in the seventeenth century. I am concerned with that marriage of Cartesian philosophy to Baconian intention whose organizing presumptions not only designed America's industrial economy and formal government but also guide the informal governance of our everyday lives, shaping our commonsense beliefs about the true, the good, and the beautiful.

3. A CRUCIAL DISTINCTION OF SCALE: The "demise" in this section's title is not that of science as an effective means for investigating the material world but that of Cartesian-Baconian science *as a ruling worldview*. I am tracking the evisceration of the once-confident expectation that science's methods could serve to adjudicate and coordinate *all* the many choices we need to make on a daily basis—that the elegance of its reasoning would soon infallibly align the morally desirable with the materially true.

4. AN ABSTRACT ASSERTION (MY THESIS IN A NUTSHELL): This demise has occurred because the "deeper grammar of values and beliefs" that calibrates scientific thinking is insufficient to the breadth of the task: it has not and cannot work as a ruling worldview, and clarifying the reasons for its failure on that scale is a crucial early step toward imagining a more effective replacement.

5. AN ETYMOLOGICAL CLUE: The word *conscience* consists of a prefix meaning *with* or *together* qualifying a root that means *knowledge*. Measured comparatively, then, science is knowledge either cleansed or bereft of

togetherness. *Cleansed* or *bereft*—choose the better word. (We always have a choice; as the thinking species, we always *have* to choose.)

6. A Metaphorical Mistake, or, The Sins of the Father, Part 1: As the founder of analytic geometry, Descartes was a mathematical genius, and when he formulated his philosophical method—the epistemological template underlying modernity's worldview—he was trying to apply mathematical principles and expectations to philosophy's enduring problems. This was a mistake, his "original sin" and so a key source of the idiocy that would periodically devil modernity's savvy. The metaphor doesn't work in crucial ways: the antiseptic certainty of mathematical proof is not a plausible expectation for philosophy's problems in the real, incarnate world.

Albert Einstein: "As far as the laws of mathematics refer to reality, they are not certain; and as far as they are certain, they do not refer to reality."[2]

7. The Method in a Nutshell: Mistrusting his education as a young man, Descartes decided he would start from scratch, completely on his own. He would begin by doubting everything that he had learned, all the traditional truths; no premise would be accepted until it had been firmly established in the mathematical sense. Point by point, conclusion built on secure conclusion, he would then construct a sequence of fixed and isolated truths, each determined once and for all like a geometric proof, until all of philosophy's problems had been so "solved." Descartes not only insisted that it was possible through his Method to begin with absolute skepticism (doubting everything) and arrive at absolute certainty (knowing everything); he also believed that a single philosopher could do so on his own—that the whole of philosophy could be solved by one person, in one lifetime, without any collaboration or reliance on tradition. A related belief that helped to fund his unchecked optimism about the purity and accessibility of truth was the assumption that our rational minds are separate from the biases of our sensing bodies.

8. A Neutral Observation Preceding a Severe Evaluation: In an epistemology presuming that the mind is fully separate from the body, that present-tense thought can be fully freed from the influence of the past, that individual problems or aspects of reality can best be studied in full isolation from all others, and that the individual thinker can succeed completely apart from the community—in such an alliance of dualism, skepticism, atomism, and radical individualism, we have the makings of a "science" fully cleansed or bereft (choose the better word) of togetherness. We have a complete rejection of *conscientious* thinking in the literal sense.

9. THE SINS OF THE FATHER, PART 2: In the extremity of expectation that attends them, all of the Method's epistemological presumptions are wrong by degree. Not only is absolute certainty an impossible goal for philosophy's problems; so too is the absolute skepticism that purportedly begins the Cartesian process. One can't doubt everything (Descartes' first step) *in order to* make an infallible judgment. Because all thought at its base floats on faith, no first mental step can be so safe. To critique and amend the very premises of one's thought is an admirable if highly elusive goal that can't plausibly extend to creating on one's own an entirely new system of belief ex nihilo. Insomuch as language is the primary medium of human thought, and insomuch as language, along with its formal artifacts (stories, adages, theories, and laws) is an inherently collective and historical creation, the desire for a self-generated philosophy is absurd on its face—an existential non sequitur.

10. AN EXTREME IRONY NOTED: Given this non sequitur, to presume that your mind is free from the influence of your body, and that your present-tense thoughts can be fully liberated from both the influence of the past and the contributions of your contemporaries, is to blind yourself to many of the actual sources of your beliefs and values. A philosopher who begins his mission by astutely noting that "the act of believing a thing is different from the act of knowing that one believes it" ironically generates an epistemology that, rather than close this gap, actually ensures that "the one act will often occur without the other." By denying the togetherness (both social and historical) that powerfully shapes our individual identities, Cartesianism makes it impossible to even approach the original goal of Western philosophy: *Know thyself.*

11. A HISTORICAL CONUNDRUM ANSWERED: How did a philosophy so flawed become so influential? The short answer is that the flaws of Cartesianism—and so, too, of modernity's scientific worldview—are primarily flaws by degree, most evident and harmful when the Method's premises are either extended beyond their due season or asserted into areas where its mathematical metaphor least applies. No one would deny, for example, that it is a useful truth-seeking tactic to try, periodically, to escape the sway of one's emotions and sensations, and to distance oneself from both the presumptions of the past and the influence of one's neighbors. But to presume that such a mental retreat can be complete and permanent rather than a temporary tactic to gain perspective—to presume its objectivity is any less of an artifice than the subjectivity of, say, a story, play, or poem—is to become trapped in a delusion. And it is this very presumption which fuels the solipsism, narcissism, and alienation that,

as exemplified by the four case studies in part 1, are the characteristic diseases of modernity.

Similarly, Descartes' methodical approach supplies an extremely effective tool for investigating and manipulating the material world, but it is largely inept when overextended to ethical problems—which by their very nature, as the word *conscience* implies, require an astute comprehension of togetherness. Ethical problems also presume an existential freedom (that we always have a choice, that we *have* to choose) implicitly denied by the tacit determinism of Descartes' mathematical metaphor.

12. THE ANSWER CONTINUED: The West's broad indoctrination into the scientific worldview was gradual, practical, and mostly unconscious. The change occurred as the new science proved materially effective and so was granted the right to redesign the pace and shape of everyday life. Two obvious and ideologically potent examples of such a redesign are the industrial factory and the rectilinear modern city. Relatively few thinkers were overtly preaching the value of modern science *as a ruling worldview,* and few citizens of the West were replacing the Bibles on their bed stands and desks with thumb-worn copies of Descartes' *Discourse* or Bacon's *Novum Organon.* But to live inside the architectural surround of the modern city, with its boxy buildings and platted grid, was to be constantly indoctrinated into the normative grammar of geometric values. And to work inside an industrial economy, whose assembly-line production became a near-literal translation of the Cartesian Method into the economic sphere, was to become habituated to that Method's biases: its isolation of parts, specialization of tasks, and mathematical metaphors—its sheer quantification of value. Inside this economic sphere, one became (and still becomes) accustomed to its presumption that *more* (efficiency, productivity, consumption, profit) must equal *better*—the incredibly crude moral compass that I have been calling *quantiphilia.*

13. A GENERALIZATION IMMEDIATELY EXEMPLIFIED: Indoctrination into any new worldview will likely occur first and most completely in those social domains where the institutions enforcing the old ruling traditions have the weakest hold. As a consequence, the pivot from medieval thought to modern logic was most rapidly and completely achieved in the New World settlement.

Alexis de Tocqueville: "America therefore is one of those countries where the precepts of Descartes are least studied and are best applied."[3]

14. A WASPISH SAYING SUDDENLY SEEMS WISE: "Mind your place"—in fact, we do, and in both the active and passive senses of that verb. Like any creature, we must adapt to our environment or die, but

as homo sapiens and homo faber *our* adaptation includes refashioning that environment after our ideas. To varying degrees, *our* place is always reshaped by our mind's preferred patterns, both architectural and ethical. Initially an abstract design constructed to serve a narrow purpose, a factory becomes an entire and enclosing sensory environment whose implicit values its daily occupants will then come to mind subconsciously even beyond that factory's walls. Given the extremity of its atomistic premises, Cartesian reasoning is especially susceptible to missing the broader influence of its own ideas—the passive minding that follows its active reshaping of our physical and social spaces. Its approach is programmatically blind to the many ethical, political, and spiritual implications encoded within the "purely" instrumental spheres that it designs.

15. IDIOT SAVANT: This blindness is a form of selective repression, an ignorance we have chosen (we always have a choice) in the delusional pursuit of a fail-safe certainty. It points to the lopsided nature of modern reasoning—a radical imbalance in its capacity to mind our place, to "check" our reality. The epistemology underlying the scientific worldview crafts a common sense that is extraordinarily adept at material description and manipulation (what-is and how-to) but obtuse at ethical and teleological accounting (whether-to and what-for). Unchecked, this perspective will boost the rationalism and materialism it radically favors, producing scientific progress and economic profit while collaterally inducing moral ignorance and spiritual cluelessness—all the solipsism, narcissism, and existential estrangement that have plagued modernity. I have been calling this lopsided mindscape, which evolved as the science of modernity was overextended into a default worldview, the Idiot Savant.

16. THE CHARACTER OF AMERICAN CARTESIANISM, LARGE AND SMALL: Insomuch as America is still that place where Descartes' precepts are least read and best applied, American culture and character should be highly susceptible to that philosophy's idiocies as well as its savvy. And insomuch as, in any culture, the character of the citizen and the character of the body politic are mutually reflective, the behaviors characteristic of the Idiot Savant ought to be evident here at both the individual and institutional levels. Further, the logic behind those behaviors ought to relate, if at some remove, to Descartes' original (and erroneous) approach to truth.

So it is that the current pressure to further free the private corporation from communal regulation (privatization) is reflective of the ongoing move to further free the private self from the restrictions of the so-called puritanical tradition (self-liberation). In each case, we are witnessing the revolt of parts, and the super-valuation of their special interests, over and against the coordinated togetherness of an organic whole—whether through the *com* of community or the *con* of conscience. And in pursuing these revolts, the privatizing company and the liberated self are mimicking in their separate domains Descartes' erroneous presumption that he could free his philosophy from both traditional thought and communal influence. Although usually found on opposite sides of our culture wars, these two radical proponents of deregulation are ultimately alike in that both believe in the hubristic folly of "self-genesis."

17. THE ELEPHANT IN THE ROOM: Commendably, science long ago began to discount its own initial presumption that its methods could solve reality once and for all. The true post-modern turn began with the physics of Bohr and Heisenberg, and with the findings of anthropology and comparative zoology. The implications of those discoveries have been percolating through the collective mindscape of the West for nearly a century. The elephant in the room, felt by all but acknowledged by few, is the simmering realization that the common sense of the West no longer "makes sense"—that the scientific worldview (our primary grammar for articulating the good, the true, and the beautiful for three centuries) fails to "mind our place" in crucial ways. For a thinking creature whose survival depends as much on the accuracy of its thought as on the acuity of its instincts, such a failure is extremely stressful, provoking a psychological crisis that modern dualism, with its rigid separation of thought from feeling, can only dimly apprehend.

18. THE ENEMIES OF OUR ENEMY ARE . . . ALSO OUR ENEMIES: The obvious implication of the previous seventeen "pieces" is that we must somehow escape and replace a scientific worldview which has proven inadequate to the complexities of our collective experience. Although one might presume otherwise, the most vociferous opponents to that worldview today—radical postmodernists and religious fundamentalists—are of little help in that vital task. This is so because, on further analysis, their movements prove to be not true alternatives but reductive remnants of the very scientism they claim to reject; each is a strictly segregated vestige (as much temperamental as intellectual) of the Method's now broken promise. Specifically, the one's nihilism and the other's fundamentalism represent the decoupling of Descartes' unjustifiable faith in an absolute skepticism from his unjustifiable expectation that, through such skepticism, we can achieve fixed and final answers to all the important questions, ethical as well as material. As decadent remnants of modern reasoning, these movements are actually worse—less true, less good, less mindful of our place—than the science they would supplant. In ways I will examine next, they exhibit much of the idiocy but little of the savvy of the worldview they attack.

Fail-Safe Certainty: The Sinful Incoherence of
Religious Fundamentalism

*Under this anointing, the words I speak cannot fall to the
ground. Under this anointing, everything I say, happens.*
—Benny Hinn, televangelist

So astute at describing and manipulating the physical world, rational materialism is, by the very nature of its exclusions, inept at the linked activities of directing moral decision-making and supplying metaphysical orientation. A fully rationalized world—in which the Cartesian division of mind
and body (and so, thought from feeling) has been projected into physical
space and into social and economic practices—is a meaningless world,
one that keeps its citizens emotionally estranged, morally inarticulate, and
spiritually bereft.

Whether tacit or overt, this form of mental governance is, finally, unendurable: as nature abhors a physical vacuum, human nature abhors a
teleological one. Driven to fill that awful maw of purposelessness, each
reductive specialty in our rationalized economy now aspires, it seems, to
the status of a spiritual practice. According to those professionals who are
most advanced within their fields, commerce is for commerce's sake, science is for science's sake, art is for art's sake alone. Practical means are
misperceived as philosophical ends, and even hobbies (quilt making, bird
watching, bass fishing, drag racing) are pursued with a zeal that recalls
nothing so much as religious observance. Addictions of all sorts run ram-
pant because the pattern of addiction supplies a fully mechanical, and
thus pathological, solution to the spiritual problem of meaninglessness.
The absence of any credible larger purpose is filled by the totemic inflation of the addictive substance or practice, with all of the addict's future
planning reductively focused on scoring the next fix or placing the next
bet, on making the next online purchase.

The rise of religious fundamentalism in America is significant because,
unlike these other faux solutions to modernity's meaninglessness, it overtly acknowledges both the ethical and the spiritual dimensions of our demise. Among the nation's many and various interest groups, fundamentalists are the most aware of, and hyper-alarmed by, the liberated self's increasing rejection of (to borrow from Melville's Bartleby) the "preference
not to." And in an attempt reenchant the American experience, they are
constantly trying to infuse the public domain with the old Judeo-Christian
symbols and narratives. But even as the fundamentalist mind-set recognizes the right problems by category, it is incapable of supplying anything

like a vital vision of reform because, contrary to its self-conception, it still believes in the rationalizing methods of the secular thinking it so passionately wishes to criticize.

As the religious historian Karen Armstrong has shown convincingly in *The Battle for God*, the recent resurgence of fundamentalism in all three of the West's Abrahamic religions has *not* been a revival of "old-time religion." On a historical scale, fundamentalism is new. It is one characteristic reaction to modernity's assault on meaningfulness—that is, to the co-opting of the sacred by the instrumental; but it is a reaction that unconsciously borrows modernity's own methods, accepting in a decadent form the epistemological grounding of the very findings it wishes to refute. And so we witness the oxymoronic invention of something called "creation science" as an attempt to prove the literal truth of the biblical account of life's origins. So, too, we watch quixotic expeditions to find the remains of Noah's ark—as if rotted wood on a mountaintop were necessary to authenticate a story already abundant with human meaning, as if only the *material* could finally redeem moral and spiritual truthfulness.

More generally, the same fantastic presumption that all human problems can be solved with certainty—the modeling of the ethical after the mathematical that began with the Method—now also arms the literalist mindscapes of all of today's fundamentalists, whether Islamic, Hebraic, or Christian. Yet, in a highly ironic resemblance to Descartes' countrymen, "the act of believing" in these scientific biases "is different from the act of knowing they believe in them, and the one act often occurs without the other."

This extreme discrepancy between the intended message and the medium of its expression is fatal to fundamentalist reasoning. Wishing to prove his case about the origins of humankind, the "creation scientist" musters an argument about fossil finds and geological formations that is little more than an exercise in wishful thinking. Even as he relies on rationalist proof (thus endorsing the determinative value of such proof), he can't really "do" rationalist thinking; his so-called investigation of the material world is permitted to discover only that which he already believes to be true. One doesn't have to be a strict advocate of the scientific worldview, as *I* clearly am not, to recognize the folly of "creation science."

But the problem doesn't end with scientific ineptitude. Because fundamentalists are biased toward rationalist expectations without knowing it, they also can't reason effectively on those spiritual and ethical matters that are, after all, their primary concerns. Recognizing the right problems but treating them with the wrong methods and temper, they tend to expect final, certain, and inflexible answers to questions that do not commonly admit to such: they are in full and often fearful flight from the ambiguities that attend the moral life. I can see the potential wisdom of asking oneself, when negotiating the moral freedom that is our lot, *what would Jesus do?* But to answer effectively, one needs to pose first a more subtle question: *How would Jesus think?* Let me be so bold as to suggest that he would not be applying mathematical methods and expectations to today's moral dilemmas. The mind in evidence in the scriptures judges through narrative and metaphorical comparison—Jesus not only *communicates through,* he *thinks in* aphorisms. The parable and not the geometric proof is his primary means for truth-testing as well as truth-telling. As models of moral and spiritual reckoning, the gospels exemplify the near antithesis to a literalist reading of the human condition.

To substantiate my claim that the fundamentalist mind does not, in general, reason effectively on ethical issues, I will turn very briefly to contemporary politics—where it is safe to say that, in general, religious fundamentalists support the political right and, in so doing, are usually allied with Wall Street's radical free marketeers. They fear the invasiveness of those marketeers' own favorite enemy, regulatory government, especially as that invasiveness is perceived to be actively promulgating "secular humanism," and they loathe the lax behavior of the liberated self that they associate with the political left. Although these perceptions are not without some basis, they egregiously misread the primary *systemic* source of moral and metaphysical indoctrination in America. It is true, for example, that public education has had a bias toward the scientific worldview, yet the overriding motive has not been to create a class of Darwinian dogmatists but to train future employees for our corporate economy. (There is no institution on earth more rationalized and materialized than the American corporation, no economy in history more dependent on rationalization than ours.)

Likewise, fundamentalists miss the obvious alliance between the morally liberated self they so loathe and the privatizing economy whose candidates receive their support. They rarely acknowledge that the rap artists and Hollywood moguls they excoriate are, in fact, usually behaving like "good business persons," adhering to the conventional ethos of today's free market—namely, that commerce should be for commerce's sake alone and that more profits must equal better. The liberated self *is* the moral mindscape preferred by our rapidly privatizing consumer economy. In each of that economy's domains, a highly efficient instrumental reason serves a fiercely focused will, which is itself subservient to an unchecked appetite, whether for the consumption of goods or the generation of profits.

Those who profess "old-time religion" in America today ought to recognize this description, because it constitutes one very traditional Judeo-
Christian explanation for why humankind is so afflicted by unhappiness.
When appetite commands will, which is then "pandered" by reason, the
inner hierarchy of faculties necessary for human happiness has been reck-
lessly inverted. America's first and most fiercely spiritual Protestants had a
simple word for this state of mind—which, they believed, so confuses our
judgment that it induces a self-perpetuating misery. They called it *sin*.

And so, when I conclude that today's fundamentalists do not, in general, reason effectively on the ethical and spiritual issues that matter most
to them, I am basing my judgment not on the standards professed by secular humanists but on those that emerge from the spiritual tradition they
would claim as their own. Highlighting the difference between "believing
a thing and knowing that one believes it," the implicit hypocrisy of the fundamentalists' alliance with a sinful Wall Street supplies one of the clearest
instances of the moral incoherence that characterizes our era.

Fail-Safe Ignorance: The Complete Capitulation
of Radical Postmodernism

My mind is like a tape recorder with one button—Erase.
—Andy Warhol

As exemplified by the "po-mo" artists and critics examined in chapter 2, the
most vociferous advocates of secular postmodernism are also unhelpful in
imagining a way out of today's incoherence; they, too, are bent instead on
reinventing the problem in another guise. As is the case with their culture-
war enemies on the religious right, these radical secularists' rejection of the
scientific worldview conceals a kind of temperamental compliance. The
demise of certainty provokes in them an ironic certainty about the total
*un*certainty of human knowledge. If we can't know it all, which had been
the presumption of Cartesian scientism, then we can know nothing at all—
the presumption of Nietzschean nihilism. The proud denial of any limits to
our knowledge merely flips into a perversely proud denial of any limits to
our ignorance. The idolatrous error that mistakes the partial disclosure of
human knowing for the whole truth is replaced by a complementary error:
the denial that such disclosures are even partially true.

Anyone who has labored on an American college campus in the last
twenty-five years has likely been subjected to a very learned lecture on the
uselessness of learned lectures, or been forced to parse a highly rationalized argument on the inherent futility of rational argumentation. All truth
statements are dismissed as expressions of cultural bias, all proclamations of

good intentions unveiled as a masquerade for sheer self-interest. Piety, loy-alty, generosity, objectivity—name your favorite virtue, secular or religious, professional or private, and each shall be exposed, via the dry dissection of an unchecked skepticism, as a mere facile front for the will to power.

I remember vividly my first encounter with this postmodern stance. After a sixteen-year absence from academic life, I managed to slip in the back door via a creative writing program. Soon thereafter, I attended a talk on the French novel where I was informed by the lecturer, himself an academic novelist, that if he had half an hour he could "prove" to us that "language only refers to itself." Although he didn't have the time that day (his lecture focused instead on the significance of an experimental novel composed without once using the letter *e*), other visiting scholars soon would. And as my initial disappointment gave way to an exasperated bore-dom at the robotic nature of the enterprise, I began to amuse myself with the observation that, if true, this po-mo claim pre-excused me from at-tending any further such lectures—which, following their own arguments, had to be solipsistic exercises in masked self-interest.

That reflexive excuse won't do here, however, where I'm obliged to tease out, if only briefly, the problematic nature of such nihilistic thinking. I'll start with this: the claim that language only refers to itself is an obvi-ous literal translation of the aphorism "the medium is the message," but one made by someone apparently unaware that McLuhan's clever coin-age was a deliberate exercise in hyperbole. Despite my academic novelist's sophisticated air and secular aestheticism, he was a literalist at heart—which is to say, a fundamentalist thinker clinging to his own version of an absolute truth, albeit a self-contradictory one: that there can be no such thing as truthfulness at all. And despite his professed antipathy to cer-tainty in knowledge, this lecturer also felt the need to "prove" (the very word he used) his own preferred version of an absolute truth. Like the sorry advocates of "creation science"—who, even as they strive to disprove the scientific worldview's theory of evolution, tacitly endorse the value of the scientific method—the radical postmodernist characteristically relies on the very rationalism whose truthfulness he claims to discount.

All of this is to say that neither the religious fundamentalist nor the secular postmodernist has escaped the formal problem I identified earlier. Although they attack modernity's worldview from opposite ends of the cul-tural spectrum, both are trapped in the very methods and temper whose authoritative findings they wish to overturn. I've addressed the dangers of the fundamentalist's inept and rigid moralism. Here, my concern is with the decadent amoralism of the radical postmodernist, for if language only refers to itself, there can be no such thing as a lie—which just so happens

to supply a convenient moral bye in a political economy increasingly dependent on the soft duplicities of salesmanship. And if all virtues merely
mask sheer self-interest, then the irksome obligation to cultivate virtue
can be dismissed from the start as a disingenuous delusion. Such stances,
one quickly sees, justify not only the ceaseless transgressions of the narcissistic self but also the "creative destruction" of the consumer corporation,
which proudly operates on the so-called principle of sheer self-interest,
and whose marketing divisions have become ever more engaged, without
embarrassment or self-restraint, in engineering deceit.

Because the adherents of radical postmodernism are commonly found
on campuses and in art studios, the usual hunting grounds of the cultural
left, their most virulent critics presume them to be anti-capitalist by association. But as should be obvious by now, the movement is, in fact, the
logical, intellectual, and ethical product of postwar capitalism. Far from a
critique of the nation's consumer economy, radical postmodernism supplies a kind of descriptive anthropology of its idolatrous mindscape and
social enclosure. The anti-truth truths the po-mo purist preaches accurately depict the emergent moral logic of an economy that, operating on
the mammonite imperative that more must equal better, is now heavily
invested in de-authenticating *any* form of regulation, political or personal,
legal or moral, that would limit the reach of its profit motive.

What proves radical about radical postmodernism, then, is not its *revolt
against* but its *conformity to* the prevailing moral logic of the day. This curious fact presents us with an apparent political paradox: the religious right,
whose proclaimed allegiance to Judeo-Christian values ought to make it
a vigorous critic of today's clearly amoral marketplace, nevertheless allies itself consistently with the free marketeers, under the umbrella of a
so-called conservatism increasingly characterized by moral incoherence.
Meanwhile, the radical postmodernists, whose amoral ideas actually do
cohere with the operating logic of our consumer economy, have been routinely demonized by that system's most passionate advocates.

After 9/11, as public debate shifted from our culture wars to the conduct of our "war on terror," attacks on radical postmodernism began to
wane. But during the previous twenty years, scarcely a week went by without the editorial pages of the *Wall Street Journal* exposing for ridicule the
latest egregious example of po-mo relativism. As a seasoned observer of
the political scene, I am well aware of the electoral gains that can be made
through cynically associating one's opponents with cultural extremism.
Still, the intensity of the ridicule suggested more personal motivations as
well, the overweening contempt of the economic right being fueled in
part at least by the hysteria of denial.

Although there was much to criticize about the po-mo stance, it did call the bluff of the free marketeers, who had (and still have) a huge stake in denying the moral consequences of modeling the whole of American life after the amoral logic of their quantiphilia. Through overtly embracing that logic, radical postmodernists were reflecting back all too exactly the privatized self being cultivated by the privatization of the American place. In the purity of their literalism, they vividly embodied the actual ethos being generated by consumer capitalism. Free of the usual moralizing gloss and patriotic sound tracks, absent the hymns to Jesus and the homilies on Jefferson routinely mustered by the self-regulating market's fiercest advocates, the nihilism of our radical postmodernists was expressing the true "soul" of a corporate economy whose daily operations were becoming both deeply anti-Christian and, through usurping the powers of elected officials, dangerously undemocratic.

No wonder the editors of the *Wall Street Journal* were hyperventilating then with manly moral contempt. Having entered the public square, their spotlit love child was exuding both a hint of mockery and the smell of decay—the rank residue of the same self-indulgent attitudes that, stoking sales, kept the cash flowing Wall Street's way.

Scapegoat the messenger, scoop up the profits.

Hopeful Humility: Embracing the Chastening of the Post-Modern Turn

The imperfect is our paradise.
—Wallace Stevens, "The Poems of Our Climate"

To summarize: America has bred two extreme but ultimately ineffective critiques of the scientific worldview, a religious fundamentalism and a radical postmodernism. Although they have emerged from opposite sides of the cultural spectrum, both are afflicted with the temper of an absolutism ironically akin to the first error of Cartesian thought: its grand promise, now clearly broken, that an initial investment in absolute skepticism could reliably result in absolute certainty. The one group worships the idol of a fail-safe knowledge, imagining that they hold something like the whole truth in their scripture-laden hands; the other bows to a fail-safe ignorance, pre-excusing themselves from the obligations of meaningful language and ethical behavior—from the burden, that is, of being truthful and good.

What these opposing groups tacitly share is an intolerance for the subtle grading and shading of the middle way. They reject those partial disclosures of human knowing that mark the bounds of our thinking species,

and by so doing they deny the double bind of vulnerability and accountability that calibrates the mental reach of a creature whose freedom and
intelligence are both inescapably real and perpetually limited. In their
scale and rigidity, both groups drastically fail to mind our place.

Nevertheless, these movements prove diagnostically useful. They came
into being for credible reasons, responding to the very real inadequacies
of a worldview in decline. Where religious fundamentalism highlights the
inherent ethical and spiritual insufficiencies of an instrumental philosophy that has been allowed to become a de facto religion, radical postmodernism illuminates the current failure of many of that philosophy's
truth-seeking forms. Ironically unaware of how "modern" they remain in
their separate allegiances to an absolute skepticism or an absolute certainty, each would-be alternative can only offer a phony rebellion—yet
their instinctive opposition to modernity is, in the grossest sense, correct.
Because even at its best, the scientific can't do the work of the conscientious, any attempt to fix modernity's errors by using its own methods alone
is, finally, a fool's errand—"jelly in a vise."[4]

Dissecting the failings of these faux alternatives to modernity's worldview proves a far easier task, however, than designing or describing an
authentic replacement. As someone raised in the second half of the twentieth century, and in a country "where the precepts of Descartes [have
been] best applied," my mind, too, has been shaped from the start by
modernity's "vise." Despite repeated efforts at reeducation, *that* child's experience is still father in subtle ways to *this* man's understanding, and the
resulting biases have led to many self-defeating attempts to "get a grip"
on a new and truly better worldview. In any case, modesty commends the
natural limits that apply to such a self-assignment. To imagine that I might
fashion on my own a new common sense for our post-modern times would
be to suffer from the same vain delusion that spurred Descartes at the
start—a solipsistic error especially ironic for someone who wants to argue
on behalf of "togetherness" in knowledge.

What I have to offer here instead is decidedly preliminary, provisional,
and incomplete: not a bulleted program or a numbered sequence of the
sort I lightly satirized in the first part of this chapter but just some of the
"pieces," intellectual and temperamental, from which a credible reformation might eventually arise. If conscientious thinking were a face, then
what follows are a few of its likely features, absent the full constellation of
internal relations necessary for any coherent identity.

PENANCE AND PURPOSE: In Malory's well-known account of the tales
of King Arthur, Guinevere asks Lancelot to pray that she might "amend
[her] misliving." *We* need to amend our mis-thinking, and we can begin by

reacknowledging the inevitable link (obscured by our tacit acceptance of modern dualism) between the mind's thought and the body's actions, including the collective actions of the body politic. For the thinking species, bad ideas have real-life consequences—devastated landscapes, despairing mindscapes, corrupt social orders. At their worst, mistaken philosophies can become lunatic governments. Americans recognize this danger today in our just condemnation of Islamic fundamentalism's oppressive regimes, but glancing backward over the precipice of the twentieth century, we have a collective responsibility to acknowledge the egregious misliving that emerged from Western modernity's own mis-thinking: the gross "collateral damage" of its broken promise in the form of the fifty to one hundred million people slaughtered by the nihilism of the Nazis and the utopianism of the Communists. Seemingly so opposed, the governments of absolute skepticism (fascist cynicism) and absolute certainty (socialist scientism) arrived at the same moral destination: the oh-so-efficient methodical mayhem of the genocidal graveyard. To revisit that graveyard is to recover a sobering sense, so easy to lose in an age of bloviating blogs, that ideas expressed are in themselves actions taken.

Or, to cite again the words of Saraswati, "every word is a sound; every sound has a meaning; and the meaning is what it does."

INTEGRATION OVER ACCUMULATION: Driven by technological change, economic consolidation, and planetary crowding, "togetherness" is already arriving whether we want it or not. Our wired, digitized global culture routinely invades all the old boundaries—between ethnicities, industries, disciplines, and art forms, between the public sphere and the private self. The world we now commonly sense and modernity's common sense—with its atomistic biases toward isolation, specialization, and individualism—no longer cohere, and such a volatile situation is especially dangerous for nations where the precepts of Descartes have been least studied and best applied. Warning: undomesticated "togetherness" (the sheer accumulation of post-modern effects) could prove disastrous, increasing the likelihood of mob rule, tyranny, monopolies, intellectual incoherence, artistic cacophony, and the demise of a morally effective individuality. The best products of modern reasoning, including the covenants of democratic practice, could be threatened along with the worst.

Thanks to our post-modern technologies, we have the "con"—what's still missing in these post-modern times is a new "science" to apprehend and direct it. The togetherness that is our inevitable future will only prove to be good, true, and beautiful if we can fashion new astute forms to evaluate and then integrate its emergent features.

More Knowledge Is Less Unless . . . : The threat of intellectual incoherence is especially relevant in that it highlights an underlying
similarity between birth of modernity and our own era. Then as now, the
West was suffering from an information overload that was being driven
by a dramatic upgrade in communications technologies. For centuries,
the primary challenge of education had been securing personal access
to the relatively few scribal manuscripts that existed. But by 1600, some
160 years after the invention of the printing press, the sheer number and
variety of available texts had exploded, and the central concern for the
scholar had flipped from accessibility to digestibility.

If one dips into Robert Burton's gargantuan *The Anatomy of Melancholy*,
first published in 1621, that transitional challenge becomes painfully obvious. The book's size, complexity, and heterogeneity of sources—more
than a thousand pages, drawn from many centuries, disciplines, languages,
and cultures, attempting to cover but a single subject—demonstrate the
limits of sheer accumulation as a plausible approach to the pursuit of
knowledge. Multiply the number of pages times the number of possible
subjects this scholarly author might have engaged in the same way and the
Renaissance goal of learning all there was to know is crushed by the sum.
Did Burton's endless examination of "melancholy" finally illuminate, confuse, or simply exhaust its contemporary readership?

At once brilliant and excessive, *Anatomy* exemplified how, after a point,
more knowledge might mean less clarity; it was an implicit plea for epistemological simplification—a project that the young Descartes, impatient
with the cluttered mindscape of a scholasticism evident on every Burton
page, had already begun. His Method in philosophy, like the Puritans'
"plain style" in both theology and everyday religious practice, was a radical
attempt to apply formal discipline to the confusing and corrupting abun-
dance of the day. Intellectual no less than economic prosperity demanded
the development of selective forms of self-discipline—those programmatic exclusions (preferences *not* to know) that would highlight, by their
absence, the more valuable truths.

Fast-forward to today and a similar challenge becomes immediately
evident. Not only is the sheer number of available texts exponentially
larger and increasing by the second; the very definition of text has been
expanded to include images and sounds, even as the accessibility of all
these modes of knowing has been made virtually instant via the web. How
do we make sense of *this* sensory and intellectual stew, where links to the
home snapshot and the Homeric epic, the anonymous slander and the
sage aphorism, may find themselves spatial neighbors in a search engine's

visual array? Once again intellectual bounty threatens to degrade into conceptual babble. Modernity's formal ways of responding to the challenge of post-Gutenberg complexity—its specialization of task and study, its endorsement of the scholarly disciplines and separate professions—are being overwhelmed by the new technologies, whose inclination instead is to mix and merge: to hybridize, not specialize.

How can the hyper-togetherness characteristic of post-modern experience coincide with the clarity of mind necessary to think truly, ethically, or beautifully? This is not merely a technical issue to be outsourced to software engineers whose filters will preselect for us, instantly and invisibly, the sorts of things we will want to know. The preferences built into their digital systems are only likely to favor the set of values that narrowly drives their own enterprise, a set now largely determined by the quantiphilia of their corporate clients. (Do *more* clicks on a website really mean that its content is *better*? And what are the consequences of the fact that the results of today's search engine, unlike those of yesterday's library catalogue, are already being "brought to us by" consumer solicitation?) If character is fate, then any change in the nature of those filters' hidden preferences will also change the likely plot line of our individual and collective destinies, and to fail to participate thoughtfully in that project of revision will cede control over what our pursuit of happiness means in actual practice.

Call to mind the dramatic differences in the forms preferred by the medieval and modern mindscapes—the ritual performance of the morality play versus the privately read realistic novel; the foundational story of Genesis versus the foundational theory of evolution; the strict hierarchies and paternalistic duties of the feudal economy versus the contractual licensing and laissez-faire morality of the free market—and then recognize that we are likely facing an equally dramatic reformation of our sense and sensibility. As in Burton's time, the new bounty of information demands a new grammar of expression to shape and direct it; what we *can do* through our new technologies will have to be disciplined by new communal understandings as to what we *should do. More* (quantity of information and the wealth its produces) will only mean *less* (quality of life) unless we can fashion a set of interrelated cultural forms that can effectively evaluate the complexities inherent in post-modern experience. For the thinking species, widespread confusion perpetually invites the calamity of anarchy.

John Milton:

> Chaos umpire sits,
> And by decision more embroils the fray
> By which he reigns.[5]

INTEGRATION OVER EXTERMINATION: The horrific history of the twentieth century insists that one crucial goal for a more conscientious thinking should be to preserve the best features of the current worldview while somehow subsuming them within a richer replacement. No more "clean slates." No more presuming that the new must exclude (read *exterminate*) the old. Two obvious candidates for preservation in some form would be the scientific method and the moralized individualism that was initiated during the Protestant Reformation, for each insists on the sort of principled self-scrutiny that can guide us in a rapidly changing world— and each, properly applied, helps to ensure the quality of democratic thought and practice.

To admit that modern science is insufficient as a ruling worldview mustn't lead to a wholesale rejection of scientific truths. The post-modern turn has reminded us that our knowledge of the world will always be incomplete and, to some degree, subjective, but when taken too far (as we have sometimes seen during the global warming debate) repeated assaults on the integrity of science will only lead to a superstitious replacement— the sort of magical thinking evident today in the nation's lotto, casino, and online gambling craze.

Likewise, we need to acknowledge how, thanks largely to our digital machinery, the conditions that once reinforced a self-reliant individualism have given way to the inherent togetherness of interactivity. But to recognize the need for a new common sense to account for this shift is not equivalent to endorsing the complete degradation of individual dignity that we now see all around us. The routine humiliation of contestants on game-show TV, the industrialized gossip of talk shows and websites, the ongoing enfeeblement of the individual will on a bogus regimen of miracle pills and self-help remedies: these are signs of a once-vital individualism in rapid decline, and without a civilized communalism to take its place.

Any projection of a plausible post-modern worldview will require a creative conservation of some of modernity's foundational strengths, for without them democracy itself will cease to exist. A new motto, then, for a more conscientious age: "To progress is to preserve."

BACKWARD IS FORWARD, TOO: Beyond preserving the best of the present-tense within the shape and pace of our future practices, a more conscientious worldview would include in its togetherness a recovery of knowledge from the more distant past. If we drop modernity's bias against cultural tradition, along with the adolescent presumption derived from this bias—that the new is necessarily improved—we are freed to treat the deeper past as a potential resource. We can explore the historical record for both cautionary tales and recuperative models; we can seek admirable examples of integrative forms created by cultures caught up in similar periods of radical transition. Two exemplary thinkers from the Western tradition quickly come to mind: Plato and Shakespeare.

In the first instance, the Greeks in Plato's day were in the midst of a climactic transformation of consciousness and culture similar to our own. After three or so centuries under the growing influence of the written word, the commonsense premises of a highly sophisticated and successful oral culture—a culture vividly captured in the *Iliad* and the *Odyssey*— were being challenged by the habits of mind natively associated with the reading and writing experiences. Unique for its day, the Greek phonetic alphabet broke down all the sounds of their spoken language (and so, too, the whole of the reality those sounds described) into a limited number of visual but nonrepresentational signs. This underlying template of a linguistic whole reduced into so many discrete and abstract pieces would eventually codify a new worldview after its image, authorizing an atomistic understanding of physical reality and an individualistic approach to social living. Further, the experience of contemplating the written word, which, unlike the spoken, persisted in time long beyond the moment of its first expression, suggested that a permanent order might exist behind the flux of experience—an order that the advanced mind might come to grasp through painstaking study.

Plato's philosophy, which emphasized those eternal truths that lay hidden behind the play of appearances, was literally *un*thinkable without the perceptual and conceptual biases inherent in phonetic literacy. Yet his writings included, as a kind of self-correction, an overt caution against the dangers of the written word, for the form he preferred above all others, the Socratic dialogue, deliberately conserved key qualities of the oral culture being left behind. Even as the dialogues promoted a worldview based on abstract analysis and rooted in the social isolation inherent in the writing and reading experiences, they retained a simulation of face-to-face conversation. In order to progress, Plato's writings were careful to preserve.[6]

Two thousand years later, Shakespeare faced the same imaginative pressures as his contemporaries, but with very different intentions and results. In sharp contrast to the Cartesian Method and the Puritan's plain style, Shakespeare's aesthetic aimed for a superabundant inclusiveness, supplying us with an exemplary instance of conscientious thinking in transitional times. The very model of an integrated togetherness, his plays mustered the means not just to list or array (as in today's collages) but to interweave artfully the era's many diverse forces. The mundane and the profound, the comic and the tragic, the medieval attitude and the modern idea—all were permitted to interact within the same imaginative arena. As we saw in *King Lear*, the disorder of the day was both expressed and contained within the nested spheres of the play's metrical, rhetorical, and narrative forms: its "most precious square of sense."

One of the great challenges of the Elizabethan era was the emergence of an analytically potent but still largely undomesticated individualism—a new and unanticipated conception of selfhood engendered by the success of the printing press. Shakespeare was the first great cartographer of this phenomenon. His many soliloquies mapped, in all its varieties, the inner mindscape being fashioned by the silent reading experience: the single self learning to speak to and of itself, worrying and complaining and, not infrequently, plotting against the duties and restraints of the prevailing social order. The emergence of this self-conscious inwardness could also be traced in the dawning popularity of the personal diary, but the Shakespearean play provided its own tacit self-corrective in the form of a mediating irony. Where the written diary was silent and secret, the soliloquy was vocal and staged; the new individualism's most private voice was being deliberately publicized, its inwardness "outed" for civic examination.

And even as the plays explored the full range and potency of this modernized psyche, they tended to side with the medieval order whose communal obligations that psyche was rejecting. Shakespeare's investigation of the day's emergent individualism included a cautionary inoculation against its psychological excesses and social dangers, as those dangers were modeled by the anarchy unleashed in *Macbeth* and *King Lear*. Like the Platonic dialogue before it, the Shakespearean drama preserved to progress.

METAPHOR AS A METAPHOR: The primary unit of truth for modernity's worldview is the irrefutable and isolated fact. When I try to imagine what shape the primary unit of conscientious thinking might take, my best guess is that it will be *like* a metaphor, for metaphorical thinking abides in togetherness in three important ways. First and most obviously, it measures by relation, not isolation, bringing apparently disparate elements together. Second, defying the division of modern dualism, the accuracy of an effective metaphor is simultaneously logical and emotional—meaning-full and feeling-filled, mind and body reunited. Finally and least obviously, even the best metaphor implicitly acknowledges its own fallibility because, to quote an old professor of mine, "every likeness implies an unlikeness." Even as a metaphor asserts its accuracy, it also admits (though perhaps *sotto voce*) its imperfections, allowing us to hold in our minds, conscientiously, likenesses and differences side by side. True to the limited reach of our lasting condition, metaphorical thinking exhibits a modesty in knowing that is the necessary antidote to modernity's fatal romance with certainty in knowledge.

A TENTATIVE TOOLBOX FOR CONSCIENTIOUS THOUGHT: The underlying grammar of modern reckoning strongly valued the literal, the sequential, and the certain, devaluing in the process those mental instruments that had, traditionally, favored their opposites—the figurative, the simultaneous, and the ambivalent. Given the demise of the scientific worldview, one might reasonably surmise that those same mental tools will be revisited and revived to create, through their native cultivation of togetherness, a more conscientious understanding of the true, the good, and the beautiful. Along with metaphor, such a post-modern toolbox might include these: *the symbol*—the literal and the metaphorical conveyed simultaneously; *rhyme and meter*—musical play and abstract sense conveyed simultaneously; *the pun* (a favorite device of both Shakespeare and Donne)—two meanings, usually with very different emotional valences, conveyed at once; *rhetorical irony*—meaning and tone fused together in tense opposition, conveying in this case, though, not a postmodern nihilism but a genuine ambivalence; and *paradox*—contradictory meanings yoked together and made to cohere, as in my titles here: backward is forward, to progress is to preserve, more knowledge is less.

HOMER'S REPUBLIC: Starting with Plato's banishing of the Homeric epics from his ideal republic (the West's first recorded culture war), rationalists have tended to discount the value of mythic thinking. They have viewed storytelling as an archaic remnant of the preliterate mind, or as a preliminary phase in the development of the child, or as an adult vacation from the hard work of real thought. But insomuch as an artful plot is a metaphor writ large and put into motion, narrative bears the same qualities of togetherness noted above, and so seems a natural mode for conscientious thought. (Nothing provides a more vivid picture of postmillennial America's cultural decline than the crudely juvenile scripts of our box office winners and TV hits, all those populist narratives mechanically produced by and for "the numbers.")

A more conscientious thought will develop new heroic myths and populist parables that, by accurately minding our post-modern place and reuniting our intellectual and emotional intelligences, will better guide our collective choices. Like the Shakespearean play, these new narratives will need to preserve even as they progress, although the elements in this case are likely to be reversed—that is, they will be advancing a new communalism that is more befitting the economic interdependence and technological interactivity of post-modern experience while still striving to protect the core integrity of American individualism. But whatever final shape these myths might take, they will certainly reawaken us to the native power of narrative in shaping consciousness and character.

George Gerbner: "If you can write a nation's stories, you needn't worry about who makes its laws."[7]

MOOD MUSIC: Because the scientific worldview wants to abstract our ideas from the bias of our emotions, it is largely unaware of the emotional tenor that its own ideas both demand and induce. Thoughts do become actions (mis-thinking, mis-living), but they do so through the agency of emotions and expectations, which is one reason why narrative thinking proves so influential. Given modern philosophy's foundational faith in a self-generating certainty, the temperament it generates all too often is hubris. And because hubristic expectations are out of scale with our given place and mental nature, they lead not only to the brutal behaviors historically associated with utopian schemes but also to the private shock and shame of failure. As most of the great tragedies and not a few of our fairytales remind us, hubris eventually and ironically generates its temperamental opposite, humiliation; time and again, the narrative climax to its expansive delusions is an implosion to despair. Whatever formal shape conscientious thinking might take, it will have to recover a more stable orbit of expectations, including an intellectual modesty rooted in the recognition that omniscience is forever beyond our reach. No more workers' paradises. No more personal happily-ever-afters. No more final solutions to philosophy's enduring questions. There's only one "end of history": extinction. To desire absolute ends and earthly ever-afters, to seek a final solution to the human condition, is to seek a premature death. *That* is the enduring lesson of the bloody century just past.

Even if we do learn to admit our mental limitations, we still would face a crucial choice in relation to them. How should we respond to—what attitude will we take toward—these inescapable restrictions with their chastening reminder of our fallible state? Does recognition of the postmodern turn "*re*turn us to our place," restore us to the Garden, in which case we might be grateful for the homecoming? Or does it "put us in our place," in which case we might resent the humiliation? Finding hope in humility, can we come to accept that "the imperfect *is* our paradise"? And can we finally find, to cite the poet's next line, "in this bitterness, delight"? . . .[8]

The goal, difficult as ever in our post-modern times, will be to better mind, to more conscientiously assess, our given place. Toward that end, I will offer one last quote, a profoundly self-descriptive joke, whose exquisite equipoise we might hold as our pole star in the crucial years to come.

Lily Tomlin: "We're all in this together—by ourselves."[9]

CHAPTER 6

Fields in Play

Conscientious Thinking Reforms the Sciences

Secondary physics is the study of "and."
—Sir Arthur Eddington

We now find ourselves in the midst of a confusing transition between worldviews. The ruling logic of a liberal modernity that has designed our scientific, economic, and political institutions is being undermined by a set of post-modern principles and tacit presumptions. We do "make sense" through the evidence of our senses, and our new digital devices have changed the ways that evidence is both arrayed and conveyed. Accelerating a process that began with the first electronic media, our use of desktops, laptops, mobile phones, and tablets with their search engines, shareware, and wiki-empowered social networking sites has been revising our default expectations about what seems natural and right in our everyday lives.

To highlight the emphasis these new devices have placed on the innate "togetherness" of human experience, I have been calling their postmodern ways of assessing the world *conscientious thinking*. Such an emphasis conflicts with the modern mind's default intention to atomize the world for specialized study and has been accompanied by an even more contentious trend: a renewed insistence on the inherent fallibility of human reasoning, even when practiced at its very best. To marry Shakespeare to Marshall McLuhan, the conscientious mind keeps finding those ways that "reason panders will" while discovering evidence that "the medium" of our thinking does indeed prefigure the likely shape of its final "message."

Given the near-total saturation of the electronic media and their subliminal restructuring of our normative patterns of perception and interaction, signs of this conscientious reasoning have been advancing in every field of formal thought and nearly every social niche, including those whose members advertise themselves as active opponents. Although we have yet to acknowledge, much less openly embrace, the ubiquity of these post-modern trends, we may be approaching one of those critical phases when, to borrow from Descartes again, the discrepancy between what people think they believe and what they actually believe has become so great that a collective shock of recognition is in the offing. Such a turn occurred early in 1776 when Thomas Paine published his aptly named pamphlet *Common Sense*, and many colonials awoke to the realization, decades in the making, that they no longer believed in the monarchy.

There are, however, significant differences between our era and theirs, the most obvious of which is that we lack the sort of repressive government whose inflexibility ironically induces revolutionary ruptures: our culture wars, though nasty, have not been violent ones. But both the impact of Paine's pamphlet and the rapid collapse of Communism do serve as reminders that, after many years of small-grained change, a categorical revision in commonsense thinking can crystallize abruptly. Rather than predict where we are on that road to Damascus, my task at this point is to establish the degree to which those prefatory changes have already occurred, and in the very fields that the modern mind-set has most respected. As the phrase "culture war" itself connotes, public attention to intellectual conflict has been drawn primarily to controversies in the arts and humanities. But as we shall see in the following quick-and-dirty survey, the post-modern turn has long been occurring within the natural and social sciences as well, with equally disturbing and confounding results.

The Natural Sciences

PHYSICS: The modern presumption that the completion of knowledge was not only possible but near at hand reached its cultural apex at the end of nineteenth century only to be challenged in the ensuing three decades by a series of transformative discoveries in anthropology, physics, literature, and the arts. Artistic truths and mathematical ones cannot *equate*, of course, but they can be metaphorically alike. Consider the use of multiple points of view in literary fiction and multiple perspectives in sculpture and painting; the cataloguing of multiple tribal beliefs, each with its own interpretation of human experience; and the double blow to the clockwork universe delivered by general relativity and quantum mechanics. Progress in each of these fields may have been following its own developmental logic, but the changes they expressed were also profoundly akin. Each was, in its own way, calling into question the notion of fixed and final truths that had calibrated the core of the scientific worldview, and their near simultaneous emergence in the early twentieth century marked the real birth of the post-modern turn toward conscientious thinking.

The revolution in physics, for example, defied the expectations of modern reasoning in numerous ways. The strict segregation of categories inherent in Newton's clockwork universe was undermined when Einstein proposed, and later experiments seemed to prove, that space and time themselves were interrelated, existing in a kind of dynamic continuum. Today, their inherent "togetherness" is so accepted within the field that the words themselves are commonly fused, practitioners exploring and debating the fundamental features of *spacetime*. Meanwhile, as physicists began to study the subatomic world, the order and behavior of material reality appeared even more alien to modern expectations. When probed with the most sensitive instruments, the structure of light became bizarrely ambivalent in the literal sense, exhibiting conscientiously qualities of both a particle and a wave. Stranger still, subatomic entities could occupy multiple places at the same time, a condition called *superposition*; and they could influence each other instantly from afar, exhibiting a "spooky" togetherness (Einstein's adjective) called *entanglement* that defied the logic of mechanical causality.[1]

The loose use of quantum mechanics' uncertainty principle by non-specialists like myself often irritates physicists today, especially when it is hijacked by those who are striving to save an unplumbable space for their version of the divine. But separate from the low comedy of our recent God wars with their dueling bumper stickers, strident court cases, and bestselling polemics largely illiterate in the reasoning of the positions they scorn, the claims first made by Werner Heisenberg in the 1920s *were* symbolically important. They signified an honorable shift in our intellectual history, a pivotal phase when modern science, through the rigorous use of its own best tools, rediscovered the reality of limits: when physicists first began to know that they couldn't "know it all"—not with the absolute certainty and pure objectivity they had previously supposed. Because at the subatomic level the act of observation became a form of participation that changed the measurable world, our assessment of the smallest units of reality couldn't be fixed and final after all. At that level, the design of each experimental protocol, the method we chose to study material reality, would predetermine the nature of reality itself.

Unlike, say, the discovery of nuclear fission in 1938, the immediate social impact of Heisenberg's principle was minimal: no war-winning weapons or transformative consumer products were fashioned from its view of the subatomic world; it didn't change the course of elections, or revise the moral management of domestic households. Yet for science itself, the implications were profound. If true, this claim fatally undermined the modern presumption that the completion of knowledge could be achieved through the cumulative addition of small-grained certainties: as a route to finality in natural philosophy, atomism was now discredited. In the realm of elementary particles, future events might be *probable* but they couldn't be *certain*, and it was at just this point, the reintroduction of uncertainty into natural philosophy, that the new *logos* of theoretical physics began to resemble the old *mythos* expressing the tragic sense of life. The postmodern turn away from some of the core expectations of modern science was also a pivoting toward *pre*-modern notions about the inherent limits of human knowledge.

Other notable thinkers, including William James and Henri Bergson, had challenged those same expectations, but Heisenberg's principle was based on actual experimental results in modern science's most prestigious field at the time, theoretical physics, which made its apparent apostasy all the more disturbing. For that reason, most physicists chose to treat the uncertainty principle as a temporary mystery, an incompletion to be fixed by a more inclusive calculation, a new "theory of everything" that would fulfill the old Cartesian promise of perfection and completion on familiar terms. Like the original atomists, many physicists continued to search for that one elementary unit out of whose innumerable pieces the whole of reality was presumed to be constructed. With all the recalcitrance of an unconscious habit, the atomizing strategy of the phonetic alphabet was still being projected onto the material world.

Yet, so far at least, the material world has stubbornly resisted the simplicity of that model. Through the use of ever-more-sophisticated instruments, the ongoing search for that one elementary unit has uncovered instead a diverse zoo of subatomic entities: quarks, leptons, fermions, and bosons, with various charges and forms of "charm." All this hard-won data keeps complicating the task of perfecting a final map, defying the sort of elegant formulations that modern science admires and prefers. Attempts to corral its diversity have led instead to exotic proposals, including the "multiverse" (the existence of multiple parallel universes) and the current reigning version of superstring theory, which requires a material world with ten spatial dimensions rather than three.

The messiness of these theories and the suspicion that their claims can never be tested experimentally have led to a conceptual revolt against the goal itself. Theoretical biologist Stuart Kaufmann, physicists Andreas

Albrecht and Lee Smolin, and the philosopher Roberto Unger have each suggested in their own way that the pursuit of a "theory of everything" is fundamentally misconceived. They argue that the modern presumption that there are immutable laws, true everywhere and forever, is itself wrong, and both Smolin and Kaufmann suggest that the physical order of the universe may be evolving over time, just as the biological order does.[2] Even Stephen Hawking, the most influential physicist of the age, conceded in 2010 that no single theory of the universe is ever likely to hold true for all places and times. Whether through the superstring approach or something else, the best we are likely to achieve, he believes, is "a family of interconnected theories, each describing its own version of reality."[3] In cosmology, then, as in pedagogy, "multilogue" has been supplanting monologue and metamorphic history challenging universal theory as the better models for authoritative thought. None of these conscientious challenges to the ruling orthodoxy are arguing that the universe is utterly unknowable, or that *all* theories are equally true; the implication instead is that even our best accounts can only be partial in both senses of that word: incomplete, and necessarily slanted by whichever methodology we choose to use.

Such revisions are telling, but because discoveries in the subatomic and telescopic realms have little immediate relevance to our everyday lives, one has a hard time making a convincing case for conscientious thinking based on the findings of physics alone. Horrible to say, but the influence of that field on contemporary consciousness and culture peaked with the invention of atomic weaponry during and after World War II. Since then—with the discovery of DNA, multiple hominid fossil finds, and the success of medical research in prolonging our lives—social influence and the prestige that goes with it have shifted to the biological sciences. Here, too, though, the characteristic elements of conscientious reasoning have been revising the prevailing thinking for years. As the primary metaphor in physics has been shifting from the isolated *atom* to the interactive *field*, the emphasis in biology has been flipping from *anatomy* to *ecology*. Wherever one turns, the same trends seem to emerge; just as "to know" is to "know *with*" in our post-modern era, one can't study biology today without thinking *sym*biotically.

EVOLUTIONARY BIOLOGY: Shifts within evolutionary theory are illustrative of this change. *The Origin of Species*, Darwin's 1859 masterpiece, was published in a Victorian England where modernity's logic ruled supreme. Reflecting the cultural common sense of the day, the theory's early proponents—including Herbert Spencer, who coined the phrase "the survival of the fittest"—reconceived nature as the marketplace writ large, interpreting life as an agonistic struggle among *biological* atoms that competed for resources and the chance to reproduce. Over the last forty years, however, that stress on atomistic competition (nature "red in tooth and claw") has been offset by a dawning recognition of the importance of cooperation in natural selection: how fitness could be achieved through strategies of togetherness. Closing the gap between human and nonhuman life, scientists were discovering that other species—not just the great apes but also dolphins, whales, wolves, and crows—were impressively intelligent (in the adaptionist ways that biologists define that term), and that the intelligence of a species was strongly correlated with its sociability. Individual competition in breeding, for example, often seemed to coexist with astute cooperation in hunting, feeding, and self-defense; and even breeding could be a collective enterprise, as within their herd or pride, female elephants and lions were observed sharing their maternal duties.

Socialization implied intraspecies communication, which, with the aid of more powerful tools, was proving to be far more prevalent than previously supposed. Whales as well as birds were found to have songs, ones that vary by group and can carry for hundreds of nautical miles. In a kind of choreographic mapping, honeybees dance to convey to their hive-mates where flowers can be found, and mute and stationary plants, when attacked by insects, emit chemical signals that warn others of their kind to take defensive measures. Even the most primitive forms of life, those supposedly solitary microbes that constitute half of the planet's biomass and most of its diversity, have now turned out to be prolific communicators. Conversing through a biochemical process called quorum sensing, bacteria are constantly taking a census of their surrounding area, and when sufficient numbers of their kind are found to be present (when a "quorum" is reached), group action is taken. As with far more sophisticated animals, microbial communication leads to social cooperation, generating coordinated shifts in collective behavior that include lighting up the ocean with bioluminescence and releasing toxins into the bloodstream of an infected host.[4]

MEDICINE: The realization that even the unicellular microbe (the atom of all life forms) is interactively communicating to explore its environment and direct group behavior has suggested an entirely new approach to the pharmaceutical treatment of infectious diseases, one that seeks to block or confuse the quorum-sensing capabilities of pathogens. A similar set of findings has been revolutionizing our understanding of cancer. In line with the atomistic biases of the modern mind-set, the prevailing model in the past for both the etiology of the disease and its treatment had been "tumor-centric." The initial presumption had been that a single cell had gone awry and, further, that one or two damaged genes had caused it to multiply uncontrollably. Following that same logic, it was presumed at first that, with the decoding of the human genome, a point-to-point map linking most cancers to a particular mutation could be drawn, leading eventually to gene-based therapies.

All this has proven to be overly simplistic, highlighting again the limits of the modern mind-set's atomistic approach to comprehending reality. At the genetic level, relatively few forms of cancer have demonstrated such a clear-cut causality—that is, with a single mutation automatically initiating the disease. The danger of most genetic errors now appears to be more probabilistic than deterministic. And not only does an intracellular chemistry far more complex than mutation alone affect the cancerous expression of genetic misinformation; evidence now exists—in the words of Joseph H. Nadeau, director of scientific development at the Institute for Systems Biology—that "the function of one particular gene sometimes depends on the specific constellation of genetic variations surrounding it."[5] Malignancy itself may depend on particular varieties of pathological "togetherness."

A like-minded shift in emphasis from atom to field has been occurring on the physiological level. Tiny tumors are proving to be more common than was formerly understood, which means that, in normal circumstances, the body must possess the biochemical means to contain them. These findings suggest that some cancers spread only when those as-yet-unknown protective processes fail, and this notion, in turn, implies a broader definition of the disease itself, one that includes not just mutating genes and a malfunctioning cell but also the overall health of the neighboring tissue. Or, to rephrase Nadeau's observation, the mass multiplication of any particular tumor "sometimes depends on the specific constellation of *physiological* variations surrounding it." That constellation may include physical injuries, infections, chronic inflammation, or the cumulative damage caused by aging. And because some of the most common current treatments, such as mastectomies and even biopsies, can generate injury and inflammation on their own, these findings challenge standard practices in troubling ways even as they suggest a whole new arena for therapeutic investigation.[6]

LAMARCKIAN GENETICS: In all of the fields examined so far, a serious reorientation has been occurring, a shift that follows the logic of the post-modern turn. A prophetic observation made in 1927 by astrophysicist Sir Arthur Eddington—that "secondary physics" would prove to be "the study of *and*"—is now also proving true for the "secondary" phases of evolution, microbiology, and medicine, as each has enriched its understanding of the living world by turning its attention from text to context, from atomistic incident to interactive environment. But as with physics, this ongoing transformation has been fitful and often fiercely contested. The conflict between the two common senses, an established but declining modern logic and an insurgent but still evolving conscientious reasoning, has been reenacted in field after field.

In evolutionary genetics, the debate between the neo-Darwinian advocates of a competitive atomism (Richard Dawkins' "selfish gene") and the new proponents of togetherness, who tend to emphasize kin and group selection, has been passionate, their highly technical arguments occasionally charged with political insinuations. In cancer research, the financial as well as psychological investment in atomistic reasoning led to a self-interested intransigence that has only recently abated. In 2008 Dr. Mina Bissell, an early advocate of the importance of a tumor's physiological environment, won the prestigious Excellence in Science award, its citation praising her for creating a paradigm shift in our fundamental understanding of the disease. But back in 1984 when she handed one of her early papers to a leading researcher in the field, his instantly dismissive response was to drop it into a wastebasket before her eyes.[7]

But no idea had been more ridiculed, no stance seemed more dead, than the claim by the early biologist Jean-Baptiste Lamarck that the features acquired through experience by one generation could be passed on to the next—a claim that, during the Cold War, seemed permanently tainted with Soviet science and its faith in the creation of a new "Soviet Man." To even entertain the possibility that acquired characteristics might be heritable was a career-killer, the equivalent to professing an ongoing belief in the existence of phlogiston or spontaneous generation. According to reigning orthodoxy, lasting changes in heritable features are solely the result of random mutations in a species' genes, as those mutations are proven to be conducive to survival over multiple generations. Evolutionary change, therefore, tends to be glacially slow and the life experiences of any single parent largely irrelevant to the physical heritage he or she passes on. Both simple and comprehensive, this theory does possess the hallmark elegance that modern science prefers. Unfortunately for its many adherents, who had tossed Lamarck's competing thesis into history's wastebasket, it now also appears to be wrong.

Epidemiological studies of a small town in Sweden, conducted by Marcus Pembrey and others, have demonstrated that the *life expectancy* of villagers has been affected in statistically significant ways by the *life experiences* of their parents and grandparents. Boys whose grandfathers suffered food shortages when they were eight to twelve years old were themselves likely to die sooner. If a woman experienced a similar shortage when very young, then her sons' daughters were also more likely to die at an earlier age. And in a finding with scary relevance to an America now afflicted with an epidemic in obesity, if a Swedish man overate as a child, his sons were four times more likely to develop diabetes and were more susceptible to heart disease as well.[8]

Important lab work has uncovered a likely physiological source of these remarkably Lamarckian results. Genetic expression, it turns out, is profoundly affected by a biochemical system of on-off switches that determine which of our twenty-five thousand protein-encoding genes are active and which are not. And because the pattern of these epigenetic switches can be both changed by life experiences and, it now seems clear, passed on through a parent's egg or sperm, the behavior of a single generation, and the material circumstances of their bad or good luck, can indeed change the probable health of their offspring.[9] Michael Skinner, a pioneer in the field, has shown that exposure to a commonly used fungicide causes epigenetic shifts that are passed on through at least four generations of rats, to the detriment of their reproductive health. In a study that may explain the behavior-based heritability of diabetes, a group of Australian scientists discovered that the pancreases of female rats, whose fathers had been deliberately overfed, contained 642 epigenetic switches in the wrong position. Meanwhile, Nadeau's Institute for Systems Biology has tracked over one hundred intracellular or behavioral traits that are affected by epigenetic change.[10]

We have only begun to map the extent, pace, and durability of these non-mutational transformations in genetic expression, much less to consider their implications for public health policy. But on the subject of interest here, their stunning ratification of a position long ridiculed by modern science provides one more example of the ongoing shift toward a more conscientious conception of reality. Following modernity's atomistic biases, as modeled in the extreme by the ideas of Richard Dawkins, the neo-Darwinian orthodoxy assumed that heritability was a process defined and determined by its smallest pieces. Just as modern cancer research had been tumor-centric, the orthodox conception of biological inheritance reductively focuses on the individual gene as a replication machine, on its "selfish" drive to persist in time, and on evolutionary change as the result of random errors in replication that just so happen to provide a survival advantage.[11]

But to recall a famous line by John Donne, even the gene, it now seems, is less an independent "island" than an integral part of a larger and multidimensional "main." The boundaries of our genetic identities are proving to be far more porous than neo-Darwinian theory allows; the benefits and dangers of the macro-environment, as directed in part by our own behavior, do seep through to interact with intracellular processes, causing durable changes in biochemical, physiological, and behavioral traits. In the words of one researcher, these discoveries and others are now "vexing" the orthodox definition of a gene "with multiple layers of complexity."[12]

A medical researcher long ago supplied a metaphor that might apply to all these fields that are now breaking away from the modern model toward a more conscientious understanding of the biological order. Arguing that malignancy was not the result of a rogue cell but a disorder of cellular organization, Dr. D. W. Smithers wrote, "Cancer is no more a disease of cells than a traffic jam is a disease of cars. A lifetime of study of the internal-combustion engine would not help anyone understand our traffic problems." The year was 1962, and although Smithers' article appeared in the *Lancet*, Britain's most prestigious medical journal, it, too, might as well have been thrown into a wastebasket. Thanks to a three-hundred-year-old predisposition to frame every problem in atomistic terms, "a lifetime of study" in the field of cancer research may have been tragically misdirected by focusing largely on the cellular "engine."[13]

SYMBIOSIS: The "traffic" of interactivity and the multiple layers of coordination that distinguish biological systems from the linear causality of clockwork mechanisms have had a powerful impact on evolution itself, and cooperation between species as well as within them is proving to be an indispensable feature of life's innate togetherness. As Princeton's Bonnie Bassler and others have demonstrated, not only can the lowly bacterium converse with its kind; it is often bilingual, possessing one chemical language for its own species and a second, more universal one to communicate with many other microorganisms. This expanded capacity to signal chemically can result in complex forms of coordinated activity among multiple species to their mutual benefit, allowing, for example, some six hundred varieties of bacteria to organize themselves into dental plaque.[14]

Other examples of evolutionary interdependency are evident in every ecological niche. Skyscraping trees exchange life-sustaining nutriments with subterranean fungi; ants protect aphids and are fed in turn by their sugary secretions; both termites and cows provide protective environments for microorganisms that then assist their hosts in absorbing food; nectar attracts the birds and bees whose anatomies have been exquisitely shaped not only to feed on but to facilitate the reproduction of flowering plants. There are at least ten times as many microbes in or on a human body as there are human cells, and many of those are vital to our survival, protecting us from ultraviolet rays, aiding in our digestion, or producing the crucial vitamins K and B12.

Not all these relationships are beneficial to both partners. Symbiosis—from the Greek *sumbiosis*, "companionship"; from *sumbion*, "living to-gether"—is a broad category that includes four kinds of co-evolving re-lationships: the predatory and the parasitic (where one species benefits while harming the other), the commensal (one benefiting while the other is unaffected), and the mutual (both benefiting, as in all the examples cited above). But whether beneficial or harmful, mutual or one-sided, symbiosis insists that evolution can only be fully understood by studying the interactive relationships *among* species—that to live at all is to live *with*, and that to live *with* is to be changed by one's biological neighbors in meaningful ways.[15]

Further "vexing" evolutionary science's initial emphasis on one-to-one relationships "with multiple layers of complexity," the field of ecology has expanded the concept of symbiosis to include the whole host of species living in any particular area, along with key elements of their physical en-vironment. And the Gaia hypothesis has completed this post-modern turn toward holistic thinking by redefining the Earth itself as a single interac-tive system: a kind of über-organism that actively sustains a range of condi-tions hospitable to all the life forms that have evolved within its biosphere. According to this theory, we are, in the most literal sense, *all* in this to-gether, not simply by ourselves. Predator and prey, slug and great ape, giant sequoia and minuscule plankton are being sustained alike by the planetary processes that regulate temperature, salinity, the balance of gases, and the rate of solar radiation. The cyclical operations of the Earth as a whole are said to resemble those of each living cell, both persisting in time through actively sustaining an inner balance between extremes.[16]

Homeostasis—this same tendency to maintain an internal equilibrium through dynamic counterbalancing—is a feature shared by all living crea-tures, and as Gregory Bateson has observed, the homeostatic character of life implies a kind of value system. Philosophers still debate the existence of "natural law," but in nature itself this much at least is clear: *more* (salt, warmth, oxygen) is only *better* up to a point, after which it can quickly be-come toxic. Both biochemically and ecologically, nature aims for *optima*, not *maxima*, which means that a political economy geared to unchecked progress and limitless profits is, at its core, unnatural. The character of biological forms, their homeostatic quality, rhymes instead with societ-ies attuned to something like the golden mean, an ideal that the most conscientious forms of post-modern reasoning are more likely to honor than did the modern sciences that preceded them.[17]

THE SCIENTIFIC METHOD: Finally, a development with disturbing implications for many fields returns us to the issue of intellectual fallibility: the reliability of some mainstream research has now been called into question. These new concerns are not limited to the corruption that occurs when corporations are the primary sponsors of research, as has long been the case with new pharmaceuticals. Even peer-reviewed studies untainted by corporate moneys and published in the most prestigious journals have been proving unreliable. All too frequently, the results of highly influential papers have either been weakened or contradicted by later studies.

For those of us attempting to improve our health by following the latest research results, this herky-jerky rhythm of assertion then reversal will seem all too familiar. Claims about the benefits of vitamin E, oat bran, bypass surgery, mammograms, daily aspirin doses, and hormonal supplements—to mention just a few of the more publicized examples—have been announced and applied only to be seriously challenged or officially reversed on further study. This anecdotal sense of the unreliability of medical research has recently received the imprimatur of science itself. Stanford epidemiologist John Ioannidis has tracked research claims in the biomedical field with shocking results that are bluntly summed up in the title of his best-known paper, "Why Most Published Research Findings Are False." In one analytical exercise, Ioannidis and his team examined the forty-nine most cited papers in the three major medical journals. The majority of these published studies were randomized controlled trials that met the highest methodological standards, yet of the initial claims that were subjected to further study, 41 percent were either directly contradicted or had the size of their correlation significantly reduced. And given that the majority of published studies are not randomized controlled trials, the numbers in general are far worse. Ioannidis has been quoted as believing that "as much as 90 percent of the published medical information that doctors rely on is flawed" in some way.[18]

This inability to replicate initially significant research findings extends beyond the field of medicine; similar problems have arisen in biology, ecology, and psychology as well. The best available explanations so far involve a belated recognition of biases built into both the normative practices of researchers themselves and the system that has arisen to reward their results. Separate from the worrisome trend of undue corporate influence, scientific publications, for example, strongly prefer positive results. (One meta-study dating back to 1959 found that 97 percent of articles published were ones that confirmed their initial hypothesis.) And because to succeed in their field researchers need to be published, there is significant pressure to cherry-pick from the available data in ways that ratify the proposition they have been testing.

To an outsider, such preferential thinking might seem an obvious instance of scientific fraud, but the data collected are often complex and ambiguous, requiring just the sort of subtle interpretation that is most susceptible to unconscious skewing. Called "selective reporting," this subliminal inclination to cite the data most favorable to one's hypothesis is—according to Canadian biologist Richard Palmer, who conducted a number of meta-studies on the subject—"everywhere in science," a discovery that both stunned and depressed him. In a published review, he summarized for his colleagues the profoundly unsettling implications for their field: "We cannot escape the troubling conclusion that some—perhaps many— cherished generalities are at best exaggerated in their biological significance and at worst a collective illusion nurtured by strong a-priori beliefs often repeated."[19]

That final phrase, "a collective illusion nurtured by strong a-priori beliefs often repeated," mirrors exactly, one can't help but note, the post-modern critique of science's faith in fixed and final truths. Even devoted researchers, true believers in the scientific method, are now finding that the intellectual objectivity they have idealized is far more elusive than they once presumed. In the hard sciences too, "reason" seems to "pander will," and merely fashionable ideas can hold sway for a time under the guise of universal truths.

This belated recognition of the subjectivity inherent in what was presumed to be the most objective results is not the most disturbing news emerging from today's laboratories. Distinct from the issues of corporate corruption, publication bias, and selective reporting, other findings call into question the very ability of the scientific method to accurately assess certain aspects of reality on a routine basis. Even some researchers who, repeating their own experiments, have every incentive to confirm their results are finding that replication is inexplicably elusive. This phenomenon, known as the "decline effect," perversely inverts the sequential progress that scientists expect: the more often an initially successful experiment is repeated, the *less* significant its original correlations become. Rather than fixed and final, the truths discovered in these cases seem to be distressingly transient, suggesting that the initial correlations may have been more random than real and highlighting the possibility that even when rigorously applied the scientific method may be, in some cases, inadequate to the task of mapping reality with the accuracy we expect from it.

A caution here: as we saw last chapter, immoderate attacks on the legitimacy of scientific knowledge present their own obvious dangers. Much of the material knowledge we have gained in the last two centuries, the very health and wealth we take for granted, are the tangible rewards of science's scrupulous investigations of the real. Yet no human practice, however useful its past, should be immune to critique. And because Ioannidis and Palmer are not po-mo nihilists or fundamentalist scolds but devoted rationalists who have been using science's own preferred methods to question the reliability of mainstream research, their doubts demand a serious response. The systemic fallibility their work has uncovered not only suggests the necessity of professional reforms such as easing the publication bias; it also poses profound questions about what we can and cannot learn through the standard techniques of modern science alone.

As currently conceived, the scientific method is inherently reductionist. It atomizes experience, presuming that through radically narrowing the number of variables present in any given design, its experiments can discover correlations (between, say, vitamin E intake and heart disease) that reliably reflect physical causation in everyday life. But as we have seen in this quick-and-dirty survey, such an approach has its limits, especially in biological systems where its models of causation are often "vexed" by "multiple layers of complexity"—that is, by the innate and interactive togetherness of the natural world. Clearly, the current version of the scientific method has allowed us to map material reality at a depth unimaginable prior to its evolution. But to cite Emerson, "under every deep another deep opens," and to explore *that* deep may require a more conscientious methodology than we currently practice.[20]

The Social Sciences

In no division of knowledge has the impact of the modern epistemology been more mixed and problematic than in the social sciences. Whether in economics, anthropology, sociology, history, psychotherapy, or political science, the modern mind-set's drive to quantify and rationalize has provided powerful new measures for apprehending human behavior even while skewing or ignoring some of the most fundamental features of our everyday experience. Too many early practitioners, inheriting the original sins of Cartesianism and applying them in fields less congenial to its logic, presumed that the study of humanity could be atomistically reduced to fixed and final facts, and that the most purely mathematical description of social as well as material reality was always the best. But the elegance of the social theories spun from their quantified data could only be won through excluding or distorting many essential human qualities. Because these sciences define what it means to be human, the contest here between modern and post-modern forms of reasoning quickly converts to political controversy.

ANTHROPOLOGY: As the scientific worldview co-opted the common sense of the West throughout the nineteenth and into the early twentieth centuries, these "mismeasures of man" became more common and dangerous. A rationalist approach that claimed to free the intellect from the influence of emotion sometimes fronted instead for the ugliest of motives, which were then all the more influential for going unacknowledged. The God that once supported the torture of heretics and the feasting of kings while the peasantry famished was being supplanted by a scientism that justified the abuse of the poor under the aegis of Social Darwinism or endorsed the segregation of races on the basis of "craniometry." The data was in, the measures of various skulls down to the last decimal, and the social scientist knew for a fact that the "dolichocephalic Aryan" was superior to the "brachycephalic Jew." He had proven that the "cranial capacity"—and so, too, according to the logic of quantiphilia, the native intelligence—of the Caucasian was categorically greater than that of the Negro.[21]

It would be a mistake to blame an entire field of study for these bigoted findings, much less for the abhorrent social policies they served to justify. After examining the same data, some early anthropologists rejected the racialist conclusions drawn, and during this same period the newly emerging field of cultural anthropology was cataloguing for the first time the richly diverse customs, artifacts, languages, and myths of preliterate peoples and tribes. These early ethnographers often gained access to their subjects through a policy of colonial expansion that was itself justified by theories of racial or cultural superiority, yet the evidence retrieved and experience gained tended to undermine those presumptions. In pursuit of the universal laws that modernity expects, anthropology's objective study of humankind was ironically discovering the inherent *subjectivity* of cultural expression. Intercultural contact both heightened into self-consciousness and called into question the ethnographer's own views and values, including the claims of his scientific profession. Here, too, the modern faith in fixed and final truths was being challenged by a new appreciation for diverse perspectives; multilogue was supplanting monologue as the better way to model reality.

As elsewhere, though, that conversion was and is contentious. The tension between modernity's pursuit of objective truths and the post-modern turn toward relativism has led to many a dispute within the profession, dividing anthropologists into feuding factions and leading, at times, to formal divisions in academic departments.[22]

HISTORY: Similar disputes have arisen over whether history either can be or should be a science in the modern sense. While the digital revolution has supplied scholars with far more data about the past as well as the facility to sort it in multiple ways, leading to new abstract frames and data-dense historical analyses, some historians have become acutely sensitive to the cultural biases built into the field's preferred methods. As the skeptical adage insists, history is typically written by the victors, and these new historians, reapplying something like the uncertainty principle to the social domain, now wonder whether what *really* happened in human affairs can ever be separable from the various subjective accounts of its participants. To the extent that history is a record of the conflicts among tribes, classes, and nation-states, isn't a narration of contention from all perspectives truer to the complete experience of any past event than a purportedly objective analysis that presumes fixed and final knowledge?

Akin to the questions posed by cultural anthropologists, these inherently post-modern doubts have generated a different sort of historical monograph. An example would be Karl Jacoby's *Shadows at Dawn*, a study of the Camp Grant Massacre in the borderlands of the Southwest where, in 1871, Anglo-Americans, Hispanic Americans, and Papago Indians conspired in the slaughter of an Apache encampment. Employing a narrative technique similar to the one used in the novels of William Faulkner and the film *Rashomon*, Jacoby examines the perspectives of all four cultures, revealing how each community interacted with the others prior to the attack and how each came to view its participation in the massacre retrospectively.[23]

This current shift away from a strictly scientific approach to history transcends both political affiliation and national boundaries. The prolific historian John Lukacs, who has defined himself as a reactionary, published an essay near the end of his long career, "Putting Man before Descartes," which asserts that "human knowledge is personal and participant" and argues "against objectivity" and for "understanding" in historical study.[24] Meanwhile, some European scholars—including France's Pierre Nora (*Realms of Memory*) and England's David Lowenthal (*Possessed by the Past*)— have been worrying about the negative impact of objective history on the foundational myths and ritual heritages of the people whose pasts those histories define. These authors insist that collective memories about public events, although often inaccurate and always subjective, are essential to the cultivation of those larger meanings and shared purposes that any thriving society requires. Consequently, a historiography that programmatically debunks the factual basis of those meanings and purposes may do more social harm than good.[25]

Implicit in all these concerns is the return to a profound debate about ruling epistemologies that was first engaged in classical Greece when Plato banned the *Iliad* and the *Odyssey* from his ideal curriculum in his *Republic*. Insisting on the superiority of rational analysis over those ritually recited narratives, Plato wanted to supplant the traditional Homeric *mythos* with the new Socratic *logos*. After the Enlightenment, a similar intention was pursued with a vengeance: as the scientific worldview took hold, knowledge was presumed to be truest and best when it was abstract and objective, not "personal and participant," and disdain for a given idea was (and often still is) commonly expressed with the dismissive phrase "it's just a myth."

But, as in so many other fields, some historians are now questioning that narrow investment in *logos* alone. Pierre Nora, for example, has made a project of preserving the once ritually recited communal memories of his homeland. In a direct reversal of Plato's curricular reform, he has been reinserting a once traditional *mythos* back into the salons and classrooms of the French Republic.[26] Even there, in very cradle of Cartesian rationalism, the post-modern mind has been busy reviving pre-modern forms.

PSYCHOTHERAPY: The evolution of psychotherapy recapitulates the ironic pattern of the modern mind-set pushing the envelope of discovery in ways that undermine its own initial premises. Here, too, the post-modern turn emerged from modernity's most diligent work. As the father of the field, Freud rigorously applied rational analysis to establish the permanent presence of *ir*rational forces in the individual psyche. His understanding of these unconscious forces was itself unconsciously framed by the prevailing metaphors of his age, among them the internal dynamics of the steam engine and the agonistic competition of the marketplace. It didn't occur to him that the repression of emotion that his theory stressed might be more an artifact of a specific cultural orientation than a universal feature of consciousness, and his approach to mental disease was, conceptually and therapeutically, atomistic at its core: just as modern medicine initially conceived of cancer as a disease of the single cell, Freudian psychiatry defined neurosis as primarily a pathology of the single self. Still, the recovery of the nonrational as a permanent and powerful feature of our minds was a conceptual breakthrough, one that disarmed the modern presumption that the human predicament could be solved on purely rational grounds alone.

By the mid-twentieth century the West was entertaining a whole host of competing theories, therapies, and philosophical approaches to the nature of the human psyche and its habitual discontents. They ranged from numerous variations on Freudian analysis to a radical behaviorism, which solved the mystery of consciousness by denying its existence, to the Gestalt therapy of Fritz and Laura Perls, who widened the definition of individual identity by insisting that the self does not exist in any meaningful way separate from the field of its interpersonal relations. The Perls asserted that, rather than a fixed entity residing "inside" each of us as discrete individuals, selfhood is created and sustained through the dynamic interplay of all its social relationships. The pattern by now ought to seem familiar. According to Gestalt therapy, the mind is *not* "its own place": psychologically as well as biologically, to live is to live *with*. As self-aware beings, we are, inextricably, "in this together" rather than primarily "by ourselves."

Later schools of thought, deriving from Jacques Lacan and Michel Foucault, also deny that a unified internal self exists. One's psyche is not only socially constructed but also multifarious and inherently unstable. Identity is best understood as a floating host of separate smaller selves, a montage of possible roles—mother, colleague, patriot, lover—with none more authentic or real than the others. American psychologist Kenneth Gergen has described today's middle-class American as "saturated" with a plethora of these possible selves, many of them modeled by the invasive imagery of TV and the Internet. As a consequence, the expression of identity has been turned into a kind of multitasking, with all the associated risks of confusion and distraction as one rapidly shifts between texting one's buddy, emailing one's boss, "friending" an old high school flame, and cheering one's child on the basketball court.[27]

An obvious implication of this characteristically post-modern shift from *atom* to *field* is that the well-being of the individual is inseparable, finally, from the ongoing mental health of the various social groups to which he belongs. Sanity, in this view, would also have an ecological dimension. Certain social niches and even entire cultures might prove predictably toxic to vulnerable individuals. In this mapping of our psychic territory, neurosis would be reconceived as *sym*-neurosis, and since the ailing mind is not simply its own place, the healing of that mind would require homeostatic adjustments within its affiliated groups. Such an approach begins to blur the differences between the psychological and the social and, if applied aggressively, would turn away from a strictly medical definition of mental disease to engage political, religious, and economic treatments as well. For that very reason, though, its current impact on actual therapeutic practices has been limited to small-scale versions like family counseling or group therapy, with the latter usually addressing the problems of like-minded individuals and not the dysfunctional dynamics of broader communal practices. In a complex capitalist society designed to fulfill modern goals and values, the social structure has been so sub-divided and specialized that a more holistic response, even if collectively desired, would be difficult to enact.

The logic of modernity still holds sway in other ways as well. This is certainly true of the dominant model for psychiatric treatment today as it is exemplified in the work of Dr. Peter Kramer. A psychotherapist affili-ated with Brown University, Kramer was a proselytizer for the most widely prescribed psychopharmaceuticals of the 1990s: the then-new family of antidepressants known as the SSRIS. In his best-selling books, he wrote openly of the "virtue of Prozac," even concluding that its synthesis was as historically significant within the field as Freud's discovery of the uncon-scious. Not merely an effective treatment for depressed patients, Prozac offered benefits that also included, according to Kramer, the opportunity to alter personality on a permanent basis; by taking the drug daily, one could initiate a "remaking of the self" in ways that would cause one to feel "better than well."[28]

Kramer was speaking out of a materialist logic which presumes that even the psyche is a strictly physical phenomenon, and mental disease a "chemical imbalance" that can be best treated by pharmaceutical inter-vention. Atomistic, mechanistic, and—with his hyperbolic claims about remaking the self—utopian, Kramer's arguments were a nearly literal ex-pression of the biases implicit in the modern mind-set, and when touted aggressively by a profit-seeking drug industry and echoed uncritically by the mainstream media, those arguments also had significant financial and personal consequences. Despite the far less publicized fact that these SSRIS can have serious side effects, including insomnia, tremors, and a diminished sex life, hundreds of millions of prescriptions have been dis-pensed and billions of dollars spent addressing our purported epidemic of depression. Yet a meta-study, reviewing thirty years of research data and published in the *Journal of the American Medical Association*, reported that, far from permanently altering personality in a positive way, the benefits of the SSRIS on depressed patients with mild to moderate symptoms "may be minimal or nonexistent" when compared with those experienced by patients taking a placebo instead.[29]

Clearly, there is a place for drugs in psychiatric treatment, especially for patients afflicted with serious mental illnesses. But for most of us, the sources of our individual anxieties and depressions are deeply interwo-ven within our social, sexual, economic, political, and spiritual practices. And because the imbalances driving our miserable moods are not simply chemical, durably "desirable . . . states of mind"—the pursuit of which Yeats defined as our "first business"—cannot be achieved solely through taking a pill.[30] One could even ask whether the very expectation that we can permanently feel "better than well" might be a primary source of the same despair that these medicines have claimed to heal—yet one more example of the toxic result of seeking *maxima* over *optima*.

ECONOMICS: In economics more than any other field, the modern mind-set has stubbornly resisted the post-modern critique. Since 1980, the most influential practitioners of the dismal science have persisted in defining their field as a pure science in the mathematical sense. As advanced by Milton Friedman, Alan Greenspan, and others, this neoclassical approach presumes that so-called economic man is a strictly rational actor who ably pursues his own material interests, and it asserts that the self-regulating market, as the sum of those actors' rational choices, flawlessly determines what is socially valuable and what is not. Once freed of inept regulation—the neoclassicists' scapegoat for every economic failure—the market's perpetual-motion prosperity machine will generate, they believe, moral as well as material improvement through the immaculate agency of enlightened self-interest.

With its emphases on atomistic individualism and a reductive rationalism (economic man as a solitary and self-interested calculation machine), and with its utopian faith that the problem of prosperity can be solved once and for all via mathematical modeling, neoclassical economics unequivocally endorses the key presumptions of the modern mind-set. As such, its reading of economic behavior ignores the nonrational dimensions of our decision-making, discounting the influence of non-economic values along with the civic institutions that foster them. And as is so often the case with rationalist thought, abstract modeling conveniently dismisses the warnings implicit in concrete history. In this case, a highly idealized view of the marketplace ignores the long and busy record of the market's failures: its inclination to corruption and propensity for *ir*rational behavior, as evidenced in boom-and-bust cycles ranging from the tulip craze in the mid-1600s to the real estate bubble in 2005. Such a record suggests that the neoclassical interpretation of human nature and culture is as inaccurate as the one supplied by Communist theory, and that, if purely applied, it will likely lead to its own implosion.

One might have thought that events as sobering as the financial meltdown in 2008 would have ended this theory's influence. But however ultimately destructive its logic proves to be, a lot of money can be made by inside players exploiting its policies, and like the killers in teenage horror films, the advocates of "enlightened self-interest" have repeatedly resurrected themselves in the aftermath of the wreckage they have wrought to threaten the body politic anew. Still, the reality of the Great Recession did generate theoretical resistance within the field, much of it reflecting one or more of the key characteristics of post-modern reasoning.

One critique, with a number of variations, has attacked the neoclassicists' overemphasis on rationalism in everyday decision-making and, in its most familiar form, has led to a revival of Keynesian economics. Public debates about John Maynard Keynes tend to center on his governmental solutions to severe economic downturns and so are polarized around the usual left-right divide in American politics. But his theories are also grounded in a psychological realism that views the market as a merely human creation and thus susceptible to our usual flaws and foibles. As a close witness to the crash of 1929, Keynes recognized that, rather than purely rational, financial speculation is a species of gambling and, as such, is vulnerable to the irrational mood swings and self-destructive reasoning found in any casino at 2:00 a.m.

Keynes' most influential book, published in 1936, focused on macroeconomic theory and policies. A separate angle of attack on hyperrationalism has emerged from the microeconomic findings of two Israeli researchers, Daniel Kahneman and Amos Tversky, whose landmark work began in the 1970s. Their experiments, which borrow the methodology of the psychology lab to study the decision-making of individual consumers, have given birth to the increasingly influential field of behavioral economics, and their results have "made clear . . . that even if we think we know what is in our own best interest, we frequently make decisions based on misinformation, myopia, and plain quirkiness."[31] Rather than neoclassical theory's super-efficient calculation machine, economic man was proving to be, to borrow the title of Dan Ariely's book, "predictably unpredictable."

Resistance has also arisen to the mathematical modeling characteristic of the neoclassical approach, including our mainstream measure of collective prosperity, the gross domestic product. The GDP presumes that the quantity of goods and services produced by any economy reliably reflects the quality of life inside its society—that *maxima* means *optima*, that *more* equals *better*. But although poverty and economic insecurity do generate considerable unhappiness, there is a limit to the equation of material quantity with communal satisfaction. A war can ramp up production, but that increase in economic activity hardly indicates a boost in collective well-being. As a consequence, reformers have crafted broader sets of indicators based on a more holistic sense of what prosperity means: on this subject, too, the post-modern mind strives to admit those "multiple layers of complexity" that the modern mind-set, bent on reduction, tends to exclude.

The best example of this approach conscientiously applied has occurred in Bhutan, whose former king, Jigme Singye Wangchuck, sponsored the creation of the Gross National Happiness index (GNH) in hopes of modernizing his small nation without sacrificing its Buddhist values. Policies in Bhutan are based on surveys that assess its people's general well-being in ways which, while valuing material progress, also try to account for other social goods such as spiritual health and cultural and ecological vitality. Although like-minded measures have been proposed in the West, similar reforms are not as easily adopted here. In multicultural democracies with a secular tradition, the public pursuit of spiritual health is an inherently controversial proposition. Meanwhile, corporate interests routinely deny accountability for policies detrimental to environmental health and communal cohesion, and the competitive race to the marketplace with the next high-tech product is not hospitable to either the pace or the politics of communal review. In America especially, neoclassical theory has not only dominated academic discussion; its logic is deeply embedded in our political and economic structures. We have no need to *plan* for the collective good, after all, if the wisdom of the invisible hand will reliably craft the sum of our self-centered actions into the stuff of social progress.

The reality of everyday life, however, tends to confound that utopian claim, and discontent with the orthodox thinking of our economic establishment has been arising across the political spectrum. Complaints about the collateral damages caused by its quantiphilia are now heard from some critics on the cultural right, who worry about the splintering of family life and the crushing of small-town economies, and from others, on the left, who are appalled by economic inequality and environmental degradation. The green economy, communitarianism, the organic and local food movements, the increasing use of the environmental impact statement, which bears a relation to Bhutan's review process—all are early signs of a more holistic reasoning struggling to revise the everyday logic of our economic life.

Whether these provisional reforms will gain sufficient traction to redefine mainstream thinking in America remains an open question. Nevertheless, and from a longer view, the overall direction of change seems clear, and its logic rejects the premises of neoclassical thought. People are not strictly rational, nor are any of their social constructions. No economy, free or planned, is equal to the whole of society. *More* in the material sense is not necessarily *better* in the social, psychological, or ethical senses. Any plausible definition of human prosperity is vexed, therefore, by multiple

layers of complexity, including elements of subjectivity not easily amena-
ble to mathematical modeling.

SOCIOLOGY: One last example of the post-modern turn eroding the
foundations of modern thought in the social sciences. Although this work
emerges from what might be best classified as sociological research, it has
implications that touch on issues vital to psychology, economics, medicine, politics, law, and ethics. The research was conducted by Nicholas
Christakis and James Fowler, and it was derived from data collected by
the Framingham Heart Study, which has been tracking the vital statistics
and psychological states of the residents of one Massachusetts town for
over five decades. The researchers were initially interested in the impact
of social contacts on health habits, and the richness of the Framingham
data allowed them to track the long-term behavior of over twelve thousand
individuals—including the original participants and their relatives, neighbors, friends, and coworkers.

The results, as reported in *Connected: The Surprising Power of Our Social
Networks and How They Shape Our Lives*, were startling and have further
undermined modernity's presumptions about the individual as a rational and self-reliant decision-maker. As clearly tracked on the researchers'
graphs, health habits spread rapidly through the separate social networks
of the Framingham population: whom one knew strongly impacted what
one chose to do—overeat or not, smoke or not—and highlighted the
power of emulation in human behavior. Further study showed that the influence of these social networks was not limited to health decisions, leading the authors to conclude,

> Our connections affect every aspect of our daily lives. How we feel,
> what we know, whom we marry, whether we fall ill, how much money we
> make, and whether we vote at all depend on the ties that bind us. Social
> networks spread generosity, happiness, and love. They are always there,
> exerting both dramatic and subtle influence over our choices, actions,
> thoughts, feelings, even desires.

More startling still,

> our connections do not end with the people we know. Beyond our social
> horizons, friends of friends of friends can start chain reactions that even-
> tually reach us, like waves from distant lands that wash up on our shores.

Our misery or happiness, our good or bad health, and our indifference or
commitment to political participation, are not only contagious; according
to Christakis and Fowler, they are mysteriously impacted at a distance by
the decisions of those we never meet. The persistence of influence within

these social networks could be traced through "three degrees of separation," so that the habits of a man's sister's neighbor's wife had a statistically significant influence on his own behavior. If she quit smoking, though out of sight and out of mind, his chances of doing the same were increased by nearly a third.[32]

Although these results are rooted in statistical analysis, the mathematical model they supply challenges the reality predicted by the pristine formulas of neoclassical theory. Along with the work of Ioannidis and Palmer on the biases in scientific research, and that of Kahneman and Tversky on consumer behavior, they fatally undermine that theory's conception of the individual as a solitary and rational calculation machine. And if economic man does not exist as such, then neither can the model of collective behavior based on him. Instead, the market's invisible hand influences our decision-making in ways that resemble the graphs reported by Christakis and Fowler: sometimes rationally, sometimes not, with the drive to conform (whether productively or self-destructively) serving as a perennial force. If even the research scientist exhibits bias on a routine basis, then objectivity is far rarer and more fragile than the proponents of enlightened self-interest suppose. And as is suggested by the contagious behavior evident in both the market's boom-bust cycles and the Framingham data, self-interest, as it is actually practiced, contains a powerful inclination to mimic those around us—a drive to belong that is not only nonrational but frequently subconscious. Although we may be capable of describing our individual behaviors on a daily basis, we remain largely in the dark about our actual motivations and the many external sources that may be shaping them—some, apparently, at a three-degree remove.

The implications of these linked findings in the natural and social sciences are profound. The evidence they have uncovered challenges long-trusted presumptions, procedures, and policies—not just the pet theories of our economic establishment but the institutionalized logic of modernity itself. In their discovery at every level from the subatomic to the macroscopic, from the chattering microbe to the web's hive mind, that "we are all in this together" connected and interacting in multiple ways, they challenge our old assumptions about the atomistic structure of both our material and social worlds. They are especially disturbing to an American nation whose political economy and moral imagination have been rooted in the belief that we are, primarily, pursuing happiness "by ourselves."

What, then, do freedom and responsibility, reward and punishment, mean—in the courts, in the market, in the home and on the street, in the

annals of fame or the accounts of the divine—if each of us is ceaselessly influenced at a subconscious level by the choices of those around us? What
does individual autonomy mean if our physical fates have been epigeneti-
cally preshaped by the sins and sufferings, the good or bad luck, of our
parents and grandparents? As humming members of the hive and history's children, how many ghosts are invisibly conspiring in each decision
we make? Who gets the credit, who the blame, and, from both a personal
and a public policy perspective, how do we initiate restorative change?

These are deeply troubling questions, and insomuch as the medium of
modern thought has been undermined along with its messages, we lack a
consensus as to how to address them. The utopian promises of the scientific worldview have been losing their luster. It no longer seems self-evident
to us that reality can be solved, strictly and finally, on rational terms alone,
and with uncertainty unleashed in nearly every field, modernity's metrics
are increasingly dogged by nihilistic doubts. If, as Gregory Bateson insisted, "the map is not the territory," why bother following maps at all?[33]

Yet, on reflection, these post-modern findings are not so strange. They
do recall, after all, some of the most eloquent claims of the *pre*-modern
age—that "reason panders will," that "no man is an island," that each of
us is instead "a part of the main"—claims that a confident modernity, in
its rush to atomize experience, had pushed aside. "If we know in what way
society is unbalanced," Simone Weil implored, "we must do what we can
to add weight to the lighter scale."[34] *Our* society's lighter scale, gaining the
weight of these older truths, has now reentered our field of vision. Yet that
field itself has changed, for the renewed emphases on social togetherness
and intellectual humility, which last prevailed in the medieval age, are
returning within a context profoundly reformed by the many discoveries
of the modern mind-set. We will never "know it all," but thanks to the
sciences born out of the Enlightenment, we do know much more than we
did before. And with "this age and the next age / engender[ing] in the
ditch," we are obliged now to fashion a new common sense from their
motley mix.[35]

CHAPTER 7

Together in the Ditch

Everyday Signs of the New Conscientiousness

One is the loneliest number that you'll ever do
Two can be as bad as one
It's the loneliest number since the number one
—Three Dog Night, "One"

Although a populist strain in American culture routinely disdains the latest claims of the intellectual class as nonsensical and impractical, as helplessly out of touch with "real life," the widespread emergence of a more conscientious style of thinking is not separate from but expressive of real changes occurring in society at large. We don't have to "live in books" (to recall Henry Ford's scornful phrase) or hide inside the charts of a laboratory to both feel and reflect the paradigm shift now well under way. Yet to feel and reflect do not always include an overt recognition of those same changes. As the findings of Christakis and Fowler stress, subconscious mimicry as well as self-conscious choice fashions who we are, and in pivotal eras "when this age and the next age engender in the ditch," an acute discrepancy arises between what people think they believe (the traditional values they continue to voice) and what they actually believe (the new values implicit in their day-to-day actions).

The need to deny that discrepancy as a means of maintaining the illusion at least of a coherent identity naturally generates great social and psychological tensions—ones that can spur the divisiveness of a culture war or even the mayhem of a civil war. But whether driven by natural catastrophes, intercultural contact, or (as in our case) homegrown technological advances, significant revisions in the prevailing patterns of everyday experience do eventually demand a reconfiguration of our communal maps in ways that close the gap between the values we profess and those we enact. And however frightening that process of admitting and refining the new preferences implicit in our everyday actions, the revisionist cartographers who undertake that task are more the heralds than the parents of the changes they depict.

I have traced this ongoing shift toward post-modern patterns of perception and comprehension in a number of ways, including the widespread emergence of conscientious thinking within the natural sciences that once were the hallmark of modern reasoning. Moving from advanced ideas to mundane behaviors, my task now is to examine how the same forces have been revising the rhythms of "real life."

The American Garden, Then and Now

Past and present are themselves alike mysterious,
but they mysteriously illuminate each other.
—Herbert W. Schneider, *The Puritan Mind*

If "significant revisions in the prevailing patterns of everyday experience" are the necessary precedent for categorical shifts in the cultural common sense, what are the revisions driving change today? . . . Memory supplies the hinge. Our current status in the transitional ditch is immeasurable, a more desirable future unimaginable without reference to the communal past from which we have sprung. So let's begin by considering the coordinates and rhythms of the following scene from our nation's formative years.

It is 1823, during that period when, after more than thirty years of independence, America's post-revolutionary identity is consolidating. The season is spring, the immediate place an open field bordered by trees and only recently cleared, with split-rail fencing marking the boundaries of its cultivation. Part of a small homestead in what we now call the Midwest, this modest plot of land is still on the fringe of the civilized settlement, still an active setting for that frontier life whose specific cast of virtues James Fenimore Cooper's romances are just beginning to memorialize, creating the first sophisticated version of an American mythos. A boy, fourteen, is currently working on this arable portion of his family's farm. Although the availability of land blurs the sharp categories of social class as they were once defined in Europe, the boy's family is largely uneducated and, after losing their previous farm in a title dispute, economically insecure. Perhaps that background serves as a motivational spur, but in any case the action here is twinned, two forms of cultivation simultaneously performed. For even as this boy is plowing the field behind the family mule, that most characteristic of preindustrial chores, he is also silently reading a book that he has managed to procure on his own initiative.

Let's imagine the scene from his perspective, its physical coordinates and mental dimensions: the open spaces; the splitting of the earth and the turning of the pages; the linear patterning of both the body and the mind, feet following the plowed rows of broken soil, eyes tracing the straight lines of printed words: back and forth, back and forth . . .

I don't have just any American boy in mind. Drawing from his lore, we are imagining here Abraham Lincoln in the slow midst of becoming one of the nation's most cherished figures. And whether actual history or representative myth, this scene does succeed in evoking many of the core elements—the literary eloquence, the lonely self-sufficiency, the ambition to improve, the social humility—that eventually will compose the admirable whole of the mature man's character. Contrary to the claim of Milton's Satan, the mind is never "its own place," nor is a man's character strictly limited to his self-conscious thoughts. The evolution of this highly desirable person is intimately linked to, though not strictly determined by, the many qualities that define the scene just described. The text of the man's character is inseparable from the *con*text of his life, from both its coordinates in physical space and the mental rhythms of its cultural time.

Consider the field's human silence and solitude, the sensory-enriched fact that this is an outside story—how nature is always close at hand, the very frame and furrow of every act. Consider the loose sociology of a democratic frontier where social standing and customs are still in flux. Or those daily habits inscribed by the preindustrial economy of the family farm and by the tenor of Western thought post–Newton, Descartes, and Locke but pre–Darwin, Freud, and Marx. Consider all the underlying biases of action and perception, the tacit schooling built into the repetitive use of the day's conventional technologies—the linear logic, for example, the back-and-forthness of both the mule-pulled plow and the printed book. Or the absence of both effective anesthesia and competent medical treatments, leading to the everyday invasions of pain and death, one's backyard still the graveyard for loved ones lost. (Lincoln's younger brother died in infancy, his mother when he was nine, his older sister in childbirth before he was twenty—a private history of loss by no means unusual among his contemporaries.) And so on.

Now fast-forward to our era and try to imagine a contemporary equivalent: the coming of age of a leader whose character will be capable of saving the day for the American project—of solving our next civil war, declared or not. Try to envision, that is, a *post*-modern Honest Abe, captured at work in one of today's conventional spaces. Insomuch as character *is* informed by context (mind shaped by place) and the conventional American scene has dramatically changed since the 1820s, this experiment quickly becomes an exercise in analogical thinking.

To begin with a notable difference, the American frontier has long since closed, the influential ethos once associated with its settlement increasingly irrelevant to the challenges of ordinary life. Both industrialized and incorporated, farming is no longer a conventional career whose underlying rhythms inform the nation's character. Rather than cultivate the earth on one's private homestead, the conventional economic earner today generates or manipulates information as a wage employee within a corporate setting, and many of those jobs are now associated with some form of salesmanship or customer relations, still relative rarities in the 1820s. Western thought is no longer just post–Darwin and Locke but also post–Einstein and Nietzsche—and, superseded by a whole host of electronic media, writing is no longer our primary means for telecommunication. The young Lincoln had to fight for access to any outside information; he was the arch exemplar of America's self-taught man, whereas today external information of all sorts, albeit much of it tainted by salesmanship, routinely invades our everyday spaces, saturating our minds at work and at play. Even as better nutrition has accelerated physical and sexual development, social maturity has been deferred, so that the age of a metaphorically equivalent boy today would need to shift forward two or three years.

And of course this national-hero-in-the-making might not be a boy. Since the 1820s, social mobility in American life has increased significantly in crucial ways (most conspicuously for non-whites and women) even as it has decreased in others (a more rigid class structure, greater economic inequality, political success more dependent than ever on personal wealth). Male or female, the conventional teen today wouldn't have experienced *any* death in the nuclear family, much less the three losses that Lincoln suffered; yet he or she very well may have been separated from one parent or the other due to divorce. And whatever the human sources of his immediate unhappiness, our post-modern Abe—unlike the antebellum one who suffered from periodic bouts of severe melancholy— might have been prescribed a psychoactive drug to stabilize his moods and keep his spirits up.

With those broad-based changes noted, the time has come to situate this hero-in-the-making within a specific setting, a plausible equivalent of the frontier farmer's field. For reasons already noted, including the closing of the frontier and the pervasive penetration of our electronic communications, the field's longitude and latitude no longer matter; but to be conventional for our era, this workaday scene will clearly have to be an inside story. So let's say this: a seventeen-year-old boy, sitting in a coffee shop in Anywhere, USA, working on a secondhand laptop that, given his economic standing, he must share with the rest of his family.

Like Lincoln before him, this boy is multitasking now, but rather than silently reading a book while plowing a field, he is helping out the homestead by creating a website for his parents' small and struggling business. Rather than moving earth while keenly absorbing a single author's printed words, he is moving information: cutting and pasting, ripping and reassembling, interweaving images and sounds along with verbal texts, drawing this multisensory mix from multiple online sources and voices, and adding links to further multiply the choices of the site's eventual visitors. Meanwhile, he listens to tunes through his headphones and interrupts his work now and then both to converse with his friends via instant messaging and to check out a social website that he has joined. There, he has posted digital photos, verbal self-descriptions, virtual diary entries, and an updated list of his favorite things and pet peeves; there, he's projected the visual pixels and verbal patterns of his most intimate self, his life an "open book" that anyone online anywhere in the world can, with his permission, access and read.

Now consider the changes implicit in such a scene and, with them, the radical revision in the shape and pace of our conventional experience since the 1820s:

- the loss of silence;
- the end to solitude (not necessarily the same as an end to loneliness);
- the rapid collapse of physical space as social impediment;
- the allied demise of the outside as a normative experience, with the everyday mind now bathing in and bounded by humanly fashioned things;
- the democratic self as perpetually publicized ("on the web") instead of protectively internalized ("in my room");
- the virtual disembodiment of both commercial labor and social engagement (the absence of touch in all our new ways of "keeping in touch");
- the accelerating decline of the printed word as our primary medium for our telecommunications and the remixing of language instead with images and sounds, conventional thought increasingly now a multisensory operation;
- the ongoing fragmentation of the fiercely focused point of view, the single author's line of thought that Lincoln was closely following (back and forth, back and forth) now giving way to multiple perspectives and interactive corrections, the elaborations and distractions of ever-branching links;
- the unanticipated and so, as yet, unassimilated Big Bang of the Internet's information explosion ("data, data everywhere, and not a form to think")

This is where we are now. We can locate the boy's coffee shop in precisely the same spot as Lincoln's Midwestern field, but that abstract equation cannot conceal the concrete transformation of our conventional experience within those same coordinates. In so many ways, this is not the same place that Lincoln knew and was nurtured by, which is why the traditional conception of the American character—long tacitly cultivated by the colonial experience and then self-consciously articulated in the post-revolutionary period—has now become an endangered species.

The American-hero-in-the-making cultivating an open field . . . the American-hero-in-the-making multitasking inside a study or store; the American mind as shaped by the mule-pulled plow and the printed book . . . the American mind *re*shaped by the personal computer and the interactive web. Compressed, this is the formidable challenge we currently face: to connect those dots, to weave together a continuity of virtues that also admits those "significant revisions in the prevailing patterns of everyday experience" detailed above. Extraordinary changes in material conditions make extraordinary demands on the moral imagination. These newer technologies will not improve our lives in the holistic sense until their undeniable powers have been revised and refined, directed to serve our higher ends.

I. The Embryonic Emergence of the Post-Modern Person

The question remains: can we successfully integrate the disruptive forces now set loose in the American garden? We can, I believe, but as to whether we will, the evidence to date is mixed at best and so demands our immediate attention. Change is everywhere and stunningly rapid. Although implicit in electronic communications from the start, conscientious thinking in the literal sense ("knowledge of or through togetherness") is now erupting in multiple domains and expressive forms. The list is long and the implications for the logic of everyday life revolutionary.

The proliferation of mobile computing devices and the explosive popularity of user-driven social networking sites like Twitter, Facebook, Instagram, and YouTube are together generating radical increases in the pace, range, and complexity of our native gregariousness. The post-modern self, it seems, is rarely "by itself" these days, and that will be the default expectation of the children raised in the Wi-Fi age, for whom the lonesome hero of our mythic past is likely to seem a strange dude indeed. The ongoing demise of the old Protestant self is a logical result of these newly prevailing patterns of perception and interaction. A few examples of that old self's demise in contemporary life will suggest the force, flavor, and overall direction of the changes under way as a new post-modern person takes center stage.

From Closed Book to Facebook

The emergence of modernity's way of assessing the world was inseparable from the rapid spread of European literacy in the late sixteenth and seventeenth centuries. Unlike conversation or public recitation, the exchange of knowledge while silently reading was occurring "in here," within the private sphere of the silent reader's own mind; it was under his or her control, in a solitary process that encouraged enhanced analysis, independent thinking, and self-reflection. To read required withdrawing one's attention from the immediate sensory and social environment, enhancing over time the lingering sense (as much a feeling as a thought) that one was, inherently, more *apart from* than *a part of* both the natural and the social worlds: that, in Lily Tomlin's terms, we were, at our core, less in this "together" than "by ourselves." This new conception of sovereign self-sufficiency was captured in its most optimistic tenor by the Elizabethan poet and courtier, Sir Edward Dyer.

> My mind to me a kingdom is;
> Such perfect joy therein I find
> That it excels all other bliss
> Which God or Nature hath assigned.[1]

Not all of Dyer's contemporaries found this new condition of psychological segregation quite so blissful, and the new internal sense of the self's rightful authority over the mind's "kingdom" frequently clashed with the subservient role that most of the educated were forced to play in a still largely feudal political economy.

So it was that, even as the print revolution extended the ideological reach of governments, literacy was cultivating the characteristic moods and messages of a newly sovereign self: its private ambitions and discrete *point* of view, its sense of social estrangement and personal entitlement, its disruptive demands for religious, economic, and political freedoms from a static social order ill-designed to grant them. The double challenge that followed was how to moralize this intellectually powerful but potentially antisocial individualism, turning the Machiavellian man into a responsible citizen, and how to reorganize society to both admit and refine the freedoms that new citizen required.

After Shakespeare's soliloquies, the literary artifacts that most clearly reveal the psychological evolution of this modern sense of self are the secular diaries and spiritual journals that began to appear in the seventeenth century. These self-reflective instruments of a newly literate middle class were not intended to be read by others, much less broadly published. As complements to the silent reading experience, they supplied instead a separate mental space where the individual could actively explore his hopes and fears, making sense of the world and of himself without threat of ridicule or official censure. As a self-generated version of the bound book, the locked diary is the mundane object that best captures the underlying character of this modernizing self: its sense of segregation and self-containment, its insistence on the dignity of privacy as both natural and right, and its consequent need to strictly control the border between personal expression and public revelation.[2]

Weakened during the TV era, that border has now been obliterated by the Internet and the ethos of transparency that has arisen with it. By 2011, there were already over 181 million active blogs online, with many thousands more added each day. As of the third quarter of 2015, Facebook had 1.55 billion active users, each adult with, on average, 338 "friends" to whom they were exposing their opinions, photos, and narrative accounts of their daily activities. In the same year, Twitter was trending toward 300 million active users who, like so many fireflies, were fighting the anonymous night of mass society by lighting up the Internet with their every whimsical opinion in 140 characters or less. Meanwhile, to entertain YouTube's 1.3 billion viewers, 432,000 hours of new videos, recording activities from amateur yodeling to self-mutilation, were being uploaded every day. The trend is unequivocal and, absent authoritarian intervention, irreversible: rather than bind, contain, and lock away its innermost thoughts and feelings, the post-modern self is driven to project them into our highly porous public sphere of virtual information. The inclination toward privacy, as encapsulated in the locked diary, has rapidly flipped into the imperative of publicity, as pursued through the web posting.[3]

Even the old medium must now submit to the new imperative of self-exposure. After rereading a boxful of her old teenage journals, Sarah Brown began sharing painful and embarrassing excerpts with a group of friends online, and this evolved in 2005 into a bar-based weekly event called "Cringe," where volunteers would read aloud from their teenage diaries, journals, letters, and poems to an appreciative crowd. Given its own Facebook page, the idea rapidly spread from Brooklyn to many other cities; Brown eventually published an anthology of representative excerpts;

and others who were drawn to the notion of outing their teenage angst created a performance piece, "Get Mortified," that has been staged in theaters from coast to coast. These diary authors and their audiences are not just laughing at the juvenile insecurities captured by their formerly secret jottings; they are also lightly mocking the ethos of privacy that kept them secret for so long. The adult fondly condescending to the child she once was coexists with the cyber-citizen condescending to the declining values of a literate modernity. In the Internet age, when transparency has become imperative and "sharing" the new norm, everyone knows that we are, primarily, all in this together rather than by ourselves.[4]

From Couple to Cluster, Pair to Pod

What does it mean in the practical sense to have 338 friends, the average number for an adult Facebook user? Although ambitious extraverts in the past did strive to sustain a wide circle of acquaintances, their ways of doing so were preshaped and constrained by the media that were available for personal communication. Prior to literacy, face-to-face conversations and messages orally conveyed secondhand through travelers were the only ways to interact with family, friends, and colleagues. Close relationships were limited to one's immediate locale, and could not be easily sustained if one party moved away. Once literacy became widespread and postal services were established, the personal letter greatly extended the reach of social interaction, making *tele*communication between family and friends practical for the first time. Many years later, the telephone added the spontaneity and emotional richness of the spoken word, transforming conversation itself into a telecommunication. In each of these instances, however, the social connection was primarily point to point, one on one—writer to reader or speaker to auditor. The grammar of interaction strongly enforced by both the weekly letter and the daily phone call was binary: we telecommunicated primarily *as a couple*—a couple of friends, a pair of lovers, siblings, or colleagues.

As their metaphorical names suggest, the Internet and the web have dramatically expanded the possible patterns for social interaction at a distance. With just a few strokes on one's keypad, any single digital message, verbal or visual, can be disseminated in multiple directions at once, potentially going viral and lighting up smartphones and home screens around the world. One-to-one communications are still common, but as the surge in blogs, podcasts, chat rooms, Listservs, interactive games, and networking sites has demonstrated, what people *can* do, thanks to technological advances, they *will* do. Intensely social creatures, human beings, it seems, will seize every opportunity to expand the range and variety of their interactions. With that expansion, the psychological shield previously mustered to protect the intimacy of the couple (whether friends or lovers) from the intrusive crowd has begun to dissolve, and the once private dialogue between pairs, like the old monologue of the diary, is increasingly shared with the larger group, clique, posse, or pod. As the old pop song put it, "one" may be "the loneliest number that you'll ever do." But in the digital era especially "two can be as bad as one. / The loneliest number since the number one."[5]

Group texts and emails, web page postings, video and photo exchanges on YouTube, Snapfish, and Instagram, smartphone apps like Google Hemisphere that allow friends to keep track of one another's geographical location in real time: the technological ease of social connectivity has magnified the urgency to make (and keep in touch with) as many friends as possible. We are becoming the paparazzi of our own lives, each Facebook update and video or "selfie" upload a new episode in a "reality TV show" staged online. This trend, too, is measurable in a way. The media-research company Nielsen reported that in 2010 Americans spent close to a quarter of their online time using social media, an astounding 43 percent increase in a single year. By 2014, time spent on those sites had crept even higher.[6]

Here, too, the question naturally arises whether *more* is necessarily *better*. Critics, doubting the depth and sincerity of the connections made via our social media, remind us that the dominant platforms are not as free as they might seem. In the cautionary words of Jaron Lanier, one of the pioneers of virtual reality, "the whole idea of fake friendship is just bait laid by the lords of the cloud to lure hypothetical advertisers" who will then try to use the voluminous data gleaned to target consumers and induce viral conformity via peer pressure.[7] And along with the joys of enhanced sociability—the "bliss" of belonging to the hive mind as opposed to Dyer's isolated kingdom—familiar forms of bad behavior like bullying, shunning, slander, exhibitionism, and fraud are also radically empowered online. A viciously vicarious mother, hiding behind an online identity, taunts the rival of her teenage daughter; a callow college freshman, mistaking cruel for cool, posts a cell phone photo of his new roommate caught in a homosexual embrace; a digital sadist, providing both emotional endorsement and practical advice, encourages a distraught woman to commit suicide. The flaws of human nature don't disappear in the fleshless precincts of the virtual world and, as on many a frontier, may actually be accentuated in the early phases of their development.

For good or for ill, though, the current shift from private monologue and intimate dialogue toward virtually accessible forms of multilogue appears to be irreversible. The emerging consensus that two can seem as lonely as one, for example, is evident in today's mating scene, where group dating, once a practice largely limited to middle school, has become popular with singles well into their twenties, and where commercial websites are turning the blind date, too, into a collective activity.[8]

From Interment to Dispersal

Few phases of life define us as profoundly as mating. Facing our inevitable mortality is one of them. Death presses us to weigh the very meaning of human identity, calling forth customs that express a culture's deepest beliefs, and so the fact that our nation is now in the midst of a dramatic shift in its mortuary practices supplies yet another sign of the transition between modern and post-modern conceptions of selfhood. Despite dualism's strict segregation of the mind from the body, the same grammar of perception and comprehension was applied to both—yea, even unto the grave. The underlying logic of the modernizing West, which atomized the social world as it did the material world, imagining each mind as "its own place," also preshaped the customary treatment of the dead. As embalming techniques improved during the nineteenth century, modernity's bound book of selfhood found its final expression in the widespread preference for preserving and encoffining the bodies of loved ones lost.

This preference was enforced in America, the most modern of nations, by religious as well as secular beliefs. Many Protestant denominations, especially those that stressed the resurrection of the flesh, shunned cremation, as most Mormons still do, and the Roman Catholic Church didn't lift its ban on the practice until 1963. For these reasons and, beneath them, a powerful identification of the lost loved one with the body that contained her or him, the percentage of the dead cremated in America each year didn't reach double digits until the 1980s. Yet, increasing each year, that number had soared to nearly 47 percent by 2014.[9]

Cremation is generally the cheaper method, so there are economic motives behind this trend, and although the issue is disputed, some believe that burning a corpse is better for the environment than embalming and burial. But both the gravity of the event and the speed of the change also reflect a significant transformation in our collective understanding of human identity. With the modern sense of the self as a closed book, as discrete and contained, "its own place," now giving way to a sense of the self as naturally intermixed with the web of the world, as projected "out there" in the field of relations, the rituals attending the self's extinction are also changing. The same mourners who, not that long ago, would have had the corpse of their beloved matriarch embalmed and buried in the family plot might be found today scattering her ashes from the mountain top where she loved to climb on summer days.

II. The Embryonic Emergence of a Post-Modern Political Economy

> There's a whole economy of kindness
> Possible in the world.
>   —Seamus Heaney, *The Cure at Troy*

As the boundary between the private and the public person has dissolved, so too has the segregation of our personal lives from the commercial world. In the early phases of the ongoing shift from print-based to electronic information, that penetration was entirely one-sided. Thanks to a regulatory model carelessly chosen in the 1920s, first radio and then TV programming (the most powerful ideological instruments of their time) were ceded to the consumer corporation. The old traveling salesman had to induce the citizen to open the door to hear his pitch; but soon, every thirteen minutes the messages of Madison Avenue were saturating millions of American households at once. The castle walls of the private home no longer protected the kingdom of the literate mind; parents were losing control over the daily flow of information their children received; and the ethos of salesmanship, which was sponsoring the entire show of radio and TV broadcasting, rapidly reshaped the American character after its ends.

The arrival of the digitized word then challenged all the prevailing models for information exchange, commercial and personal: the letter, the phone call, the book, the album, the movie, the newspaper, the sales transaction, the professional and civic service would never be the same. The Internet supplied an entirely new place to interact, to talk and shop, and one—initially at least—that was not controlled by the mega-corporation. Soon, the passive consumers of information in the TV age could broadcast their own messages; file-sharing threatened corporate control over the flow of copyrighted information; and the fundamental structure of our political economy began to submit to the same post-modern logic that was changing our traditional conceptions of friendship, mating, and burial. Again, a few examples from a variety of professions and businesses will have to stand as representative of the rapidly proliferating changes now under way.

From Independent to Interactive Authorship

Although writing is profoundly associated with the evolution of atomistic individualism and the secular sanctification of the lonely genius, its practice today is also being drawn toward more conscientious means and methods. Again, technology has been driving this shift in the prevailing forms of authorship. Placeless, weightless, and nearly instantaneous, the digitized word both empowers and endorses enhanced forms of collaboration—of writing *through* "togetherness." The speed and ease of sharing drafts online, the tracking software that facilitates group editing, and the now default practice of inviting responses to website postings (thereby initiating collective conversations in something close to real time) have together been shifting the underlying grammar of writerly expression from linear, static, and monologic (modern) to resonant, interactive, and multilogic (post-modern). And given the co-optive power of cyber technology, this new inclination toward interactive collaboration is becoming normative in a relative blink of historical time.

Contemporary screenwriting, for example, has begun to adopt similar methods. Commercial filmmaking has always been a collective enterprise, of course. Under the old studio system, the Dream Factory (as the name itself attests) drew on multiple specialists to manufacture, assemble, and test its products, with many minds contributing to any single release. Scripts were not much different in this regard: in a common case, a novel by a fiction writer would be adopted by a separate screenwriter, after which the studio might hire a series of "script doctors" to improve the plot, pacing, or dialogue. But such rescripting was usually serial, not so much cooperative as competitive, whereas today the process of authorship is becoming more truly interactive in the post-modern sense. A "Bucket Brigade" of some of the industry's most successful comedic actors, writers, and directors—including Ben Stiller, Judd Apatow, Will Ferrell, and Sacha Baron Cohen—routinely volunteer to improve one another's films. They read the separate drafts of one another's scripts, attend trial readings and rough cuts, and then supply detailed notes with suggestions for improvement.[10]

This cooperative process produces a different sort of product. Rather than funneling the humor through (and focus the camera on) a single major character, these comedies tend to be ensemble pieces. And just as the lonely genius of authorship surrenders some of its authority to the talented tribe of co-professionals and the spotlight on the star widens to include the ensemble cast, the individual lines in the final screenplay are open to further revision by the actors themselves. Encouraging improvisation, the filmmakers allow the *atom* of the printed word to be influenced by the *field* of the multisensory set—the text by its *con*text—with the intention of generating a humor that seems more spontaneous and natural. On the serious side of the aisle, some of cable TV's most impressive serial dramas, such as *The Wire, The Sopranos,* and *Breaking Bad* have combined a supervising sensibility with an influential stable of talented producers, writers, and directors; more generally, the sheer pace and scale of TV production demands extensive collaboration.

Still, the turn toward interactive authorship is by no means complete, and an anecdote from my academic life exemplifies the ironies that arise in these transitional times. Two years before facing tenure review, a colleague reported to me that he was meeting on a regular basis with a few of his fellow junior faculty to work on the book whose acceptance or rejection would determine his professional fate. This wasn't collaboration in the intellectual sense. Although all were in the humanities, they were employed by different departments, and each assistant professor was the sole author of his own book in progress. Indeed, to proceed otherwise would have been reckless, for everyone knew that our administration, despite occasional claims to the contrary, still strongly favored "original scholarship." Yet these were also people who, coming of age with the Internet, were accustomed to its ethos of interactive sharing; so, despite the apparent irrationality of the practice, they continue to meet, working on their separate manuscripts silently side by side, trying to bridge the discrepancy between their now customary expectation of "togetherness" and the need to write and create, as their institution still demanded, "by themselves."

The contradictions implicit in this scene call to mind the oft-cited observation by Jürgen Habermas that "modernism is dominant but dead"— a claim that could be made with equal accuracy about medievalism in the early 1600s when the newly emerging sovereign self was still being squelched by an institutional common sense hostile to individualism.[11]

From Newton's Apple to Galaxy Zoo

In the previous chapter I surveyed some profound changes in the prevailing patterns of scientific thinking as a more conscientious form of reasoning has taken hold. The same logic underlying these newer maps and theories has been driving significant shifts in the *social* process of scientific discovery. Here, too, the model of the lonely genius is giving way to an ethos of collaboration and the collective savvy of the online crowd.

In 2007, Kevin Schawinski faced a daunting task: as a graduate student in astronomy at Oxford, he needed to examine some fifty thousand images of galaxies and classify each one according to its formation. Computers could not be trusted to assess them accurately, and the sheer number of man-hours he faced to complete the project seemed oppressive. So, at the suggestion of a friend, he created a website that posted the images, provided a brief tutorial in how to assess them, and then invited any amateur astronomers who might be online to assist him. Thanks in part to publicity provided by the BBC, the response was immediate and overwhelming, so much so that the server storing the images had a meltdown. Rather than the few dozen volunteers Schawinski had anticipated, thousands were pitching in, reaching a capacity to classify as many as seventy thousand images per hour during the first day. This mass collaboration completed Schawinski's apparently laborious task in a relative instant, and it was such a success that the website, dubbed Galaxy Zoo, was made available to other projects. In less than three years, "more than 275,000 users [had] made nearly 75 million classifications of one million different images," assisting numerous astronomers in their studies: an effort that would have taken any single investigator hundreds of years.[12]

Given its obvious success, this model of inviting the amateur masses to become co-participants in scientific discovery is now being applied in other fields, even as advanced scientists themselves are interactively sharing results and collaboratively producing new knowledge through the use of increasingly sophisticated digital networks, databases, and forums.[13] Some of these sites, such as InnoCentive's global network of two hundred thousand scientists, are commercial: there, corporations can post specific technical problems, eBay style, with freelancing researchers competing to solve them for a fee. Other sites, such as the Human Genome Project and philanthropist Paul Allen's Brain Atlas, are structured more on the open-source model of nonprofit sharing. Together, these examples suggest two basic alternatives—the market or mall versus the civic commons—for organizing these new fields of gregarious investigation. But in both cases, the everyday practices of scientific research are being radically changed by the new speed and range of interactivity. Online, potential partnerships can be scouted easily; national boundaries and institutional restrictions are less of an issue; and a rich, rapid, and multifocal exchange of preliminary information can accelerate the process of final discovery by years.

There will always be a need for the fallen apple of individual inspiration when exploring the nature of the material world, but because inspiration feeds on communal exchange, this new "zoo" of digitally enhanced collaboration is sure to expand rapidly in the decades to come. Meanwhile, both for good and for ill, parallel transformations can be found in nearly every other field or avocation—from American ministers sharing sermons online with new churches in Africa and NGOs collaborating globally on their philanthropic projects, to pedophiles and terrorists exchanging technical tips for their criminal acts and boosting each other's spirits with the toxic bravado of their self-justifications.

From Credentialed Expertise to Crowd-Sourced Consensus

The metrical stress in our collective reading of Tomlin's joke has clearly flipped. More and more, we are now living our lives in a kind of virtual togetherness, posing the vital question as to whether the etymological meaning of conscientious thinking will now be enhanced by the traditional one. Can these various new fields of gregarious interaction be successfully infused with the voice of conscience as the old social atom eventually was? Can their cybernetically juiced *virtù* (Machiavelli's term for a forceful but amoral effectiveness) acquire both the temperamental intention and the evaluative intelligence necessary for a post-modern version of *virtue* to prevail? And which movements will hasten that conversion in the way that the Protestant Reformation once did?

The online, open-source encyclopedia Wikipedia has supplied an early example of the ethical challenges implicit in the newer technologies and the interactive authorship they routinely empower. For someone with my inclination toward solitary research, the nearly instant creation of this collaborative repository of knowledge seemed miraculous at the time. Founded in 2001 and utilizing software that allows anyone with Internet access to add or edit an official entry, this project had acquired 1.8 million articles in two hundred languages in less than five years, with many more added each day and all generated by thousands of self-appointed volunteers. (By 2016, the number of articles had increased to over five million in English alone.) Meanwhile, older entries are being edited all the time, providing an ever-growing, ever-morphing, utterly accessible, and openly contestable body of official knowledge. The sheer quantity of the information and the speed with which it is being gathered are mightily impressive. But neither *more* nor *faster* necessarily means *better*, and the site's qualitative problems have been obvious from the start, linked as they are to its self-professed strengths. Given its ethical commitment to open access—the Golden Rule of the web ethos—Wikipedia has been susceptible to amateur incompetence, personal vendettas, and political and professional bias.[14]

The virtual community that both uses and maintains the site is aware of these weaknesses and has been working to address them. Committees of volunteers strive to review new entries and vet the many editorial changes being made to older ones, with the intention of correcting factual errors, adjudicating disputes, or simply highlighting which articles lack sufficient documentation. Contributors can be banned from the site for repeated instances of bad behavior when editing entries, as was the case for members of the Church of Scientology in 2009. Through these efforts to police the process, Wikipedia's volunteer caretakers have been striving to infuse the collaborative field of their virtual encyclopedia with an effective conscience—this time, however, the inner voice of the anguished Hamlet and the spiritual diaries of the Protestant self have been replaced by the interactive, online deliberations of the editorial collective.

Such efforts only matter, however, if their good intentions prove effective—in this case, if they enhance the overall truthfulness of the site's information, which is the traditional virtue that encyclopedias aspire to— and there is, in fact, some evidence to support that hopeful claim. As early as 2005, the respected journal *Nature* compared scientific entries from Wikipedia with its commercial rival *Encyclopedia Britannica* and, to the surprise of many, found no significant differences in their quality.[15] Now compare their histories and economic models—at the time, *Britannica* was 248 years old, Wikipedia less than 5; the former was only accessible for a fee and the product of paid experts in the various fields, the latter entirely free and the creation of mostly amateur volunteers—and the revolutionary power of the open-source model becomes clear.

As one of the most successful examples of that model, Wikipedia challenges many of the underlying presumptions of liberal modernity, either reversing or, more often, confounding its grammar of values. On the topic of knowledge itself, for example, the site's epistemology—in contradistinction to *Britannica*'s, which was born during the Enlightenment—strongly prefers *consensus* (the wisdom of the gregarious field) over *credentials* (the genius of the specialist atom). The nature of the truth-seeking process it endorses is assuming an inherently conscientious shape and tenor.

Accumulation to Affiliation

If we view Wikipedia as a political economy and ask which of the twentieth century's dominant ideologies its operational logic resembles, the disorienting answer proves to be *both and neither*. In that the site seems to be endorsing the collective over the individual and operates according to the well-known Marxist ideal "from each according to his ability, to each according to his needs," one would be tempted to say that the site is inherently communist. Yet, at the same time, it is totally committed to the democratic ideal of individual free choice, and rigorously rejects the coercive tactics that have characterized all Communist regimes in actual practice.

Viewing the site from a different angle, one might say that its endorsement of individual freedom and its faith in the self-correcting nature of the open-source process (so many hundreds of thousands of individual decisions, with only minimal top-down regulation, achieving a highly desirable social end) resembles nothing so much as an idealized version of the free market—*except* (and this can't be stressed enough) unlike the commercial marketplace, this enterprise is not being driven by the profit motive. Like most of the open-source sites and systems, Wikipedia aggressively pursues *aggregation* (togetherness) absent the intention of *accumulation* in the financial sense. Against the privatizing trend of our day, Mammon holds no sway here, and in his place, the primary motive for donating one's time and intelligence to maintain this labor-intensive enterprise appears to be the inherent value of gregariousness itself. At Wikipedia's virtual meeting place, *aggregation* is being pursued for the natural rewards of social *affiliation* and, too, out of a sense of *philanthropy*. The vast majority of its contributors are being motivated by the very real and allied pleasures that arise from joining a group and from co-participating with it in the generation of a new and valuable resource for the community at large.[16]

Most analysts today believe that central among the many practical flaws leading to the Soviet Union's sudden collapse was its inability to adapt to the digital revolution. Although China is laboring hard today to prove the exception, authoritarian governments have been especially vulnerable to the Internet because its technology decentralizes communications, making it harder to censor their regimes' opponents. As cyber-technology has been enhanced, so has its inherent threat to authoritarian rule. In 2011, the dynamic combination of mobile computing devices, social networking sites, and large numbers of youth trained in their use led to the overthrow of the Ben Ali and Mubarak regimes in Tunisia and Egypt in less than a month's time, making the Soviet Union's earlier implosion seem slow by comparison.

That cyber-technology would destabilize *all* modern forms of social order, however, was not apparent at first. In the self-congratulatory celebrations that followed the collapse of the Soviet empire, there was little recognition that the PC would also prove incompatible with certain crucial features of capitalism's own regime. With the rise of the Internet, the web, shareware, and the open-source movement more generally, however, computerization's twofold threat to the prevailing economic system soon became evident. First, the Internet's decentralization of telecommunications potentially undermined corporate America's control over the flow of information and entertainment—its previous license, in the broadcast era, to "sponsor the show" and so to generate programming that was not only "brought to us by" but also "for" its commercial sponsors. Second, the ease, instancy, and sheer economy of the Internet's decentralized distribution network threatened the existence of many a corporate middleman who had become part of the consumer economy's highly profitable "delivery system."

Under Communism, the government wanted to come between individuals to assure and enforce political obedience. Its notorious bureaucracies may have been highly inefficient in the economic sense, but at each way station in the long process of getting anything at all approved or accomplished, individuals were forced to acknowledge the government's near total control over their everyday lives. And because the Communist Party's primary intention in actual practice was the assertion of political power and not the generation of economic plenty, its own (if often despicable) ends were being served by the system. In consumer capitalism's regime, it is the private corporation that wants to come between individual citizens, not to enforce political obedience but to collect a fee for distributing its goods and services. That fee is justifiable when the corporation is supplying something uniquely valuable—either a new necessary product or a more efficient connection between producers and consumers, as the mail-order catalogue once did for rural Americans. And that fee is fair when the rate charged is being regulated by a truly free and competitive market.

But as the no-bid pig-out for Iraq reconstruction projects demonstrated, it is a fantasy to presume that corporations themselves want competition. As money machines, they are designed to pursue one thing: money, the *more* of which is always presumed to be *better*. When left unchecked by the sorts of regulations that assure competition, those same money machines will be the first to prevent any real improvement in the creation or distribution of goods and services if it threatens their coffers. Contrary to the old GE jingle, profit, and not "progress," is unregulated capitalism's "most important product"—which is why when a new and initially unregulated technology arrives, a monopoly or near monopoly (U.S. Steel, Standard Oil, Microsoft, Google, or Facebook) usually arises to dominate the scene.

Hence the corporate world's panicky reaction to the emergence of file-sharing in the 1990s. In the pre-Internet economy, adults and kids alike had always shared their infoproducts, lending their detective novels or top-ten LPs to a friend or neighbor without threat of being sued by Bantam Books or Capitol Records. The difference between now and then, of course, is one of *virtù*, one of scale. As it does with every aspect of communications, cyber-technology puts the very human inclination to share (a key feature of our innate "togetherness") on steroids. To upload your favorite film or CD onto a file-sharing site makes it potentially accessible to many thousands of hitherto unknown "friends and neighbors." Let's be clear, however, about what was really being defended by the entertainment industry's aggressive lawsuits and their successful lobbying for anti-piracy legislation. Rather than protecting the "creativity of the artist," as was hypocritically claimed, recording companies and film studios were rushing in to defend the profitability of a delivery system that was being rendered obsolete before their eyes.

To further clarify the forces driving this obsolescence, we can turn back to the competition between the file-sharing operation of Wikipedia and the proprietary model of *Encyclopedia Britannica*. In the not too distant past, a hardbound set of *Britannica* sold for $1,600; when I checked its online website in 2015, the list price for its "deluxe" digital version was $19.95. That precipitous decrease, eightyfold in a virtual blink of historical time, highlights the astonishing efficiency of cyber-technology and the economic reason why digital commerce is bound to supersede its older rivals in many fields. Even with that radical reduction in price, Britannica faced a marketing problem, for its primary competitor was offering a similar service for free. The customer who trusted the old epistemological model (the credentials of hired expertise) over Wikipedia's new one (the crowd-sourced consensus of the volunteer field) still might choose to purchase Britannica's product. But as *Nature*'s 2005 survey suggests, it is no longer clear to an objective observer that modernity's faith in the innate superiority of individual expertise is justifiable—a reservation confirmed in detail by each of the four case studies that opened this book.[17]

The crisis confronting Britannica—that the product they have been delivering for a fee, motivated by financial accumulation, is now being delivered for free out of philanthropic affiliation alone—also haunts the computer industry itself, and the way this has played out there clarifies both the enormous benefits and the very real dangers currently present in our digitizing economy. Here it is necessary to distinguish between the sorts of behaviors that have characterized the success of the dominant players. I don't believe that it is possible, for example, to imagine the PC revolution without the innovations of Intel or its equivalent; the ever-improving speed and mnemonic capacity of the microchip have fueled the whole enterprise from the start. It is entirely possible, however, and some would say preferable, to imagine that revolution occurring without Microsoft, which has dominated the software side of the digital revolution more completely than has any single hardware manufacturer. Although its products were neither the first nor the best at any stage along the way, astute and relentless corporate maneuvering, including an early alliance with IBM, allowed Microsoft to monopolize the PC's own delivery system—so much so that even as late as 2015 more than 90 percent of the world's desktops and laptops were still running on its Windows operating system.[18] That advantage, ruthlessly wielded, permitted the company to thrive despite its failure to anticipate the five most significant innovations in personal computing in the last fifteen years: the Internet browser, the search engine, the smartphone, social networking, and cloud computing.

The relevant irony here is that Microsoft's ongoing profitability (over $5.2 billion in the first quarter of 2013) is still largely dependent on its Windows franchise when the quality of that operating system is more than matched by a free alternative.[19] Like Wikipedia's website, Linux's operating system is managed by a nonprofit foundation and is open-source in both senses of the term: it is constantly being upgraded by an ad hoc community of software engineers, who offer their improvements without charging a fee ("from each according to his ability"), and it is available for anyone to use whether or not they contribute to the cause ("to each according to his needs").

Linux works and it works well. Its ongoing evolution is a technological and sociological success story that is also proving to be a marketplace one. Started by a single software engineer, Linus Torvalds, in 1991, Linux is now the largest software project in the world, generating some twenty-seven hundred thousand new lines of code every year, and feeding a fifty-billion-dollar economy of computer services that run everything from gaming devices and cable boxes to nuclear power plants and traffic control systems.[20] As the public turns away from desktops and laptops, where Windows still holds sway, to smartphones, netbooks, and tablets, Linux may yet become the world's dominant operating system.

More to the point here, where we are analyzing cyber-technology's influence on political reasoning, the character of Linux calls into doubt the fundamental premise of the privatization movement—its claim that the profit motive alone provides the key to our social as well as material progress. The success of Linux suggests instead that our native gregariousness may be just as creative as our natural avidity. It begs us to consider whether philanthropic cooperation, as it now can be practiced through our much enhanced communications networks, might be more efficient and productive in some endeavors than modernity's old model of marketplace competition, not to mention more conducive to our democratic values.

From Privatization to Collaboration to . . . Privatization?

What these developments propose is not a full rejection of the competitive marketplace but a significant reconsideration of its proper place and proportion in American life. Corporate capitalism earns its fee when it generates a socially beneficial product that wouldn't have existed otherwise, as is clearly the case today with microchips, whose development required huge initial capital investments. And it earns its fee when it finds new ways to enhance the flow of goods and services between producers and consumers. Earlier I mentioned the mail-order catalogue, which was invented by Sears in the late nineteenth century, as a historical example of such an enhancement. Utilizing both the new profit-driven railroad system and the federal government's postal service—note the implicit partnership between private and public enterprises—the Sears catalogue creatively completed a significantly improved delivery system, one that linked rural Americans with the nation's urban manufacturers to the benefit of both. In our current economy, the search engine, as developed by Google, Yahoo, and others, has now supplied us with a radically upgraded version of that system. Indeed the analogy works almost perfectly, with the Internet service provider taking the place of the private railroad, the publicly created and supported web playing the part of the postal service, and the search engine itself serving as a mega-version of the mail-order catalogue by supplying access to a seemingly endless digital warehouse of products and services.

Not only has the search engine's creative completion of our Internet-based delivery system radically increased the pace, range, scale, and facility of interconnectedness between consumers and producers; its technology is so efficient that it can provide a highly valuable public service at the same time. Unlike the mail-order catalogue these same engines can connect us to nearly all of the *non*commercial information on the web, providing a potentially significant educational benefit to the public at large. Still, there are serious concerns as to whether this apparently sunny merger of civic service with corporate profit will prove beneficial down the line. Among them is the fear that commercial websites are being treated preferentially. What is the inner grammar of values driving these search engines' algorithms and therefore determining the resulting ranks of their searches? What have they been designed to prefer? Are they being operated *conscientiously* in the full sense of the term, or are they being dominated by a partiality that favors the profit motive alone? And are they really "free" when we may be forfeiting our privacy when accessing their information?

Similar issues haunt Facebook, whose rapid rise to near monopoly status as the first globally accepted social networking site may threaten Google's financial standing. Like Google, nearly all of Facebook's revenues come from the advertising industry, and for that very reason, its executives have repeatedly fiddled with the site's default privacy settings in attempts to gather more information about its users, which then might be packaged and sold to corporate marketeers. Mimicking one of Microsoft's favorite tactics, Facebook has often made it difficult for the average user to opt out of those new default settings, generating an involuntary transparency where the loss of privacy is less freely chosen than technologically imposed.

Stepping back to view the ongoing development of the online world, we can see broader reasons for concern as the radical empowerments of digital communication have become increasingly privatized, often under the control of just a few corporations. Initially, the Internet, a government creation that was cheap to use and publicly accessible, supplied a chance to circumvent corporate control over mass communications. But although it retains that potential, many of the newly dominant services and sites are now returning us to the status quo of the broadcast era, when nearly every show was being "brought to us by" one form or another of commercial solicitation. Just as the civic square was co-opted and replaced by the enclosed mall, our initially unbounded virtual commons is now being gated and enclosed, monetized and marketized according to the usual precepts of quantiphilia.

Neither the postal service nor the telephone, nor for that matter the first email accounts—earlier dramatic upgrades in personal communications—required either forfeiting privacy or exposure to advertising in order to be utilized. Communicating through Facebook now does, and the same worry applies to the commercial search engine as it replaces the public library as the first place to turn for information. Initially, many people hoped that the Internet's assault on the corporate middleman would redound to the benefit of the creative artist, with musicians and authors winning direct access to their audiences, and with the efficiencies of digital communication proving financially rewarding to both. Instead, corporate giants like Apple and Amazon have been creating and monopolizing new delivery systems that, coming again between creators and consumers, redirect much of the money in their own direction.

In a political economy revised to value a richer range of human motives, the influence of the market would fade away in those domains where it was no longer needed due to the inherent efficiency of our new technologies and the tonic generosity of their many users. Such a fading away may soon be the case for commercial encyclopedias, and it probably should be the case for PC operating systems. But, to indulge in understatement, Microsoft will not go gently into the good night; it will rage, rage against the dying of its monopoly. And the privatization movement more generally is aggressively driving our political economy in the opposite direction— away from any renewed conception of ethical equilibrium and toward a fanatical idealization of the profit motive alone. Given its avid character, today's corporate quantiphilia not only refuses to disappear where it is no longer needed; it is actively engaged in expanding its base by inserting itself where it was *never* needed. Just as the most radical version of scientific socialism was driven to come between individuals to politically control every human interaction, today's radical version of scientific capitalism is now striving to come between today's cyber-citizens with the aim of monetizing our every transaction.

As a result, we face a new generation of corporate middlemen intruding into the natural intercourse of everyday life with their bars and gates and shrink-wrapping machines, charging tolls and fees for goods and services that were once commerce-free. When battered or puzzled by life, we used to turn to our friends who, motivated by the reciprocity of mutual affection, would offer the solace of their best advice. Now we're advised to hire a "personal coach." Once upon a time when the country went to war, it depended on the voluntary, self-sacrificial devotion of its citizenry to service that effort. Now, supplanting patriotic devotion with financial incentives, America increasingly depends on "private contractors"—but a mercenary by any other name smells as foul.

A new concern is the explosive growth of the so-called sharing or gig economy, which, digitally driven, is radically accelerating the already worrisome disassociation of the American corporation from its traditional responsibilities to its employees. For the last thirty years, our most successful tech companies have been outsourcing much of their work, either sending it overseas (although the design, production, and sales of Apple products require some one million workers worldwide, less than 10 percent are actual Apple employees)[21] or hiring temporary help at home (a favorite tactic of Microsoft, some two-thirds of whose one hundred seventy-one thousand employees are contract workers).[22] And now companies like Uber, TaskRabbit, and InnoCentive have taken that trend one step further. "Disrupting" the taxi, home repair, and research industries, respectively, they provide "sharing apps" that connect freelance drivers, servicemen, and researchers to those consumers or businesses that wish to employ their services. These new companies typically collect a fee for their cyber match-making without admitting any further obligations to either the consumer of those services or the freelancer who supplies them. As a consequence, they radically reduce their own overhead by avoiding many of the costs— liability insurance, paid sick and vacation days, Social Security payments, healthcare and pension contributions—that are commonly borne by their older competitors such as limousine services and carpentry shops. Given a chance by these new apps to exploit the hyper-connectivity of the web, more freelancing Americans do get to be the "CEOs" of their own one-man or -woman operations, and a relative few may do very well in the process. But many more are now finding themselves without the security, benefits, or income provided by traditional employment. Nor can they easily return to those traditional jobs when these digitally empowered middlemen are putting the companies that once provided them out of business.

And just as many large corporations have been divesting themselves from their old obligations to permanent employees, they also have been fleeing their financial obligations to the nation and states they once called home. In 2013, the amount of American corporate profits parked over-seas to avoid federal taxes topped $2.1 trillion. GE was first on that list (110 billion), Microsoft second (76.4 billion), and Apple fifth (54.4 billion).[23] Meanwhile, at the state and local level, some of those same companies have periodically threatened to transplant themselves elsewhere if local officials won't bend to their will. In 2013, Boeing used just such a threat to bully Washington's state legislature into giving them an estimated $8.7 billion of long-term tax relief, the largest such deal on record.[24] (At the same time, and using the same threat, the airplane manufacturer coerced their unionized machinists into giving up their old pension plan.) Boeing is a profitable corporation. These cuts made at the expense of both their employees and the citizenry of their home state weren't needed to save the company from ruin; rather, heeding the overweening demands of quan-tiphilia, they were pursued to boost the bottom line for their sharehold-ers, and for the very executives who demanded the deals.

Meanwhile, the state of Washington was in the midst of a constitutional crisis due to underfunding its K-12 education system and needed money desperately to initiate court-mandated reforms. If Boeing and Microsoft (another highly profitable local company) hadn't used their political clout to drastically reduce the taxes they owed, that funding crisis would have been eased, if not fully solved. The egregious failure of their corporations to contribute their fair share, however, didn't prevent Boeing spokesmen and Bill Gates, in particular, from lecturing state officials on the inadequacies of the education system. Or to demand changes in the content of the courses that system offered, favoring those subjects (science, technology, engineering, and math) that were key to their own industries. As school budgets, already strapped, adjusted to those demands, tuition at the state's public universities soared, humanities' offerings shrank, and at a middle school in Everett (home to Boeing's largest assembly plant), a new course in building robots was funded by cutting all courses in the visual arts.

And so it goes under the self-interested rule of the Idiot Savant.

Alternately worrisome and encouraging, the examples surveyed throughout this chapter clarify the fateful choices that we collectively face as our nation completes its conversion to the new machinery of post-modernity, transforming in the process the shape and pace of our everyday lives. The long evolving but now rapidly accelerating turn toward togetherness generated by our use of these machines has been changing our beliefs in actual practice, if not yet formal profession, and as the demise of modern America's original ethos proceeds apace, the vital question remains as to which specific configuration of values will take its place. The radically enhanced forms of collaboration utilized by Linux, Wikipedia, and Galaxy Zoo highlight what is promising about our post-modern place and the behaviors it empowers. They demonstrate how, through infusing the web's power with both democratic practices and humanitarian intentions, the *more* of our new togetherness might be made *better* in the holistic sense. Reminding us that the inclination toward philanthropic affiliation is as fundamental to our natures as self-centered appetite, they "add their weight to the lighter scale," countering our political economy's still dominant but ultimately deadly obsession with financial accumulation alone.

CHAPTER 8

Marrying the Monster

Hopes and Fears for the Post-Modern Era

> The problem of grace is fundamentally a problem of integration.
> —Gregory Bateson, *Steps to an Ecology of Mind*

Even when self-induced, cultural change is a risky affair. Because beliefs are dear to the thinking species, the social analogues to our physical instincts, all transitions between ruling worldviews are fraught with fear and churned by the riptides of dissension and confusion. If the "center cannot hold"—as Yeats so clearly foretold in 1920 when, in the aftermath of the First World War, the West was already primed to generate the next—then "mere anarchy is loosed upon the world."[1] As populations grow and armaments improve, the potential scope of the anarchy "loosed" also increases, yet the underlying story of self-generated turmoil retains its basic shape.

Ceaselessly inventive, we are (paradox approaching) the one "naturally artifactual" species. It is in our nature to *mind our place* in both the active and the passive senses of that phrase. We project the inventions of our minds to extend our powers, transforming in the process the environment that surrounds us. But those same inventions then change how we experience our everyday places in collateral ways that we often can't predict and that redirect our behavior beneath the radar of our self-conscious intentions. More specifically, significant changes in the ways we *perceive* both the word and the world (whether through writing, printing, the telescope, television, or the smartphone) undermine the descriptive accuracy and so, too, eventually the prescriptive authority of the conventional ways that we *conceived* of the world prior to their application. Patterns once perceived as beautiful begin to seem grotesque. In the Don Quixote syndrome, the old configuration of the heroic character is construed instead as comically inept. And even as methods long trusted to calculate the truth appear to miscompute, the replacements proposed by the new prevailing technologies can seem to those raised on the older methods crude, uncivilized, or disorienting. Soon our cleverness outpaces our wisdom, and in the absence of consensus "the best lack all conviction, while the worst are filled with passionate intensity."

This is a generalized version of the concrete story we have been living through for a century now, as the logic of a modernity deeply ingrained in our collective life has been challenged by the powers set loose by the proliferating use of our *post*-modern machines. It is the story I have been dramatizing and analyzing throughout these pages.

I. Reviewing the Argument

Henry Ford, Andy Warhol, Harold Bloom, the Media Lab's crew . . . the first the most successful entrepreneur of his era, the second the most influential visual artist of his, the third and the fourth employed at the most prestigious institutions in their fields of expertise, literary criticism and artificial intelligence: for all their intellectual excesses, these were, I have been arguing, representative men. Advanced by a technical savvy in the narrow sense, their most dubious ideas—a commerce of disingenuousness, an aesthetics of *an*esthesia, a solipsistic criticism, and a science expecting to resurrect the dead—were both reflecting and advancing a "map of the territory" that descended from modernity. And although this map was bearing less and less resemblance to the outlines of reality, its dubious plotting was shared by the exceptional and average thinker alike.

The Media Lab's quest to manufacture a "friend" may have been an elaborate exercise in self-deception, as I argued in chapter 4. But AI's broader ambition to pass the Turing test—to reach that point when a discerning observer could no longer differentiate a living mind from its cybernetic simulation—was perfectly at home in a Virtual America where spin, packaging, and public relations increasingly defined social reality. Warhol's project of blurring art-making with product placement was but a self-conscious extension of the commercialization of everyday life that was characteristic of the postwar era. Despite Bloom's elitist stance, his habit of reducing the rich experience of great literature to a rote reflection of his pet theories was clearly akin to the viewing habits of millions of ordinary Americans who were tuning in channels and websites that reliably confirmed their social views, the "news" now customized into a flattering reflection of the same old biases. And these attempts to produce a simulation of reality exactly attuned to one's prejudicial fantasies recalled Henry Ford's predigital attempt to reconstruct history as *he* wanted it to be, neatly divided into separate moral spheres of heroic Gentiles engineering progress and parasitical Jews corrupting our youth.

In a nation where, as de Tocqueville observed, "the precepts of Descartes [were] least studied and best applied," the Cartesian expectation of completion and perfection demanded satisfaction, and when reality, too big and abundant to be so biddable, failed to comply, the anxious modern mind was inclined to fashion various versions of "its own place" as a self-deceiving substitute: Ford's Greenfield Village, Warhol's safely "empty room," the purported desire of Bloom's canonical author to be "elsewhere, in a time and a place of [his] own," the digital technowomb of Negroponte's "cognitive physical environment." Submitting to the same fantasy of total sovereignty that Hamlet considered only to refuse, each of these thinkers found a way to bind himself inside a conceptual "nutshell" where he could then proclaim himself "the king of infinite space."

Empowered by decades of marketing campaigns and seemingly justified by the sudden collapse of global Communism, this same inclination toward a fantastic self-regard had fully infected the American establishment by the turn of the millennium. Both the perennial problems of political governance and the economic turmoil of the boom-bust cycle had been, we were promised by our prize-winning experts, permanently solved. Our Cold War victory was not just another chapter, then, in the ceaseless story of human conflicts but the "end of history" on American terms while our new mastery of economic theory guaranteed unending prosperity for all—chipper predictions that were quickly shredded by 9/11 and the Great Recession.

That even our best and brightest "should think so wrongly" suggested a fundamental failure in the cultural common sense, and as we saw in chapter 5, these devastating miscalculations were logical in their own way. The germ of their erroneous thinking was present at the birth of modernity itself, encoded inside its newly evolving "scientific" worldview. Adopting a method suggested by that era's key technologies, the modern mind was characterized by a new commitment to atomize experience for magnified study, and this strategy of isolation for intense analysis led to a crisp division of the present from the past, the part from the whole, reason from emotion, the self from its community, and humanity from the natural world.

Operating on the allied assumptions that reality could be reduced to an elementary unit and that the individual mind was "its own place," modern reasoning did supply a powerful design for the reformation of medieval life, but one whose justifiable promises of material progress were shadowed from the start by social and psychological dangers. When left unchecked, this scientific perspective would boost the rationalism and materialism it radically favored while collaterally inducing moral disingenuousness and emotional estrangement.

Shifts in worldview are inherently contentious. The often violent struggle to reform the institutions of the West in ways that could accommodate the new atomization of social thought and practice lasted more than two centuries, finally resulting in an entrepreneurial economy and various forms of democratic rule whose hard-won checks and balances licensed the *savvy* of the modern mind-set while restraining the *idiocy* of its potential excesses. These solutions to the problems of human governance, however, didn't mark "the end," or even the beginning of the end, "of history." They were agile adaptations to the cultural conditions of a specific era, and those conditions themselves were bound to change. Over time and ironically, modernity's innate inventiveness generated new technologies that so revised the prevailing patterns of everyday life that modernity itself was ceasing to make sense. The key agents driving this change were the electronic media, and their radical revision in the pace and shape of our daily perceptions and social interactions quickly led to new conceptions about reality itself. As seen in the rapid emergence of relativity, quantum theory, cubist painting, comparative anthropology, and novels favoring multiple points of view, the West's primary metaphor for mapping reality had already begun to flip from *atom* to *field* by the 1920s.

I have been calling this post-modern way of gauging the world *conscientious thinking*, and have defined its approach as one that preferentially seeks "knowledge of or through togetherness." As we saw in chapter 6, conscientious thinking's turn away from atom, text, and figure toward field, context, and visual ground can now be found in all divisions of the sciences. From cosmology to microbiology, from macroeconomics to cancer care, multilogue has been replacing monologue, metamorphic history supplanting universal theory as the better models for authoritative thought. And as we are coming to think, so too are we beginning to behave. With the publicly accessible blog supplanting the private diary, the scattering of ashes replacing the embalmed corpse, and a new belief in consensus challenging modernity's faith in individual expertise, the same trend toward "togetherness" has been rapidly revising our social customs.

The shift in emphasis from isolated incidents to interactive environments has been inseparable from a like-minded change in the methods preferred for intellectual investigation. Collaborative, interdisciplinary, multisensory, multicultural: in various ways and combinations, the conscientious mind aims to express or contain thought *with* feeling, the sciences *with* the arts, the visual *with* the auditory, the familiar *with* the foreign, the present *with* the past, this medium or genre *with* that. To the modern mind, these new mongrel mixes can seem ugly, amoral, atonal, incoherent—monstrous even. (Whether they *are* monstrous or merely *seem* monstrous is and should be a worrying question.) But whatever the final quality of this or that project, they are as a group aiming to redress the isolation-unto-alienation that was so characteristic of modern thought and practice, a collateral result of its habitual atomizing.

This potential reintegration of the self with society and humanity with nature is one of the most promising aspects of the post-modern turn. Yet to receive anew the consolations of belonging is inseparable from minding the obligations that attend them. This need for a renewed accountability recalls my second reason for selecting conscientious thinking as the best possible label for the new common sense that is still evolving. Not only do its etymological origins (knowing *with*) accurately describe the native tactics of the post-modern mind; its primary definition (a thinking that is "governed by . . . the dictates of conscience") redirects even the most advanced forms of intellectual pursuit to the perennial problems of virtue and value. It insists, after Yeats, that "the first business" of our arts and sciences should be to "paint or describe desirable people, places, states of mind," even as it reminds us that our ideas, once applied, can have consequences far beyond their original intentions.[2]

As such, this new common sense would reject the moral immunity of specialization—art for art's sake, "pure" science, corporate quantiphilia's narrow obsession with the bottom line—and would provide as well a temperamental correction to the habitual arrogance of modern scientism. Instead, conscientious thinking at its best would counterbalance an enduring hope for rational progress (sparing the best of modern reasoning) with an intellectual humility that was more characteristic of the pre-modern era. No mere superstitious cowering before the unknown, this humility would be grounded in one of the most significant findings of the post-modern turn: the discovery, in fields as diverse as physics, physiology, classics, and anthropology, of the inherent limits of objective knowledge.

Although shocking to minds raised on the modern doctrine of perpetual progress, this humbling news that we will never "know it all" is finally more a gift than a punishment. Rather than license us to quit the search for the good, the true, and the beautiful—the stance of the po-mo nihilist—the post-modern turn's timely reminder of their inherent fragility should spur us into a heightened vigilance. Freed from the lazy guarantees of the utopian dream, which is constantly seeking "systems so perfect that no one will need to be good," we are brought back to the ceaseless struggle of striving to be truthful, striving to be good, ever alert for divergent patterns and hidden motives, including our own.[3] Since the human predicament can't, after all, be *scientifically* solved, it must be *conscientiously* engaged, moment by moment, day after day.

II. The Perils and Promise of Our Transitional Era

> With hope of better mingling fear of worse,
> Let us too, echoing his uncertain tale,
> Cry sorrow, sorrow—yet let good prevail!
> —Aeschylus, *Agamemnon*

The Perils of an Undomesticated Postmodernity

My working definition of conscientious thinking combines a realistic assessment of emerging trends in thought and practice with an idealistic guide, tentatively sketched, for a new common sense that can adopt and refine these post-modern preferences while still preserving the best of modern reasoning. We have no guarantee, though, that such a happy marriage is in the offing—that what *should* occur, a civilizing conscientiousness, *will* occur.

Undomesticated, the sheer assertion of post-modern effects could prove disastrous, inducing further bouts of confusion and dissension, more culture wars and even civil wars. As we saw with radical postmodernism, the rediscovery of the inherent subjectivity of human knowledge can easily lead to a nihilism that cynically justifies the worst behaviors. Likewise, the inclination toward togetherness in all things is a trend with dangerous as well as delightful potentialities. Our enhanced capacity to retribalize via our social networking sites doesn't in itself assure the quality of the new tribes formed. The wannabe terrorist as well as the cancer victim can now easily find his own "community" online; the hive mind that empowers the peaceful protest for democratic rights can also organize the thugs sent in by a regime to break it up. And even if that regime is overthrown, as was the case with the Arab Spring in 2011, the pace of the power to "disrupt" the old system through digital communications is not likely to be matched by the formation of new and stable democratic institutions, leading instead to anarchy (as in Syria's vicious civil war) or the reactionary return to authoritarianism (as in General el-Sisi's pseudo-democratic Egypt).

Nor should we underestimate the challenges now posed to a consciousness and culture deeply encoded with the moral logic of liberal modernity. In its rediscovery at every level from the subatomic to the macroscopic that "we are all in this together" connected and interacting in multiple ways, the post-modern turn profoundly undermines long-standing presumptions about our own social and psychological worlds. In doubting the truth of atomistic individualism—that the single mind can *ever* be "its own place"—conscientious thinking is especially disturbing to an American nation whose political economy and moral imagination have been rooted in the belief that we are, primarily, pursuing happiness "by ourselves."

If each of us is influenced at a subconscious level by the choices of those around us, as some social scientists have now found; if our physical fates have been preshaped by both the freely chosen behavior and the circumstantial luck of our parents and grandparents, as recent studies in epidemiology seem to have proven; and if our digitized tools expose, even as they enhance, the collaborative nature of human creativity, then what do individual autonomy and responsibility really mean? If we are not acting primarily "by ourselves," then how should merit and accountability be assessed—in our schools, in our courts, in our professional rankings? How should rewards be distributed in our marketplace, and how can desirable social change be best enacted?

The Perils of a Reactionary Modernity

Insomuch as the questions posed above challenge a commonsense way of assessing the world centuries in the making, they are deeply disturbing and have triggered in some quarters a fear and loathing that rigidly rejects the cultural implications of the post-modern turn, even as the technologies driving those same changes are avidly embraced. In our transitional era, the perils of a radical postmodernism coexist with those of a reactionary reassertion of modern principles. Indeed, given the social status and economic power of those who have most benefited from modernity's establishment, the latter may be the more imminent danger.

The reactionary resistance of modern reasoning, its refusal to go gently into the good night of cultural obsolescence, can be found in many fields. As Neo-Darwinism's most adamant advocate, Richard Dawkins likes to imagine himself as a beacon of progress defending an ever-advancing rational science against the superstitious fantasies of fundamentalist religion. But although it is easy to appear progressive when comparing oneself to the prophets of the Rapture, Dawkins' own thinking hasn't really advanced, clinging instead to its origins in the now archaic Old Testament of the modern epistemology. The evidence assessed or the field analyzed may change, but his paradigm for interpretation has remained largely the same. He is ever the reductionist bound to a version of reality that was first being formalized in Descartes' day: as physical evolution is best conceived through the competitive persistence of the "selfish gene," cultural evolution is best understood as the self-replication of various bits of ideas and behavior called "memes." Dawkins' mapping of our territory is *viral* in the literal sense that he presumes that the most elementary particles of physical and social life will provide the best explanatory key. As someone who relentlessly atomizes each subject he studies, he brings a nineteenth-century sensibility to a twenty-first-century evidentiary scene.

Although the truth claims of evolutionists like Dawkins have usually entered the public arena only insomuch as they have contributed to the tedious revival of the old feud between science and religion, the opinions of our entrepreneurial technologists have a more global hold on the public imagination. Because their inventions amaze and wealth astounds, their thoughts even on subjects foreign to their field are presumed to be oracular—hence, the toxic influence of Henry Ford's "ideas and ideals . . . for the good of all" on European politics and, more recently, the submissive acceptance of Bill Gates' pronouncements on public education despite his foundation's dismal record in the field. As we saw when analyzing MIT's Media Lab, the narrow nature of technological savvy, its inability to think conscientiously in both senses of that phrase, makes it highly susceptible to the dangerous idiocies of utopian hubris.

It is no small irony, then, that the architects of our *post*-modern machines continue to promote the most characteristic delusions of the modern mind-set, mistaking the virtual for the actual and the mind as "its own place," and proselytizing newer versions of the radical rationalist's utopian schemes. As preached today by high-tech inventor Raymond Kurzweil and others, the same ditzy dreams of divine authority that deluded the first generation of AI engineers have been passed on to Google's Larry Page and PayPal's Peter Thiel. In the giddy precincts of Silicon Valley where twentysomething billionaires summon their simulated kingdoms-to-come out of the pixie dust of their algorithms, faith in the imminent arrival of the so-called Singularity is widespread. These futurists believe that our computers are about to become both self-replicating and recursively self-improving, and that growing more powerful at an ever faster rate, they soon will generate a new and "living" species of superhuman intelligence. Expanding the old mission favored by the Media Lab, these high-tech wizards aim to "seize the design initiative" from evolution itself and, supplanting biology with their cyber technologies, upgrade *themselves* into *Homo sapiens* 2.0. Through this merging of their minds with their smart machines, they believe, like Hans Moravec before them, that they can fully flee the pain and finally solve the puzzle of the human predicament. Once again, thanks to a technical fix on the grandest of scales, the end of history, philosophy, and even mortality is close at hand.[4]

Not only do the utopian delusions characteristic of the modern mindset continue to find a home in our *post*-modern industries; these entrepreneurs' dreams of an immortal future coexist with a reactionary nostalgia for an atomistic individualism that never existed in the purity they imagine, and whose more moderate forms, so crucial to the early success of the American experiment, are being rapidly eroded by the same digital revolution they have been advancing. After members of the military (ironically that most *collective* of national institutions), the employees of Microsoft and Google supplied the greatest number of individual contributions to libertarian candidate Ron Paul's 2008 presidential campaign.[5] Even as they were rushing to install the next generation of social networking sites, further empowering the hive mind, these high-tech execs were supporting a political philosophy that archaically insists that we are still, primarily, "in this . . . by ourselves."

Touting Horatio Alger heroes in a wiki-driven age, our most influential "thinking men [have been] thinking wrongly" once again, which is why their specialized savvy, overly valued and misapplied, now threatens the health of the body politic. You are not likely to hear this at Davos, where our leaders are schooled by the Delphic pronouncements of digitally enriched CEOs. But at the level of everyday experience (as distinct from our self-conscious understanding of that experience) the post-modern turn has already occurred, and as the primary model for both the psyche and society has flipped from atom to field, so too has the ethical crisis most needing to be resolved. Where early modernity confronted the problem of how to moralize a rationally empowered but socially estranged individualism, we now face the challenge of how to moralize a technologically enhanced but still undomesticated collectivity, especially the highly efficient but sociopathic mega-corporation. These highly specialized money machines are mustering all the aggregating powers of today's new technologies while avoiding the emotional affiliations and ethical responsibilities that ought to attend them. Through their acquisitions, mergers, invasive marketing, global outsourcing, and digital surveillance, they assert the sheer force of organizational togetherness without operating *for* togetherness in the richest sense.

Properly understood, today's large corporation is a kind of Machiavellian collective. Like most of the institutions born in the modern era, it thinks scientifically instead of conscientiously, applying ever more efficient techniques for purely self-centered purposes. For that reason, ceding political power to corporate interests, whether overtly through privatizing governmental services or covertly through radical deregulation, is bound to prove socially destructive.

The Potential Promise of Conscientious Reforms

Gauged to the isolation implicit in both silent reading and frontier settlement, America's once super-effective "lonesome hero" can't solve *these* problems, save *this* day. Nor can his professional analogues, those thinkers raised on the narrow savvy of specialization. We need a new configuration of heroic intervention, one better attuned to the post-modern truths now emerging. The readings of climatology; the findings of communications studies; the global flow charts and tissue residues of industrial pollution; the genetic mappings of our species' genealogical tree; the tragedies of the once distant suffering now instantly accessible on our mobile screens; and the symbolic sum and substance of them all, the image of the Earth as seen from space, one garden after all, one cloud-draped sphere of blue and green gracefully spinning in the emptiness of space: "what instruments we have agree."[6] Each of our islands—each person and profession, each private place and nation-state—does share in the fate of a larger main.

This rediscovery of our native interconnectedness—that even the most distant bell, whether warning or mourning, still tolls for us—is part of our era's true and lasting news. Yet to integrate that news into our everyday practices does demand a revision of our commonsense thinking and institutional character. As potentially painful as it is perplexing, such a project of self-reformation is the proper task of the moral imagination, and real hope exists wherever we can find people who are striving to reestablish a new equilibrium by adding "weight to the lighter scale." As we saw with Wikipedia, Linux, Galaxy Zoo, and the open-source movement more generally, such a homeostatic effort can take the form of humanizing and democratizing our most powerful new technologies. We can witness it, too, in the commercial boycotts organized by both the left and the right, the environmental movement, and "socially responsible" investment funds, all of which are striving to infuse today's money machines with a renewed awareness of what their products and services actually *do* when released into the world.

Another hopeful turn has been the recent emergence of the Benefits Corporation, some version of which has now been legalized in thirty states. Although still profit-seeking, the "B corp" also formally pledges to pursue socially beneficial goals—carbon-neutral manufacturing, for example, or donating a portion of its profits or products to the developing world. Further, they agree to have their adherence to those goals evaluated by an outside nonprofit and can be held accountable by their shareholders if they fail to meet their ethical benchmarks as well as the usual financial ones. Because investors are choosing a company with such an overtly diversified mission—one that begins to resemble conscientious thinking in the richest sense—these legal entities are far less susceptible to corporate practices that are bent on maximizing profits without regard to their communal impact. There are now over a thousand B corps in America, including Etsy, Patagonia, and Warby Parker, and although they represent only a small percentage of American businesses, their emergence does highlight the formal ways by which the core institutions of capitalism might eventually acquire a collective conscience.[7]

At the same time, a counter but not necessarily contradictory set of reforms is taking place in the field of philanthropy. In transitional eras, the primary challenge to the moral imagination is finding the best ways, as in the fairy tales of old, to marry the monster unleashed by the latest technologies. As in all true marriages, the transformation involved will be mutual and bidirectional, civilizing both partners. So it is that one can express the primary cultural crisis of early modernity in two ways, each accurate and neither complete without its complement. One can say that the challenge then was how to moralize the new individualism, infusing its acutely atomistic intelligence with the voice of virtue; *and* one can say that the challenge then was how to modernize the medieval mind-set by infusing it with the new powers native to that same intelligence. And what was true of modernity's *atom* is now true of post-modernity's *field.* Just as those movements cited above have been trying moralize the new sites of corporate and cybernetic togetherness by counterbalancing their emphasis on sheer accumulation with the duties and pleasures of philanthropic affiliation, other organizations have been striving to *post-modernize* philanthropy itself by enhancing its authority with either the tools of the digital age or the tactics of the contemporary marketplace.

A brief sampling of these projects should suggest the scope and character of the reforms under way. The Satellite Sentinel Project—a collaboration between Google, the United Nations, Harvard, and a few NGOs funded by "philanthrocelebrities" like George Clooney, Brad Pitt, and Matt Damon—uses satellite imagery to publicize heretofore hidden incidents of genocidal violence: political evil becomes that much harder to pursue when its acts are exposed in something close to real time.[8] Ushahidi, a Kenyan-born NGO, has created a crisis-mapping website that, using the power of social networking, can organize rapid responses to natural disasters such as Haiti's earthquake in 2010. These high-tech ventures are complemented by more commercially directed forms of social entrepreneurship. Some, modeled after Bangladeshi economist Muhammad Yunus' nonprofit micro-loan program, assist the Third World poor by lending them the re-sources to purchase farmland or to enter the marketplace with their own small businesses. And then there is the work of a foundation established by Bill Clinton that tries to coordinate global social needs with traditional corporate practices by generating "public goods markets." In 2003, this group managed to convince key figures in the pharmaceutical industry that, through economies of scale, they could drastically reduce the price on their AIDS drugs for the Third World poor and still make a profit.

At this early stage, one can't say whether these various programs will succeed in recovering an ethical equilibrium sufficiently powerful to save the age from its toxic excesses. There certainly are dangers in commer-cializing charitable work, for "monetizing" the good may leave it vulnera-ble to those same market forces that have razed the natural environment, split the nuclear family, and debased the quality of our cultural life more generally. The recent emergence of "philanthrocapitalism"—a movement that demands a conversion to the operating principles of quantiphilia in exchange for large donations—is a particularly disturbing development. Although it should go without saying that the same CEO culture which drove the global economy off the cliff is not likely to save the day for pub-lic education, philanthrocapitalists like Gates and Eli Broad (who made his billions in the very industries that caused the crash) have used their foundations to control the national agenda for school reform.[9] On the other side of the equation, product boycotts and socially responsible in-vestment funds have been only marginally effective in their attempts to reform corporate behavior. The B corp, although promising, remains a relative rarity, and as impressive as the inventions of the open-source movement have been, mainstream corporate interests have succeeded to date in either limiting or co-opting their potentially transformative impact on the character of our political economy.

Surveying the current scene, one can't help but conclude that the danger posed by a reactionary modernity remains formidable indeed. If the most powerful private organizations on the planet continue to have no conscience themselves, and if we continue to allow these same corpo-rate bodies to usurp the authority of the democratic institutions that once checked their excesses, then one doesn't have to possess the prophetic powers of a Yeats or Melville to predict that widespread social wreckage will ensue.

Still, one can see in these various programs the collective mindscape hard at work on the problem. They are striving at least to marry the monster and, through a reintegration of technological *virtù* with philanthropic values, to initiate the transition into a newly coherent consciousness and culture. In them, we can see glints and gleamings of the sort of conscientious thinking that, making sense of our current predicament, might gracefully integrate the forces set loose in our post-modern age.

Fairy Tale Endings

Of this much we can be sure, though: a correction of one sort or another will eventually occur. The self-conscious attempts at moderating reform listed above may seem awkward, even threatening to some, but if they don't succeed, the *un*conscious ones presently astir will prove far more destructive. As our fairy tales once reminded us, no tribe or hero can long survive the unnatural presumption that *more must equal better.* When any society forgets its origins in the natural world and defies the ecology of checks and balances that directs the instinctual, it triggers a reaction even more severe than its own violations. The "wrath to come" *will* come, Melville's monstrous whale turning back to crush the keel and sink the ship of our communal expectations.

Over-pursue the goal of scientific control and we end up instead, abracadabra, with an increasingly magical worldview, touting our imminent escape from the fate of death. Proclaim that "pain is the only evil" and initiate a campaign to banish it therapeutically or pharmaceutically, and that now-demonized dimension of human experience returns, valorized in the cheesy embrace of talk-show victimhood, or it rebounds as "erotic" in the robotic rituals of sadomasochistic sex.[10] Overemphasize the plausible reach of personal liberty, and we invite the punitive redress of addiction and compulsion. Disdain the spiritual experience and the ethical intention for the material explanation and the technical fix, and we beckon the return of religiosity and moralism on their crudest terms: the lockstep literalism and graceless intolerance of today's various fundamentalisms. Believe Descartes' promise, expecting to solve all of philosophy's perennial problems, and the sheer impossibility of the project eventually induces instead the nihilism of the radical postmodernist. We flip from know-it-all to know-nothing-at-all in a virtual blink of historical time.

A very familiar if unforgiving logic has been driving these whipsawing inversions, an existential mechanism as old as Eden and as current as the bursting of the housing bubble. The ironic reversals of classical tragedy still apply in our post-modern times—to arrogant nations as well as to overreaching individuals. And these excessive corrections do, after all, make a crude kind of sense. Although wrong by degree, the gross reversals noted here are mostly right in their overall direction. Eroticizing suffering is a perverse solution to the happy-talk delusions of popular culture, yet pain is a real and purposeful part of human nature and so must be allowed a meaningful place in the American story. Addiction enforces an especially hellish psychological imprisonment, yet individual freedom *is* paradoxically dependent on a submission to habits and the acceptance of limits. Yes, the rigid beliefs of today's fundamentalists ironically enact the very idolatry their scripture forbids; but the rational materialist worldview they oppose is, finally, a dehumanizing philosophy incapable of providing any higher meaning to our lives, and just as nature abhors a material vacuum, human nature abhors a spiritual one. Although the nihilism so playfully pronounced by the radical postmodernist does supply an easy alibi to avoid the agonizing trials of moral and metaphysical thinking, the Enlightenment expectation of a scientific certainty in human affairs has been an exceptionally disastrous delusion, complicit in crimes on a once unthinkable scale, and our conventional thinking desperately needs a re-infusion of humility.

When taken as a whole—crudely juxtaposed, unrestrained, and un-assimilated—these reactionary adjustments do seem monstrous. Today's body politic emerges from the oceanic dark of the collective unconscious like some thunder-footed beast out of Tokyo Bay. Such a menacing and repulsive image is characteristic, however, of every epochal transition in human consciousness and culture, every middle phase in the embryonic articulation of a new identity.

This was true of early modernity's Machiavellian man, at once so vital and so venal, as irresistible as he was appalling. And it was also true of his contemporary enemy (and secret brother), that early version of the Protestant self which viewed its own emerging inner powers as potentially appalling: "Was ever heart like mine? / A sty of filth, a trough of washing swill, / A dunghill pit, a puddle of mere slime."[11] Yet the rough makings of democracy's well-tuned citizen—at once materially ambitious and morally self-disciplined, so beautifully aligned to express and refine the powers unleashed by modernity's new place—abided embryonically in *both* those figures, the Machiavellian schemer perpetually on the make and the Protestant seeker pathologically obsessed with his own fallen state. Transitional periods such as theirs and ours demand a graceful integration of those crude-but-vital traits unleashed by their technological innovations, and in the early modern era, the West was awaiting the mutually self-moderating marriage of the Machiavellian man's egregious self-promotion with the early Puritan's excessive self-loathing.

That particular conception of equilibrium is easy enough to see when glancing backward, but its equivalent is harder to fathom today while we are mired in the ditch of our transitional confusion. The grounds for modernity's worldview are collapsing all around us. The logic of its once-dominant science—atomizing and objectifying, individualizing and specializing—no longer describes our current place and so can't effectively prescribe our best behavior there. Meanwhile, as we saw in chapter 5, the alternatives proposed by the most energetic opponents of modern science often seem worse than those they would replace.

Still, when I allow myself to step back from the fray and assess our body politic as an alien anthropologist might, I do begin to glimpse something like the shadowy shape of a new coherence: a terrible beauty struggling to be born. From that remove, it becomes easier to see how even the crude corrections of the reactionary religionist and the radical postmodernist may be pointing us in the right overall direction. In our era of togetherness, we do need to amend modernity's overemphasis on the rational and the material by refocusing our attention on the ethical and the spiritual, and we do need new intellectual and aesthetic forms to express and refine the changes now invading our everyday lives. Somewhere, and not "over the rainbow," these radical reimaginings might mix and merge to their and our mutual betterment.

Certainly some odd pairings are now afoot, and ones that defy the lockjaw oppositions of our culture wars. Some evangelical Christians, increasingly concerned about global warming, industrial pollution, and the threat of mass extinctions, have allied themselves with environmental scientists. Hold that image in mind for a moment: the Darwinian biologist and the born-again Baptist breaking bread together in a common cause, call it ecology or "creation care"; then type into YouTube's search window this juxtaposition of the seemingly incongruous: *Christian* and *hip-hop*. Not only will you find there black rappers using the same bone-shaking beats to aggressively sermonize about their love of the Lord; you can also spy white and Asian youth groups dancing ecstatically to hip-hop music, engaging in a form of choreographic worship oddly reminiscent of the preclassical Greeks. Although these various performances draw from two opposing traditions, this is neither the vulgar and violent revolt of gangsta rap nor the staid and still worship of my Methodist youth, when the body remained benched on pillowless pews and the soul sought release in the silent prayers of the self's secret room.

For someone of my cast of mind, these vivid videos prove unsettling. Hectoring and didactic, hip-hop's songs can seem alien to a literary sensibility trained to favor quiet reflection, subtle emotions, and nuanced analysis. The evangelical dancing does seem a measure more alluring, but although I left the church as soon as I left for college, I was sucker-punched with sadness while watching these videos, struck by the realization that the old hymns I once loved are going the way of the medieval chant.

But all things fall, and my nostalgia, too—I labor now to remind myself—is the enemy of truth, the heart's sappy propaganda. And when I force myself to heed my own analysis, I do seem to glimpse in the oral, choral, rhythmic, and collective nature of those young dancers' worship the resonant togetherness of a genuine spirituality struggling to recast itself in post-modern terms. The imperfect, after all, is *our* paradise, and these are, perhaps, the early rough drafts of conscientious thinking in actual practice.

Orestes Agonistes

In the perpetual present tense of the fairy tale, the monster awaits our transformative kiss. And when the time finally comes, the secret source of his climactic metamorphosis into a prince won't be found in the rituals of magic but in the revisions wrought by the moral imagination: their rearticulation of the monster's crude powers into a better, more beautiful form. The wild wolf at the door is another version of ourselves, and in the undisneyfied version of the nursery rhyme, the third little pig must eat the rough beast to domesticate its spirit of unbridled appetite.

Such symbolic acts are the mythic mind's way of informing us that, in the fitful evolution of human consciousness and culture, the problem of grace *is* fundamentally a problem of integration. And if asked, after all these pages of contemplation, whether we can successfully integrate the crudely appetitive forces now set loose in post-modern America, I wouldn't hesitate to say yes, ever careful to maintain, though, the crucial distinction between *can* and *will.*

The fate of the free is to suffer that distinction, the simmering uncertainty of the conditional, but the resources available for this anxious task of self-reformation are far richer than our rationalizing minds are prepared to comprehend. Backward *is* forward, too. The long-ago past is still whispering warmly into the sleeves of our sleeping ears, and if we're willing to heed its mythic dreams, we will find there models of successful renewal as well as cautionary tales of cultural collapse. Once upon a time, America's royal subjects did, after all, reimagine themselves into a democratic citizenry, completing in the process the West's long transition between the medieval and modern mind-sets. And the ancient Greeks and Jews, whose core beliefs still inform ours, have also left behind a rich record of internal crises confronted and resolved—further proof that, contrary to the boast of Henry Ford and all the techno-utopians now cast in his mold, we *do* "need history very bad."

No surprise, then, that the most hopeful work I know on the crucial subject of cultural rebirth is one of the oldest in the Western tradition. Although Aeschylus was born some twenty-five hundred years ago, we can observe in the rich and arresting narrative of his *Oresteia* the whole cyclical process of cultural demise and eventual renewal within a new set of social and psychological forms. Hundreds of years of Greek history are compressed as the long and agonizing crisis of transformation from an oral common sense to a literate one is completed at last. Although the nominal time frame never changes, we are transported in spirit (in just some 140 pages) from the archaic age of Homer's Trojan War to the classical period of Socrates.

The story begins with a terrible irony. Something is rotten in the city-state of Argos, and a sense of dread pervades what would otherwise seem an apt occasion for celebration: Agamemnon's triumphant return after conquering Troy. Soon enough the source of that inarticulate fear is revealed when the returning king is slain by his wife, who is then murdered in turn by her avenging son, Orestes. Yet this demise into domestic and political anarchy, reminiscent of *King Lear*, eventually ends with a renewed conception of equilibrium. In the translation I prefer, "God and Fate are reconciled," and the final word of the third and final play is "joy."[12]

For once, in Seamus Heaney's lovely words, "hope and history rhyme," and that rare conjunction has been earned through a graceful but nevertheless still global reformation of the old consciousness and culture.[13] Condensed into the story of a single mythic family, a historical crisis centuries in the making has been artfully enacted and beautifully resolved. A new domestic, judicial, and spiritual order has been imagined, one in which the sovereignty of sheer vengeance has been transferred to deliberative reason, and the very core of democratic practice, the jury system, has been established.

Key to this climactic triumph over self-induced chaos was the way the Greek imagination managed to marry continuity to change. Just as the new aesthetic form of the Greek drama retained elements of the ancient religious rituals out of which it evolved, the new moral order announced in the third play savvily adopts, even as it subordinates, the potent spirit of the old regime. There *is* a secret sharing that underlies human experience, metaphorically aligning then-and-there with here-and-now. We *can* find lasting principles of design, as well as enduring flaws to avoid, in our ancient chronicles and mythic lore.

To read these plays is to recognize that even twenty-five hundred years ago *backward was forward too*, and that cultural progress had to proceed through integration, not extermination. In the perpetual present tense of the play, the old gods must still be given their due. The urge to vengeance, after all, is not an alien visitation but a native expression of our emotional intelligence. To want to kill those who have slain our beloved daughters or fathers is a natural reaction—a true measure of the devastating loss we feel—and to simply deny the existence of that primordial desire would only invite its return in a more monstrous form, the wolf once again raging at our door.

And so in the climax of the final play, those old spiritual personifications of ferocious vengeance, the terrifying Furies, are not banished but absorbed. Although their sovereignty over the daily operations of the Greek imagination is being transferred to a new generation of more reasonable gods, these "dread and friendly Powers" are allotted their own special place, the "exalted sanctuary" of a subterranean cave. They remain within the bounds of the new city-state of Athens and, just as crucially, within the reach of the new Apollonian consciousness that minds it. Both acknowledged and suppressed, the wolfish appetite for vengeance has been successfully domesticated.

The Greek invention of the fully phonetic alphabet was one of the most pivotal events in the cultural evolution of our species: the widespread literacy unleashed by this new verbal technology not only greatly magnified humanity's preexisting powers; it also disrupted and eventually destroyed the artful inner logic of the old oral tribe. Intellectual progress triggered social regress as, for a significant period in Greek life, the center failed to hold. All things seemed to fall, including the old covenantal graces, yet the elements for a new coherence were eventually found and the human garden, in a Greek accent, was built again.

Now, in the ongoing aftermath of the electronic revolution, we are facing an equivalent crisis in self-conception, and the question remains whether we can fashion a renewal as successful as the one Aeschylus depicted. Other than to continue in disingenuous denial, we have no choice but to try. As in the Chinese curse, we have been born to "interesting times"—into an era demanding that we "paint or describe" a new configuration of "desirable persons, places, states of mind."

In every field, from physics to fiction, the news is the same: we now know, or *ought* to know, that the human condition cannot be scientifically solved—that it must, instead, be conscientiously engaged, moment by moment, day after day. In the current phase of our imperfect earthly paradise, modernity is in decline, post-modernity has arrived, and roughly conceived in our messy ditch, their hybrid monster still awaits our transformative kiss. None of us shall prove exempt, no techno-womb can spare us, from the hell to come if we fail this latest test of our moral imaginations. The warning bell is tolling: we are in *this* fix together, not simply by ourselves.

Notes

INTRODUCTION. A Key to the Map

Chapter epigraph: Václav Havel, *Disturbing the Peace* (London: Faber and Faber, 1990), 181.

1. J. C. Fournier, et. al., "Antidepressant Drug Effects and Depression Severity," *Journal of American Medicine*, January 6, 2010.

2. For a history of the uses and abuses of antidepressant prescriptions see David Healy, *The Antidepressant Era* (Cambridge: Harvard University Press, 1999).

3. Christopher Lasch, *The Revolt of the Elites and the Betrayal of Democracy* (New York: W.W. Norton, 1995).

4. Sophocles, *Antigone*, trans. E. F. Watling (New York: Penguin Classics, 1947), line 271.

CHAPTER 1. Our Lord Ford

Chapter epigraph: Sophocles, *Antigone*, trans. E. F. Watling (New York: Penguin Classics, 1947), line 271.

1. *Chicago Tribune*, May 25, 1916, in an interview with Charles Wheeler, as cited in Allan Nevins and Frank Ernest Hill, *Ford: Expansion and Challenge, 1915–33* (New York: Charles Scribner's Sons, 1957), 138, and in Carol W. Gelderman, *Henry Ford: The Wayward Capitalist* (New York: Dial Press, 1981), 177.

2. Gelderman, *Henry Ford*, 177.

3. Francis Fukuyama, *The End of History and the Last Man* (New York: Free Press, 1992), xi.

4. One of the fundamental precepts of the Cartesian approach, the atomistic reductionism of his Rule V—"we reduce complex and obscure propositions step by step to simpler ones, and then, by retracing our steps, try to rise from intuition

of all of the simplest ones to all the rest"—supplied the procedural model for both scientific study and modern manufacture, each of which breaks down a whole into discrete parts and then sequentially reassembles them. See René Descartes, *Rules for the Direction of the Mind*, in *Descartes—Philosophical Writings*, ed. Elizabeth Anscombe and Peter Thomas Geach (Indianapolis: Bobbs-Merrill, 1971), 157.

5. Gelderman, *Henry Ford*, 177.

6. Albert Lee, *Henry Ford and the Jews* (New York: Stein and Day, 1980), 3.

7. David Lanier Lewis, *The Public Image of Henry Ford: An American Folk Hero* (Detroit: Wayne State University Press, 1976), 135.

8. Lewis, *The Public Image of Henry Ford*, 139; Lee, *Henry Ford and the Jews*, 14, 27–34.

9. Lee, *Henry Ford and the Jews*, 14.

10. Gelderman, *Henry Ford*, 217–241; Lee, *Henry Ford and the Jews*, 45–64.

11. Lee, *Henry Ford and the Jews*, 52, 79, 113–14; Lewis, *The Public Image of Henry Ford*, 143.

12. Lee, *Henry Ford and the Jews*, 33.

13. Gelderman, *Henry Ford*, 99–100.

14. Lee, *Henry Ford and the Jews*, 8.

15. Lewis, *The Public Image of Henry Ford*, 212–13.

16. Lewis, *The Public Image of Henry Ford*, 218.

17. Lewis, *The Public Image of Henry Ford*, 96.

18. Gelderman, *Henry Ford*, 157–92.

19. "flivver": a small cheap automobile. The slang word evolved at the time of the Model T's success, and the Flivver King was a nickname applied to Ford both positively and pejoratively.

20. Gelderman, *Henry Ford*, 221–22.

21. Gelderman, *Henry Ford*, 276–77.

22. Gelderman, *Henry Ford*, 289; Gary Wills, *Reagan's America*, (New York: Penguin, 1988), 442–43.

23. Wills, *Reagan's America*, 440–47.

24. Lewis, *The Public Image of Henry Ford*, 106.

25. Wills, *Reagan's America*, 444.

26. Gelderman, *Henry Ford*, 286.

27. William Butler Yeats, "The Second Coming," *Selected Poems and Two Plays of William Butler Yeats* (New York: Macmillan, 1962), 91.

28. David Bosworth, "The Cultural Contradictions of Philanthrocapitalism," *Society*, September/October 2011, 382–88.

29. F. Scott Fitzgerald, *The Great Gatsby* (Charles Scribner's Sons, 1925), 100.

CHAPTER 2. Echo and Narcissus

Chapter epigraph: Robert Hughes, *The Shock of the New* (New York: Knopf, 1991), 9.

1. Gregg Toppo and Paul Overberg, "Census: More Americans Are Living Alone Today," *USA Today*, August 28, 2013.

2. New York: Harcourt Jovanovich, 1975.

3. Quoted in Jean Baudrillard, "Pop—An Art of Consumption?" in *Post-Pop Art*, ed. Paul Taylor (Boston: MIT Press, 1989), 40.

4. Robert I. Fitzhenry, ed., *The Harper Book of Quotations*, 3rd ed. (New York: Harper-Collins, 1993), 88.

5. Harriet Zinnes, "David James Sibbit," *New Art Examiner* 19 (1992): n.p.

6. Peter Plagens, "The Great Impersonator," *Newsweek*, April 6, 1992, p. 62.

7. Plagens, "The Great Impersonator," 62.

8. Taylor Holiday, "Hannah Wilke, in Her Prime," *Wall Street Journal*, October 21, 1996, A20.

9. See, for example, David Littlejohn, "Who Is Jeff Koons and Why Are People Saying Such Terrible Things about Him?" *Art News* (1993): 90–94.

10. Christopher Lasch, *The Culture of Narcissism: American Life in an Age of Diminishing Expectations* (New York: Norton, 1979).

11. Indeed, the link may go back to the very origins of capitalism. As long ago as 1831, Thomas Carlyle, one of the earliest and harshest critics of the new industrial economy, was noting a subtler version of the same syndrome: obsessive self-consciousness and mechanistic behavior. See his essay "Characteristics" in *Critical and Miscellaneous Essay* (New York: AMS Press, 1969), 3:1–43.

12. Also collected in *Post-Pop Art*, 171–89.

13. Baudrillard, "Beyond the Vanishing Point in Art," 172.

14. Baudrillard, "Beyond the Vanishing Point in Art," 178.

15. See "The Gadget Lover: Narcissus as Narcosis" in McLuhan's *Understanding Media: The Extensions of Man* (New York: McGraw-Hill, 1964), 41–47.

16. When Picasso died and Warhol read that he had left behind some four thousand masterpieces, his first reaction was to attempt to make four thousand "masterpieces" in a single day. In his jealous desire to best another master, the Factory owner was once again borrowing the values of industrial manufacture. As quantity replaced quality with da Vinci ("Thirty Are Better than One"), efficiency would replace quality with Picasso: *faster is better.* See *The Philosophy of Andy Warhol*, 148.

17. Maggie Scarf describes narcissistic personality disorder as follows: "The narcissistic person is, nevertheless, deeply injured at the core and suffering from sorely depleted supplies of self-esteem. His overweening grandiosity is, for this reason, intermingled with a sense of inner emptiness and painful feelings of unworthiness, despair and desolation" ("The Mind of the Unabomber," *New Republic*, June 10, 1996, p. 22). Also see Christopher Lasch, "The Narcissistic Personality of Our Time" in *The Culture of Narcissism*, 21–51.

18. On the opening page of chapter 1 in *The Philosophy of Andy Warhol*, Warhol briefly reports that he suffered a nervous breakdown three years in a row, at the ages of eight, nine, and ten, each time at the start of summer vacation. He describes the condition as St. Vitus' dance, which, according to *ScienceBlogs*, is a convulsive disorder "characterised by involuntary and uncoordinated movements of the face, hands and feet" usually occurring in early life. (See "St. Vitus's Dance," August 13, 2007, http://scienceblogs.com/neurophilosophy/2007/08/13/st-vituss-dance/.) In his usual flight from interpretation, Warhol writes that he doesn't "know what this meant," but it is easy to imagine a personality (and an aesthetic)

constructed in defense against such a potentially humiliating loss of control. As the narcissist invents a grandiosity to hide his inner sense of worthlessness, Warhol assumes a frigidity to contain and conceal his actual hypersensitivity; the passive mask guards against the reemergence of the twitching face of the bedridden child.

19. A loss of sensation *with* loss of consciousness is far too threatening an option for someone as terrified of death as Warhol was.

20. William Butler Yeats, "Lapis Lazuli," *Selected Poems and Two Plays by William Butler Yeats* (New York: Macmillan, 1962), 159–60.

21. Baudrillard, "Pop," 178–79.

22. Ecclesiastes 9:11, NIV.

23. Baudrillard, "Pop," 185.

24. Another way of phrasing this within the chapter's own terms: by sparing us the intellectual and emotional tension of perceiving differences, the postmodern approach spares us the obligation of making a difference.

25. Yeats, "Those Images," *Selected Poems and Two Plays by William Butler Yeats,* 172.

26. Yeats, "Under Ben Bulben," *Selected Poems and Two Plays by William Butler Yeats,* 192.

CHAPTER 3. Flatter-Fest

Chapter epigraph: "Si Dieu nous a faits à son image, nous le lui avons bien rendu," *Voltaire's Notebooks,* ed. Theodore Besterman (Geneva: *Institut et Musée Voltaire, 1952), 231.*

1. Herbert W. Schneider, *The Puritan Mind* (University of Michigan Press, 1966), 3.

2. William Irwin Thompson, *The American Replacement of Nature* (New York: Doubleday, 1991), 78.

3. Harold Bloom, *The Western Canon: The Books and School of the Ages* (New York: Harcourt Brace, 1994), 34.

4. *Boston Review,* April/May 1998.

5. Harold Bloom, *Shakespeare: The Invention of the Human* (New York: Riverhead Books, 1998), xvii.

6. Bloom, *The Western Canon,* 40.

7. Bloom, *The Western Canon,* 7.

8. Bloom, *The Western Canon,* 4.

9. Bloom, *The Western Canon,* 30.

10. Bloom, *The Western Canon* 7.

11. Bloom, *The Western Canon,* 12.

12. Bloom, *The Western Canon,* 30.

13. Bloom, *The Western Canon,* 10–11.

14. Bloom, *The Western Canon,* 67–69.

15. Bloom, *The Western Canon,* 66–67.

16. The most comic-horrific instance of this perverse aesthetic value system put to work in the real world occurred when Hitler, that Wagner-obsessed Romantic

megalomaniac, instructed his minion architect, Albert Speer, to design buildings that would make beautiful ruins. Alas, he soon transformed all of Europe into his own operatic set—a stage where, among the Wagnerian ruins, millions of real people wandered and wept. See the 1991 documentary by Swedish director Peter Cohen, *Architecture of Doom.*

17. Bloom, *The Western Canon*, 68.

18. William Shakespeare, *King Lear*, in *William Shakespeare, Selected Plays* (Franklin Center: Franklin Library, 1981): 1.1.52–53.

19. *King Lear.* 1.1.57.

20. *King Lear.* 1.1.74–76.

21. *King Lear.* 1.1.236–37.

22. Bloom, *The Western Canon*, 66.

23. Bloom, *Shakespeare*, 477–79.

24. *King Lear.* 5.3.290.

25. *King Lear.* 5.3.302–4.

26. *King Lear.* 5.3.305–8.

27. T. S. Eliot, "Yeats," in *Yeats: A Collection of Critical Essays*, ed. John Unterecker (Englewood Cliffs: Prentice Hall, 1963), 61.

28. Seamus Heaney, *The Redress of Poetry* (New York: Farrar, Straus and Giroux, 1995), 190.

29. Isaiah 2:8, KJV.

30. William Hazlitt, *Selected Writings* (Oxford: Oxford University Press, 1991), 323–34.

CHAPTER 4. Boxed In

Chapter epigraph: Robert W. Rydell, "Century of Progress Exposition," Encyclopedia of Chicago website, http://www.encyclopedia.chicagohistory.org /pages/225.html.

1. Leon R. Kass, "The Wisdom of Repugnance," *New Republic*, June 2, 1997.

2. J. B. Watson, "Psychology as the Behaviorist Views It," *Psychology Review* 20: 158–77.

3. William Wordsworth, *Prelude*, Book 2, 216–19.

4. William Hazlitt, "On Mr. Wordsworth's 'Excursion,'" *Lectures on the English Poets* (New York: Russell and Russell), 352–53.

5. William Irwin Thompson, *The American Replacement of Nature* (New York: Doubleday 1991), 130.

6. Jonathan Chait, "Prophet Motive," *New Republic*, March 31, 1997.

7. Hans Moravec, *Mind Children: The Future of Robot and Human Intelligence* (Cambridge: Harvard University Press, 1988), 180.

8. Nina Burleigh, "Cyberwonks," *Spy*, April 1993.

9. Saraswati was an Indian spiritual leader, the quote supplied to me by a member of the School of Practical Philosophy that follows his teachings. His series of observations linking word to sound, sound to meaning, and meaning to practical activity acutely captures a key difference between oral and literate traditions of

thought. For Saraswati, working out of a religious tradition that still emphasizes face-to-face teaching, language spoken *is* action taken, with all the social, political, ethical, and spiritual resonance that implies.

10. Steven Levy, *Artificial Life: The Quest for a New Creation* (New York: Pantheon Books, 1992), 347.

11. Although Einstein predicted that mass could be converted to energy at the start of the century, it wasn't until 1939, when Hahn and Strassmann discovered the potential for a chain reaction in uranium, that the idea of a nuclear bomb became feasible.

12. Stewart Brand, *The Media Lab: Inventing the Future at M.I.T.* (New York: Penguin, 1988), 6–9.

13. Although Brand's book is an informative piece of journalism, the objectivity of his judgment is tainted by the origins of the project. At his own request, he came to the Media Lab not as a journalist but as a consultant, a temporary paid employee. His admission of collaboration in the preface—that Negroponte "helped see the entire project through from my original book proposal to final draft, and the rough design of the cover and the color photo sections are his"—suggests a problematical relationship that few scholars or investigatory journalists would have sustained. Brand's claim that Negroponte "had much of the work of a co-author with none of the control of one" seems disingenuous and ironically reflects Negroponte's own disingenuous account of robotic intelligence as benign servant which will be critiqued in the pages to come. See xii–xv.

14. Brand, *Media Lab*, 132.

15. Brand, *Media Lab*, 55.

16. Nicholas Negroponte, *The Architecture Machine: Toward a More Human Environment* (MIT Press, Cambridge, 1970), in an unnumbered preface.

17. Negroponte, *The Architecture Machine*, 7.

18. Negroponte, *The Architecture Machine*, 13.

19. Nicholas Negroponte, *Being Digital* (New York: Knopf, 1995), 233.

20. Negroponte, *Being Digital*, 233.

21. Thompson, *American Replacement of Nature*, 128.

22. Nicholas Negroponte, *Soft Architecture Machines* (Cambridge: MIT Press, 1975), 1.

23. Negroponte, *Soft Architecture Machines*, 102.

24. Negroponte, *Soft Architecture Machines*, 103.

25. Negroponte, *Soft Architecture Machines*, 109.

26. Negroponte, *Soft Architecture Machines*, 5.

27. See Philip Wylie, "Common Women," in *A Generation of Vipers* (New York: Rinehart, 1942), 184–204. Wylie's prose, composed in the hyperbole of high dudgeon, caused a stir. In a much later book on the sixties youth "rebellion," he more clearly allied momism with consumerism. See *The Sons and Daughters of Mom* (New York: Doubleday, 1971), 41–55.

28. William Hazlitt, "On Mr. Wordsworth's 'Excursion,'" *Lectures on The English Poets* (New York: Russell and Russell, 1841), 356–57.

29. Hazlitt, "On Mr. Wordsworth's 'Excursion,'" 356.

30. Negroponte, *Soft Architecture Machines*, 1.

31. Negroponte, *Being Digital*, 218.

32. Negroponte's desire mirrors that of the obsessive fan. See Martin Scorcese's film *King of Comedy*, where the fan and wannabe comedian, played by Robert DeNiro, kidnaps the star he admires, holding him as a literal "captive audience."

33. Even Brand's defense of the Lab ("It inflates hubris and then mocks it." [228]) echoes one of the standard defenses of postmodern art, framing each corrupt gesture and investment in vanity as intentional—a "parody"—and so immune to critique.

34. Negroponte, *Soft Architecture Machines*, 5.

35. This warning that "artificial life," with a will all its own, might eventually revolt against its human creators, is hardly new. The caution was being voiced in the very cradle of techno-optimism. The year was 1818, the author was Mary Shelley, and the lab—awaiting funding from major corporations—was Dr. Frankenstein's. The first thing *his* intelligent machine demanded, and with a vengeance, was the comfort of some company. The new Adam, like the old, was desperate for a date.

36. William Shakespeare, *The Tempest*, 2.1.

37. The symbolic turning point for Europe's conversion from a religious to a scientific worldview is usually ascribed to the reign of Charles V of France (1364–80), who recalibrated public life by switching from canonical hours to the mechanical clock. Smaller, privately owned clocks became more prevalent in the seventeenth century, and their adoption paralleled an increasing preference for precise and regular measurement in all fields, especially commerce. Newton's *Principia Mathematica* was published in 1687.

38. Brand, *Media Lab*, 188, 200.

39. Levy, *Artificial Life*, 346.

40. The full quote is, "It [our fixation on technological progress] creates an *appetite for immortality* on the one hand. It threatens *universal extinction* on the other. Technology is lust removed from nature." See Don DeLillo, *White Noise* (New York: Viking Penguin, 1985), 285.

41. Lawrence Durrell, *Justine* (New York: Pocket Cardinal, 1961), 250.

INTERMISSION. Between Common Senses

Chapter epigraph: Quotation found in W. S. Merwin, *Asian Figures* (New York: Atheneum, 1973), 37.

1. The danger of the West's utopian pursuit of the self-regulating market has not gone unnoted. In a trenchant analysis that, nevertheless, was ignored by the West's political and economic establishment, Karl Polanyi argued back in 1944 that the self-regulating market is not a natural feature of human society; that the mechanisms required by that market system are inherently detrimental to traditional values and the social relations they govern; that those mechanisms are

pursued through the proselytizing of an ideology that sanctifies property rights and condones poverty, and often have to be instituted through violent means; and finally that rather than being truly self-regulating, such markets have historically lurched from disaster to disaster. See Karl Polanyi, *The Great Transformation: The Political and Economic Origins of Our Time* (Boston: Beacon Press, 1944 [1957]).

2. See William Blake's poem, "The New Jerusalem," accessed at Poetry EServer, June 28, 2016, http://poetry.eserver.org/new-jerusalem.html.

3. "Afghanistan and other troubled countries cry out for the sort of enlightened foreign administration once provided by self-confident Englishmen in jodhpurs and pith helmets. . . . To turn Iraq into a beacon of hope for the oppressed peoples of the Middle East: Now that would be a historic war aim." See Max Boot, "The Case for American Empire: The Most Realistic Response to Terrorism Is for America to Embrace Its Imperial Role," *Weekly Standard*, October 15, 2001.

4. "How dreadful it is when the right judge judges wrong!" A sentry protesting Creon's harsh rule in Sophocles' "Antigone." See *The Oedipus Cycle*, trans. by Dudley Fitts and Robert Fitzgerald (New York: Harcourt, Brace Jovanovich, 1967), 198.

CHAPTER 5. Conscientious Thinking

Chapter epigraph: René Descartes, *Discourse on Method*, in *Descartes: Philosophical Writings* (Indianapolis: Bobbs-Merrill, 1971), 24–25.

1. Marshall McLuhan, *Understanding Media* (New York: New American Library, 1964), 277.

2. Albert Einstein, "Geometry and Experience," in *Readings in the Philosophy of Science*, ed. Herbert Feigl and Mary Brodbeck (New York: Appleton-Century-Crofts, 1953), 189.

3. Alexis de Tocqueville, *Democracy in America*, vol. 2 (New York: Vintage, 1945), 3–4.

4. W. S. Merwin, *Asian Figures* (New York: Atheneum, 1973), 59. These "figures" are the American poet Merwin's translations of otherwise anonymous Asian aphorisms. "Jelly in a vise" is Japanese in origin.

5. John Milton, *Paradise Lost*, bk. 2, lines 907–10.

6. Eric Havelock, *Preface to Plato* (Cambridge: Harvard University Press, 1963). Havelock was the first to delineate the connection between the underlying structure of the phonetic alphabet and the rise of Greek philosophy.

7. George Gerbner, "TV or Not TV?" *Bill Moyer's Journal*, April 29, 1979.

8. See Wallace Stevens' poem, "The Poems of Our Climate." Note, too, that *Eden* in Hebrew means *delight*. The naming of the physical site simultaneously signals a psychological state, the loss of the Garden (as I argued in chapter 5) not just the forfeiture of a particular place but the rupture of a harmonious relationship between the human mind and the place it occupies.

9. Robert I. Fitzhenry, ed., *The Harper Book of Quotations*, third ed. (New York: HarperCollins, 1993), 266.

CHAPTER 6. Fields in Play

Chapter epigraph: Arthur Eddington, *The Nature of the Physical World* (Ann Arbor: University of Michigan Press, 1958), 103–4. The context of the excerpt is as follows: "We often think that when we have completed our study of one we know all about two, because 'two' is 'one and one.' We forget that we have still to make a study of 'and.' Secondary physics is the study of 'and'—that is to say, of organization."

1. Einstein and other notable physicists of the day had difficulty accepting the sheer strangeness of quantum mechanics. For a concise summary of the theory see Clive Cookson and Chris Nuttall, "Making Sense of a 'Nonsensical World,'" *FT.com*, September 16, 2010.

2. Adam Frank, "Who Wrote the Book of Physics?" *Discover*, April 2010.

3. Stephen Hawking and Leonard Mlodinow, "The (Elusive) Theory of Everything," *Scientific American*, October 2010.

4. Natalie Angier, "Listening to Bacteria," *Smithsonian*, August 2010.

5. Stephen S. Hall, "Revolution Postponed," *Scientific American*, July 2010.

6. Gina Kolata, "Forty Years' War: Old Ideas Spur New Approaches to Cancer Fight," *New York Times*, December 29, 2009.

7. Kolata, "Forty Years' War."

8. Sharon Begley, "Sins of the Grandfathers," *Newsweek*, November 8, 2010.

9. Begley, "Sins of the Grandfathers."

10. Hall, "Revolution Postponed."

11. Richard Dawkins, *The Selfish Gene* (New York: Oxford University Press, 1976).

12. Hall, "Revolution Postponed."

13. As quoted in Kolata, "Forty Years' War."

14. Angier, "Listening to Bacteria."

15. For an excellent, thorough examination of the new and more "conscientious" trends in evolutionary theory see Eva Jablonka and Marion J. Lamb, *Evolution in Four Dimensions: Genetic, Epigenetic, Behavioral, and Symbolic Variation in the History of Life* (Cambridge: MIT Press, 2005).

16. The Gaia hypothesis was first proposed by British scientist James Lovelock, under a different name, earth feedback hypothesis, and was changed later at the suggestion of Lovelock's friend, the noted author William Golding. Once again the post-modern *logos* demonstrated its affinity for a pre-modern *mythos*. See Lovelock, *In Search of Gaia* (Princeton, N.J.: Princeton University Press, 2009).

17. "In biology there are no values that have the characteristic that if something is good, then more of something will be better. Economists seem to think that this is true of money but, if they are right, money is thereby shown to be certainly unbiological and perhaps antibiological. . . . For the rest, good things come in optima, not maxima." See Gregory Bateson, *A Sacred Unity: Further Steps to an Ecology of Mind*, ed. Ronald E. Donaldson (New York: Cornelia & Michael Bessie Books, 1991), 297. The polymath Bateson, who had experience in zoology, anthropology,

psychotherapy, and communications theory, explored the grounds for a new epistemology in which all perception and, therefore, all knowledge was rooted in "togetherness." Or as Bateson phrased it, "while I can know nothing about any individual thing in itself, I *can* know something about *relations between things.*" See Gregory Bateson and Mary Catherine Bateson, *Angels Fear: Toward an Epistemology of the Sacred* (Cresskill, N.J.: Hampton Press, 2005), 157.

18. David H. Freedman, "Lies, Damned Lies, and Medical Science," *Atlantic,* November 2010.

19. Richard Palmer, QUASI-REPLICATION AND THE CONTRACT OF ERROR: Lessons from Sex Ratios, Heritabilities and Fluctuating Asymmetry," *Annual Review of Ecology and Systematics,* as quoted in Jonah Lehrer, "The Truth Wears Off," *New Yorker,* December 13, 2010.

20. Ralph Waldo Emerson, "Circles," in *Selected Essays* (Chicago: Peoples Book Club, 1949), 205.

21. Stephen Jay Gould, *The Mismeasure of Man* (New York: Norton, 1996).

22. In 1997, Stanford's anthropology faculty democratically acknowledged their intramural strife by voting to split into two departments along the lines noted above. In 2007, the university's administration ordered them to reunite.

23. Karl Jacoby, *Shadows at Dawn* (New York: Penguin, 2008).

24. John Lukacs, "Against Objectivity: Putting Man Before Descartes," *American Scholar,* Winter 2009.

25. Gordon S. Wood, "No Thanks for the Memories," *New York Review of Books,* January 13, 2011.

26. Wood, "No Thanks for the Memories."

27. See Kenneth J. Gergen, *The Saturated Self: The Dilemmas of Identity in Contemporary Life* (New York: Basic Books, 1991) and *Relational Being: Beyond Self and Community* (New York: Oxford University Press, 2009).

28. Peter D. Kramer, *Listening to Prozac* (New York: Viking, 1993). In the final words of the paperback edition, Kramer actually equated the importance of the discovery of the SSRIS with Freud's discovery of the unconscious.

29. Thomas Bodenheimer, "An Uneasy Alliance: Clinical Investigators and the Pharmaceutical Industry," *New England Journal of Medicine,* May 18, 2000.

30. "It is our first business to paint, or describe, desirable persons, places, states of mind." See W. B. Yeats, *Essays and Introductions* (London: MacMillan, 1961), ix–x.

31. For a pointed analysis and critique of behavioral economics and "happiness studies" see Alan Wolfe, "Hedonic Man," *New Republic,* July 9, 2008.

32. Nicholas A. Christakis and James H. Fowler, *Connected: The Surprising Power of Social Networks and How They Shape Our Lives* (New York: Little, Brown, 2009), 7.

33. Gregory Bateson, *Mind and Nature: A Necessary Unity* (New York: Dutton, 1979), ch. 2.

34. Simone Weil, *Gravity and Grace* (London: Routledge, 1963), 151.

35. "Because this age and the next age / Engender in the ditch, / No man

can know a happy man / From any passing wretch." From "The Old Stone Cross," Yeats, *Selected Poems and Two Plays of William Butler Yeats* (New York: Macmillan, 1962), 172.

CHAPTER 7. Together in the Ditch

Epigraph: Three Dog Night, "One," on *One*, ANC-Dunhill, 1969.

1. As a contemporary of Shakespeare's, a friend to Sir Philip Sidney and a fellow courtier, Edward Dyer lived at the height of England's literary Renaissance. His poetry was much admired in his time, but little of it has survived. And although "My Mind to Me a Kingdom Is," is commonly attributed to him, his authorship of it is by no means certain.

2. The two great cross-Atlantic examples of the emergence of the private diary in the seventeenth century are the ones kept by Samuel Pepys (1633–1703), a Member of Parliament, and Samuel Sewall (1652–1730), a judge in the Massachusetts Bay Colony, who participated, much to his later shame, in the Salem witchcraft trials.

3. For the number of blogs see "Buzz in the Blogosphere: Millions More Bloggers and Blog Readers," *Newswire*, March 8, 2012, http://www.nielsen.com /us/en/insights/news/2012/buzz-in-the-blogosphere-millions-more-bloggers -and-blog-readers.html.

For Facebook see "Number of monthly active Facebook users worldwide," http://www.statista.com/statistics/264810/number-of-monthly-active-facebook -users-worldwide/.

For Twitter see "Number of monthly active Twitter users worldwide," http:// www.statista.com/statistics/282087/number-of-monthly-active-twitter-users/.

For YouTube see "YouTube Statistics," http://www.statisticbrain.com /youtube-statistics/.

4. For the history and schedule of Sarah Brown's "Cringe" readings, which, as of 2014, were still occurring monthly in New York and London, see "Que Sera Sera: Cringe," http://www.queserasera.org/cringe.html. The "Get Mortified" crew has turned the concept into a multidivisional industry with films, books, and a TV interview show on the Sundance channel as well as their live performances.

See "The Mortified Yearbook," accessed February 28, 2014, https://web .archive.org/web/20140228205725/http://www.getmortified.com/about /yearbook.php.

5. Three Dog Night, "One."

6. See Andrew Keen, "Sharing Is a Trap," *Wired Magazine*, April 3, 2011. The statistics for online social media use had crept up to 28 percent by 2013. See Shea Bennett, "28% of Time Spent Online is Social Networking," *Social Times*, January 27, 2015, http://www.adweek.com/socialtimes/time-spent-online/613474.

7. Jaron Lanier, *You Are Not a Gadget: A Manifesto* (New York: Alfred A. Knopf, 2009), 54.

8. There are, of course, websites set up now to facilitate this trend of group dating—for example, Grouper (www.joingrouper.com).

9. Elizabeth Lucas, "Popularity of Cremation on Rise in U.S.," *Scripps Howard News Service*, April 4, 2010. For the 2014 rate, see "Industry Statistical Information," Cremation Association of North America website, accessed May 26, 2016, http://www.cremationassociation.org/?page=IndustryStatistics.

10. Tad Friend, "First Banana," *New Yorker*, July 5, 2010.

11. Jürgen Habermas, "Modernity vs. Postmodernity," *New German Critique* 22 (Winter 1981).

12. Don Tapscott and Anthony D. Williams, *Macrowikinomics* (New York: Penguin, 2010), 157–59.

13. These new opportunities for mass collaboration between the professional investigator and the amateur crowd are being shadowed by a dramatic increase in the cooperation between scientists themselves. According to a study conducted by the Santa Fe Institute, the average number of authors of scientific papers has doubled and tripled in certain fields. See Don Tapscott and Anthony D. Williams, *Macrowikinomics*, 159–62.

14. For a concise analysis of the early history of Wikipedia see Marshall Poe, "The Hive," *Atlantic*, September 1, 2006. For the number of articles in English, see "Wikipedia:Size of Wikipedia," https://en.wikipedia.org/wiki/Wikipedia:Size_of_Wikipedia.

15. "Internet Encyclopedias Go Head to Head," *Nature*, December 15, 2005. Surveying fifty articles on scientific topics, the study found 2.9 errors per article in Britannica and 3.9 in Wikipedia. Other later studies have had similar results on academic topics. See Natalie Wolchover, "How Accurate Is Wikipedia?" LiveScience, January 24, 2011, http://www.livescience.com/32950-how-accurate-is-wikipedia.html.

16. Wikipedia "may well be the greatest effort in voluntary collaboration of any kind" in human history. See Poe, "The Hive."

17. In 2012 Britannica ceased publishing their hardbound version.

18. For Windows statistics, see Ben Z. Gottesman, "Readers' Choice Awards 2015: Laptops and Desktops," *PC Mag*, February 25, 2015, http://www.pcmag.com/article2/0,2817,2477288,00.asp.

19. David Goldman, "Microsoft Profit Jumps 17%," *Cannoned*, October 24, 2013, http://money.cnn.com/2013/10/24/technology/enterprise/microsoft-earnings/.

20. Don Tapscott and Anthony D. Williams, *Macrowikinomics*, 68–72.

21. See Noam Scheiber, "Growth in the 'Gig Economy' Fuels Work Force Anxieties," *New York Times*, July 12, 2015.

22. See Todd Bishop, "Microsoft's Contractor Crackdown," *Geekwire*, July 21, 2014, http://www.geekwire.com/2014/microsoft-takes-big-swipe-shadow-workforce/.

23. Kevin Drawbaugh and Patrick Temple-West, "Untaxed U.S. Corporate Profits Held Overseas Top $2.1 Trillion," *Reuters*, April 8, 2014, http://www.reuters.com/article/us-usa-tax-offshore-idUSBREA3729V20140409.

24. Despite the deal, Boeing announced eleven months later that it was transferring two thousand high-paying engineering positions out of the state. See Reid Wilson, "After Huge Tax Incentive Package, Boeing Still Ships Jobs Out of Washington," *Washington Post*, October 8, 2014.

CHAPTER 8. Marrying the Monster

Chapter epigraph: Gregory Bateson, *Steps to an Ecology of Mind* (Chicago: University of Chicago Press, 2000), 129.

1. Yeats, "The Second Coming," *Selected Poems and Two Plays of William Butler Yeats* (New York: Macmillan, 1962), 91.

2. W. B. Yeats, *Essays and Introductions* (London: MacMillan, 1961), ix–x.

3. T. S. Eliot, "Choruses from 'The Rock,'" *T.S. Eliot Collected Poems, 1909–1962* (New York: Harcourt, Brace & World, 1963), 160.

4. For a summary of the beliefs of these techno-utopians see Ashlee Vance, "Merely Human? That's So Yesterday," *New York Times*, June 14, 2010.

5. Vance, "Merely Human?"

6. W. H. Auden, "In Memory of W. B. Yeats," *Selected Poetry of W. H. Auden* (New York: Modern Library, 1958), 52.

7. For a concise summary of the B corporation movement see James Surowiecki, "Companies with Benefits," *New Yorker*, August 4, 2014.

8. For the history of the Satellite Sentinel Project, see "Our Story," Satellite Sentinel Project website, accessed May 26, 2016, http://www.satsentinel.org/our-story. For information on Ushahidi see "About Ushahidi," accessed May 26, 2016, http://www.ushahidi.com/about.

9. For my take on the disastrous influence of mega-philanthropists like Broad and Gates on educational reform, see David Bosworth, "The Cultural Contradictions of Philanthrocapitalism," *Society*, Autumn 2011, 382–88.

10. The quote is from Jeremy Bentham, whose version of utilitarianism supplies the purest example of the reduction of moral issues into material problems. See Jeremy Bentham, *An Introduction to Principles of Morals and Legislation*; ch. 10 ("Of Motives"), article 10: "Now, pleasure is in *itself* a good: nay, even setting aside immunity from pain, the only good: pain is in itself an evil, and, indeed, without exception, the only evil."

11. Edward Taylor, "Still I Complain, I Am Complaining Still," in *Major American Poets*, ed. Oscar Williams and Edwin Honig (New York: The New American Library, 1962), 38.

12. Aeschylus, *The Oresteian Trilogy*, trans. Philip Vellacott (Baltimore: Penguin Books, 1961).

13. Seamus Heaney, *The Cure at Troy* (London: Faber, 1990), 77.

Index

Abstract Expressionism, 50

academia: Harold Bloom's literary criticism, 5, 6, 64–81, 92, 117, 122; increase in collaboration within, 232n13; Media Lab (MIT) born out of, 6, 96–98, 100–103, 110–11, 113; natural sciences paradigm shift within, 151–63, 173–74; scientific worldview challenged by radical postmodernists in, 137–40; social sciences paradigm shift within, 163–75

accountability: conscientious thinking's role in renewed, 205; dialogue of knowing's dual demand for creativity and, 57; how to assess, 207; of King Lear's role in Cordelia's death, 76–78; meritocracy's flight from, 2–3; scientific self-deception versus scientific, 85–86

Adam and Eve story, 53–54, 55

Aeschylus, 206

aesthetics of anesthesia, 50–53

Agamemnon (Aeschylus), 206

Albrecht, Andreas, 153–54

Alger, Horatio, 21, 209

Algonquin culture, 111–12, 113

Allen, Paul, 189

American Bar Association, 92

American democracy: consequences of the subversion of, 115–16; liberal modernity's corruptions of, 14–16; Media Lab's pseudo-dedication to, 96–98; need for post-modern reclaiming of, 10; negative response to mean-spiritedness by, 66; postmodern tactics challenging the psychological grounding for, 49; revision or supersession of, 31–32; technological imperative's threat to, 105–8. See also freedom; politics; United States

American Garden: comparing post-revolutionary and modern life in, 176–80; embryonic emergence of post-modern person and, 180–86; increased social mobility in, 178; reconsideration of the competitive marketplace in, 196–200; revision of conventional experience since the 1820s in, 179; significance of the loss of, 228n8, 229n9. See also Paradise

American idealism: Henry Ford as representing a revision in, 84–85; Ford's "pacifist fascist" inspired by ignorant form of, 20–21. See also idealism

American meritocracy: broad complicity in mismanagement of, 2–3; the failures of, 1–2; scientific capitalism as subversion of, 33–35, 37, 114–20

American Revolution, 26